The History Written on the Classical Greek Bo

T0382027

This book challenges historians of all periods to come to terms with the distortions that they systematically introduce into their work by relying on what has been written on paper, without looking at what was and was not written on the body. Historians use textual evidence to try to understand what people did in the past. But in interpreting that textual evidence they make assumptions about what past peoples could see. In particular they make assumptions about the way in which the classifications of language were visible to the eye, as well as conceivable in the mind. This book is concerned with the ways in which texts relating to classical Greece, and in particular to classical Athens, classified people, and with the extent to which those classifications could be seen by the eye. It compares the qualities distinguished in texts with those distinguished in sculpture and painted pottery and emphasises the frequent invisibility of the categories upon which historians have laid most stress – the citizen, the free person, the foreigner, even the god. The frequent impossibility of seeing who belonged to which category has major political, social and theological implications which are variously explored here. It also has implications for how history is written which go far beyond the case of classical Greece. Nothing short of a revolution in what historians are prepared to treat as source material will be required to take account of the findings of this book.

ROBIN OSBORNE is Professor of Ancient History at the University of Cambridge, a Fellow and Senior Tutor of King's College, and a Fellow of the British Academy. His research ranges broadly across Greek history, Greek archaeology and the history of Greek art. Along with numerous edited and co-edited volumes, he has written monographs on Demos: the Discovery of Classical Attika (Cambridge, 1985), Classical Landscape with Figures: the Ancient Greek City and its Countryside (1987), Greece in the Making, 1200–479 BC (1996, 2nd edn 2009), Archaic and Classical Greek Art (1998) and Greek History (2004). A collection of his papers has been published as Athens and Athenian Democracy (Cambridge, 2010). This book was written as a contribution to a project on 'Changing Beliefs of the Human Body' funded by the Leverhulme Trust.

The History Written on the Classical Greek Body

ROBIN OSBORNE

CAMBRIDGE
UNIVERSITY PRESS

CAMBRIDGE
UNIVERSITY PRESS

University Printing House, Cambridge CB2 8BS, United Kingdom

One Liberty Plaza, 20th Floor, New York, NY 10006, USA

477 Williamstown Road, Port Melbourne, VIC 3207, Australia

314-321, 3rd Floor, Plot 3, Splendor Forum, Jasola District Centre, New Delhi - 110025, India

79 Anson Road, #06-04/06, Singapore 079906

Cambridge University Press is part of the University of Cambridge.

It furthers the University's mission by disseminating knowledge in the pursuit of education, learning and research at the highest international levels of excellence.

www.cambridge.org
Information on this title: www.cambridge.org/9780521176705

© Robin Osborne 2011

First published 2011

A catalogue record for this publication is available from the British Library

Library of Congress Cataloging in Publication data
Osborne, Robin, 1957–
The history written on the classical Greek body / Robin Osborne.
  p. cm.
Includes bibliographical references and index.
ISBN 978-1-107-00320-0 (hbk.) – ISBN 978-0-521-17670-5 (pbk.)
1. Human body – Social aspects – Greece – History – To 1500 – Historiography.
2. Greece – History – To 146 B.C. – Historiography. 3. Social classes – Greece –
History – To 1500 – Historiography. 4. Greece – Social conditions – Historiography.
5. Human body – Social aspects – Greece – History – To 1500 – Sources. 6. Greece –
History – To 146 B.C. – Sources. 7. Social classes – Greece – History – To 1500 – Sources.
8. Greece – Social conditions – Sources. 9. Historiography – Psychological aspects.
10. Historiography – Social aspects. I. Title.
DF78.O83   2011
938.0072 – dc22   2011008370

ISBN 978-1-107-00320-0 Hardback
ISBN 978-0-521-17670-5 Paperback

Contents

Illustrations

Preface

Many histories have been and could be written on the classical Greek body. That I have written this particular history is owed in the first instance to the initiative of my colleague John Robb, who enlisted me to be part of a research project on 'Changing Beliefs of the Human Body from the Palaeolithic to Modern Medical Anthropology', and to the generosity of the Leverhulme Foundation in funding that project. In second place it is due to the kind invitation of the Wiles Trust to deliver the Wiles Lectures at Queen's University Belfast in May 2008. For any historian the invitation to deliver Wiles Lectures is an honour and a privilege, but for an ancient historian it is a particularly daunting prospect to follow the trail blazed by E. R. Dodds, whose *Pagan and Christian in an Age of Anxiety* (Cambridge, 1965), and M. I. Finley, whose *Politics in the Ancient World* (Cambridge, 1983) formed the Wiles Lectures in 1963 and 1980 respectively.

It is the precious peculiarity of the Wiles Lectures that not only are the lectures extensively discussed but the members of the History Department at Queen's are joined for those discussions by scholars invited from elsewhere. I am therefore most grateful not only to David Hayton, David Whitehead and the Queen's University department but to Roger Brock, Ashley Clements, James Davidson, Nick Fisher, Lin Foxhall, Oswyn Murray, Boris Rankov, Claire Taylor and Stephen Todd, who gave up a week of their own research time to listen to these lectures and debate their ideas and arguments. They will see from the text that follows how much I am in their debt.

This book has grown out of research and teaching ancient Greek history and Greek art and archaeology over many years. But this particular development of my ideas has been stimulated by the rich academic interactions of my Cambridge environment, both within the Leverhulme research project and outside it. More conversations than I can reasonably record have left their mark on my text and on my vision. I am particularly grateful to Catherine Osborne, Michael Squire and Caroline Vout for reading and commenting on drafts of the lectures and the additional chapters of this book. My research assistants, Ben Keim and Philippa Steele, played an invaluable part in preparing the book for publication, and Philippa prepared the index. I am grateful to them, and to the valiant copy-editor, Jan Chapman.

Abbreviations

ABL	C. H. Haspels (1936) *Attic Black-figure Lekythoi.* Paris.
ARV	J. D. Beazley (1963) *Attic Red-figure Vase-painters.* Second edition. Oxford.
Bekker, *Anecdota Graeca*	I. Bekker (1814–21) *Anecdota Graeca.* 3 vols. Berlin.
CAT	C. W. Clairmont (1993) *Classical Attic Tombstones.* 8 vols. Kilchberg.
GDI	F. Bechtel and others (eds.) (1884–8) *Sammlung der griechischen Dialekt-Inschriften.* 5 vols. Göttingen.
IG	*Inscriptiones Graecae.* Berlin.
LGPN	P. M. Fraser and others (eds.) (1987–) *Lexicon of Greek Personal Names.* 5 vols. to date. Oxford.
LIMC	L. Kahil and others (eds.) (1981–99) *Lexicon iconographicum mythologiae classicae.* 17 vols. Zurich.
ML	R. Meiggs and D. M. Lewis (eds.) (1969) *A Selection of Greek Historical Inscriptions to the End of the Fifth Century BC.* Oxford. Revised edition (1988).
RO	P. J. Rhodes and R. Osborne (eds.) (2003) *Greek Historical Inscriptions 404–323 BC.* Oxford.
SEG	*Supplementum epigraphicum Graecum* (1923–)
SIG	W. Dittenberger (ed.) (1915–24) *Sylloge Inscriptionum Graecarum.* Third edition. Leipzig.

Introduction

'Don't you think it's strange that life, described as so rich and full, a
camel-trail of adventure, should shrink to this coin-sized world? A head
on one side, a story on the other. Someone you loved and what
happened. That's all there is when you dig in your pockets. The most
significant thing is someone else's face. What else is embossed on your
hands but her?'[1]

This is a book about how we write history. It is also a book about why we
need the history of the body. But it is not a history of the body. It is about
the history written on the body – and the history *not* written on the body.
In particular it is a book about how the history written on the classical
Greek body rewrites the history, archaeology and art history of classical
Greece. Although classical Greece, and in particular classical Athens, is
my example here, I hope to engage not only those interested in ancient
Greece, but also all those interested in the place of the body in history
and archaeology; for my fundamental concern is with the history that we
construct on the basis of oral and written discourse and how that differs
from the history that can be written on the basis of the body that is seen.
I explore how oral and written discourse in classical Athens constructed
beliefs about the body, and how those beliefs compared with the beliefs
supported by the body that was seen and sensed. I am concerned both to
map ways in which beliefs about the classical body changed during the
period from the sixth to the fourth centuries BC, and with changing our
beliefs about the human body during that period.

We can no longer hear what Greeks said nor see what they saw. We rely
upon texts to convey their verbal discourse and on sculpture and painted
pottery to indicate what they saw. To write about how Greeks spoke and
what they saw is to write about art and text. There has been a great deal of
recent writing about the relationship between art and text, both in general

---

[1] Winterson (1992) 189.

and in antiquity.[2] This writing has all been concerned with how visual representations deal with stories told in literature and how literature describes what the artist represents or what the eye sees. My concern with art and text here is quite different. For my concern is with how texts write about the world as seen and experienced, not with how they write about the world as depicted in art; and similarly my concern is with the evidence the visual arts give us for how the world was perceived, not with how they react to texts. And curiously this is not a comparison with which scholars have much concerned themselves – the 'art and text' debate passes it by.

This book not only explores different discursive frameworks but inserts itself into several different discourses. Few readers are likely to be equally interested in all the theoretical and substantive issues that I explore, and I therefore offer a short guide here to the structure and substance of the argument, so that readers who have particular interests in one aspect or another of the book can locate quickly the part of the book in which they are interested and understand why I write about the various topics I discuss in the book as I do.

The first chapter explores the consequences of basing history upon what people say and write, investigating the peculiar character of language and the differences between the way in which words and the way in which images communicate. I argue that the structures required by language are necessarily more formal than those required by images, and that the fundamentally arbitrary relationship between words and things means that words require and produce classifications which images, which are not entirely arbitrary signs, are always liable to undermine. This matters, I maintain, for the historian since people live their lives not simply according to the dictates of the word but according to their observations of the world around them.

The second chapter explores the difference between modern classifications of the classical body, with their obsessions with its muscularity, contrasting with ancient classifications of the body, which stress its articulation. I argue that if we are to understand the place of the body in classical Greece we must understand the ways in which the different classification led to different assessments of how to treat the body properly and of what the body was good for. And I also argue that properly to understand ancient

---

[2] For the theoretical questions see above all the work of W. J. T. Mitchell (e.g. 1986, 1994). For Greece and Rome see Himmelmann (1967), Snodgrass (1982), Goldhill and Osborne (1994), Elsner (1996), Snodgrass (1998), Stansbury-O'Donnell (1999), Small (2003), Giuliani (2003), Woodford (2003), Elsner (2007), Taplin (2007), Squire (2009), Platt (2010).

representations of the body in painting and sculpture we need to be able to see the body in the terms in which the Greek artists themselves saw it. Art as well as text record reality selectively, and if we are to distinguish what history was written by classical Greeks upon the body we must understand the classificatory grid which Greek writers and artists imposed upon the world.

If the second chapter takes its lead from writers, the third chapter takes its lead from the visual arts. Here I ask which features of the human body Greek artists most regularly focus upon, and I seek to isolate which questions about individuals are appropriately answered by observing those features. I suggest that here again we can find a parallelism between the visual arts and classical texts when we look at the way in which such ancient studies of the world as Theophrastus' *Characters* are constructed.

The classifications of the world by classical Greek legal discourse have been afforded privileged status by historians who have been concerned above all with political history. In Chapters 4 and 5 I direct my attention in turn to the division between citizen and non-citizen and between Greek and foreigner. I point out how ambiguities in modern use of 'citizen' have their origin in ancient ambiguities and suggest, by a lengthy analysis of the use of citizen terminology in ancient texts, that the division between those who could and those who could not vote was of rather minor importance most of the time in a city such as classical Athens, and that what people felt that they needed to know was how a person related to the rest of the community. The failure of artists to show any interest in marking citizen status or the qualities of age required to be a citizen or perform particular citizen functions both reinforces this observation and suggests that the distinctions of law offer no indication of the distinctions by which people guided their way among those they met.

Foreignness is, I demonstrate in Chapter 5, variously shown on Athenian monuments, but the features that discriminate the foreign are most frequently features of culture, not nature, and are deployed as often to show role-playing by individuals who there is no reason to think were of non-Greek origin as they are to indicate those who were not born in Greek-speaking families. There is much evidence that Athens was a cosmopolitan community, but neither pots nor grave stelai offer a snapshot of that community. Rather they show how the foreign was good to think with, and how Athenians and non-Athenians alike manipulated exotic visual as well as verbal vocabulary in order to make social statements negotiate particular social positions.

Those sceptical about the invisibility of these legal and popular classifications might wonder whether, however little it is flagged in images, foreignness was not in fact something betrayed by details of appearance, clothing, speech and manners. No such suspicion arises in the case of the polluted, with whom I am concerned in Chapter 6. When a man whose past actions have left him impure arrives in a community, that community has no way of seeing his state and depends entirely on his self-declaration. So why did Greek communities convince themselves that certain actions or being present in certain situations left a person 'impure' and requiring special treatment? In this chapter I explore the ways in which scholars have in the past explained notions of pollution; I pay attention to its curious history and argue that notions of pollution work hand in hand with the mechanisms of the law to reach those areas of community concern that law cannot effectively reach.

Chapter 7 turns to another, even more fundamental, distinction of religious status which was not immediately visible – the distinction between mortal and immortal, human and god. Here my concern is with how the images of the gods change over time, and with the implications of the different relationships between the images of the bodies of the gods and the images of the bodies of mortal men and women for what can be thought about the nature of the gods.

In the final chapter I look at the implications of the findings of the earlier chapters. What difference does it make to how we understand the classical Greek world that very little of what is central to conventional histories was written on the body? I try to show both the importance of the invisible distinctions to the ordering of the Greek city, and how different the social history of classical Athens looks when the invisibility of those categorical distinctions is taken into account.

The implications of this book extend beyond classical Greece. The discrepancy between what is said and written, which insists upon putting bodies into categories, and the evidence of what is seen, where no such categorical divisions are required, is one to be found in every society. Historians of every society work from texts and employ images almost only to illustrate what they regard as established from the texts. Archaeologists, or at least those concerned with prehistory, are forced to rely upon material evidence, upon interpretation of what can be seen rather than what can be read. Historians complain that archaeologists give only descriptions; archaeologists find historians exclusively concerned with politics and unable or unwilling to look at other areas of life. The different features of the different evidence used by archaeologists and historians does much to illuminate this sterile debate.[3] But as long as history is concerned with the past as lived, and not merely the past as recorded in texts, historians need to find ways of getting beyond the limits of those texts. I hope to have shown in this book not only why that is the case, but also how that can be done.

[3] For recent attempts to stir up or resolve the tension compare Whitley (2001) Preface and Part I, the contributors to Sauer (2004), and Smith (2006).

1 | Writing history on the classical body

The history incorporated in words, and the history embodied in images

It is conventional to observe that we talk of 'history' in two quite different senses. 'History' is the past, but it is also writing about the past. Not only writing about the past, but writing based on past writing. What distinguishes historians from archaeologists is that they study the past on the basis of the evidence of texts, rather than of material remains.[1] Even when historians do the 'cultural history' of material culture, they either study texts about material culture or treat the products of material culture as texts, as documentary evidence. Archaeologists, on the other hand, when they do cultural history, describe those cultural products.[2] The past that archaeologists and historians study is not the same past.

The different approach of archaeologists and of historians is masked by the fact that most of the time they study different periods of the past. Archaeologists concentrate their efforts upon those periods of the past for which there is little or no textual evidence, upon what is sometimes called 'prehistory'.[3] Historians operate only with those past societies which have left written records. This distinction applies even to the History of Art. For the History of Art as a discipline studied in university departments of that name concentrates upon the art of literate societies. Study of the art of non-literate societies is left to courses in 'the anthropology of art' or courses in 'world art', whose comparative framework requires art objects to be withdrawn from their detailed context, treated as if outside history.

---

[1] Cf. 'L'histoire se fait avec des textes', Fustel de Coulanges cited by Marrou (1954) 77, cited by Hartog (1980) 381; 'History is developed in the continuity of signs left by scriptural activities: it is satisfied with arranging them, composing a single text from the thousands of written fragments in which already expressed is that labor which constructs time . . .', de Certeau (1988) 210.

[2] For a case for turning archaeology into cultural history see Morris (2000) 3–17, but Morris seems to me to neglect the biases built into basing history upon texts.

[3] Such a limitation of archaeology to periods for which oral or written evidence is lacking goes back at least as far as Thucydides. See Hornblower (1987) 91–2.

The Greek and Roman worlds have long been a strange anomaly here, the object of attention both of a special breed of archaeologists, 'classical archaeologists', often regarded with suspicion by 'real' archaeologists, and of a special breed of historians, 'ancient historians'. 'Real' archaeologists regard classical archaeology as too dominated by the agenda set by ancient texts.[4] Rather than interpreting the remains of antiquity in the context of archaeological assemblages, it is suggested, classical archaeologists interpret them according to an agenda derived from Pliny's *Natural History*, the Roman encyclopaedia which includes histories of both sculpture and painting. This Plinian agenda privileges the creator over the creation and the aesthetic over the functional. Art historians regard classical archaeologists as antediluvian because their art history has remained so largely formalist, since they are kept both by surviving material and by their own inclinations from making the study of works of classical art the study of contemporary written evidence about them and their creation. Meanwhile 'modern' historians regard 'ancient' historians with suspicion because they have so little archived material and spend so much time rewriting literary histories.

Precisely because of the peculiar development of ancient history and of classical archaeology, however, the Greek and Roman world provides an ideal ground for the investigation of the effect of privileging a particular source material when writing about the past. In this book I want to ask what is at stake in the claim that *History*, the story of the past written on the basis of the evidence of texts, is *history*, is the past itself.[5] What would the past look like if we took as our evidence not what people said but what people saw?

From classical antiquity onwards, some historians, at least, have been very conscious that what they do is produce literature. Indeed in the wake of Hayden White, historians have become more self-conscious about the writtenness of history, and more prepared to acknowledge that it is the historian who gives the past a plot.[6] But acknowledgement often substitutes for analysis of the nature of the issue. Historians, and this is equally true of 'ancient' and of 'modern' historians, still rarely discuss, in anything more than a desultory way, the effects of drawing upon texts as the sole source, or at least the highly privileged source, for knowledge of the past.[7]

---

[4] See further Osborne and Alcock (2007).

[5] My question and my answer are related to Joan Kelly's famous question 'Did women have a renaissance?' (Kelly 1977).

[6] White (1978), (1987).

[7] Cf. Marrou (1954) 77: 'si l'histoire ne se fait pas uniquement avec des textes, elle se fait surtout avec des textes, dont rien ne peut remplacer la précision'.

Meanwhile archaeologists, including classical archaeologists, often write as if the strongest claim material culture has is that it fills a gap in what we happen to know from texts, for instance by giving evidence for the lower classes.[8]

My concern in this book is to draw attention to the ways in which we limit our understanding of the past if we restrict ourselves to, or unduly privilege, what we can know from texts. For all that textual communication holds a central place in our lives, we do not know the world in which we live purely on the basis of what we are told in speech or writing, and we need not know the past purely on the basis of written texts. We live in a sensuous world, and it is worth trying to understand how their sensuous world impacted upon people in the past, their relations and their actions.

The problem with texts with which I will grapple in this book is not, primarily at least, the problem that any text is crafted by an author, and so any description an act of persuasion. Important though it is to acknowledge the partiality of all writing, such partiality is an inevitable and happy consequence of texts being personal, not impersonal products. We should celebrate, rather than regret, that our engagement with texts is an engagement with people, with the authors of texts, just as we should celebrate, rather than regret, that we only ever interpret the world that we hear with our own ears or see with our own eyes.[9]

The problem with which I will grapple here is rather that an author is crafted by his or her text.[10] The world of writing is always a world that is already classified. The giving of names, the putting into language, is classification. A language which made no distinctions would not communicate. But the distinctions made by language have to be based on distinctions

---

[8] Cf. Clarke (2003) for the pursuit of the lower classes in Roman art; Given (2004) 162 gives a strong theoretical justification for uncovering the strategies of the oppressed through survey and excavation: 'Thanks to the archaeology of the colonized, it is possible to understand the lives and experiences of people like this. They were not statistics or the objects of some deeply implicated bureaucrat, but real people who used actual material culture in tangible contexts. The objects, structures and landscapes that enveloped their lives were the means of their repression and the tools of their resistance.'

[9] It is vain to try to know the world only through objects, to the exclusion of texts, or to deny that artists and other creators of material objects also craft a world-view into the objects that they create. For a powerful critique of the possibility of knowing the world through the senses see Plato's famous analogy in the *Republic* between our perception of the world and the perception of shadows projected onto the wall of a cave. For a useful review of ancient appreciations and critiques of the power and limitations of the sense of sight see Jay (1993) ch. 1.

[10] I am not here concerned to explore ancient Greek views on the power and limitations of texts; on that see recently Männlein-Robert (2007), Tueller (2008) ch. 1.

always already made. 'In linguistic communication "world" is disclosed.'[11] When we convey to others, who are not present, what we see or hear or taste or smell or feel, then we must find a way of linking our sensations to the sensations experienced by others. To do that involves breaking down the continuum of sensation, placing our sensations within a structure that is already understood. It is the beauty, but also the limitation, of language that it provides that structure.

This need to give things an order if we are to share experiences was famously stressed by Foucault in *Les mots et les choses*. For Foucault, it was only once the visible world of natural history had been limited and filtered by having a structure imposed upon it that it became possible for it to be transcribed into language.[12] And that structure, as he illustrated in his preface with the famous discussion of the 'certain Chinese encyclopaedia' of Borges, must itself be part of a larger structure. The individual categories of the Chinese encyclopaedia are none of them unreasonable – 'sucking pigs', 'sirens' and 'stray dogs' can all potentially find a place in a taxonomy dividing real and imaginary animals according to species and relationship to men. But to find such categories alongside 'innumerable', 'drawn with a very fine camel-hair brush', 'having just broken the water pitcher' or 'that from a long way off look like flies' defies comprehension, because we can devise no broader structure in which all these groups can be made to relate to each other. We can imagine perfectly comprehensible discussions of each of these categories individually, but put together they offer us no understanding of the class of animals as a whole, or indeed of any world which they might inhabit.

Borges' fantasy encyclopaedia causes both laughter and unease. As Foucault observes, '*Heterotopias* are disturbing, probably because they secretly undermine language . . . because they destroy "syntax" in advance, and not only the syntax with which we construct sentences but also that less apparent syntax which causes words and things (next to and also opposite one another) to "hold together".'[13] Our unease with Borges' encyclopaedia has two roots. One is the thought that there might be a world which is so incommensurable with ours that we cannot conceive of the larger structure in which structuring knowledge in this way would make sense. The other is the thought that actually this world is not so different, that

---

[11] Gadamer (1975) 404.

[12] Foucault (2002[1970]) 147; cf. 150 'Structure is that designation of the visible which, by means of a kind of pre-linguistic sifting, enables it to be transcribed into language.' We might, however, question the existence, indeed the possibility, of a sifting that is entirely 'pre-linguistic'.

[13] Foucault (2002[1970]) xix.

the structures of our knowledge, which we think self-evident, are really just as artificial, except that we cannot see that. But our laughter comes from our awareness that Borges' encyclopaedia could not really exist, that there can be no such world because language is made up not simply of names that categorise but of a syntax that establishes relations between words. It is syntax which guarantees that if one category is constituted by animals 'drawn with a very fine camel-hair brush', it must be possible to have another category of animals not drawn with such a brush, or drawn with a less fine brush, or with some other implement, or not drawn but otherwise depicted. It is syntax which guarantees that if there is a category of animals 'having just broken the water pitcher', there must be a category of animals which have not just broken the water pitcher, or have done something else to a water pitcher or have simply just done some range of other things.

Borges' encyclopaedia illustrates by reversal the way in which language creates a world both of possible things and of possible relations between things. When we look at a male person and decide how to refer to him we have no choice but to slot him into, or at least relate him to, one or other preordained categories. If current language offers us 'boy', 'youth' or 'man', we will write onto this figure the distinctions that those terms imply. The world transcribed into, and constantly reinforced by, this language is a world where boys and youths and men are, for all their potential overlap, distinct groups. That becomes a truth about the world, a truth established by definition but not arbitrarily. Where we put the line between a boy and a youth, or a youth and a man, may be arbitrary, and the boundaries may be fuzzy, but the possibility of being 'not a youth' requires there to be boys and men. Of course, we can signal our difficulties about classification in any particular case, but the linguistic tradition in which we participate requires us to segregate.

It is not by chance that Borges' fantasy encyclopaedia is itself classified as Chinese. If we are tempted to think that there might be a world with such a classificatory system, we are so tempted because we know that different linguistic communities classify the world differently. Given that Chinese characters work quite differently from Western alphabets, the temptation to think that their language might be quite different is particularly strong.[14] The German philosopher Gadamer noted that 'learning a foreign language . . . gives one a new standpoint in regard to the view of the

---

[14] On the question of whether Chinese does work differently and whether one can translate, in particular from ancient Greek to Chinese, see Reding (2004) esp. p. 48; Wardy (2000).

world one had held hitherto'.[15] One can, the suggestion is, occupy various
standpoints to the world by adopting foreign attitudes of mind without
forgetting one's own view of the world. Indeed Gadamer sees it as a feature
of man that he can 'rise above the particular habitat in which he happens to
find himself'.[16] But however much these different views of the world differ
in the things that they name, the 'syntax' of the world is not challenged. A
language which had no distinct word for a young man, which had no 'youth'
and used only 'boy' and 'man', would indeed offer a different view of the
world, but it would still be a view in which male human beings were divided
into those who did and did not have certain qualities. A language which
had no distinct word for 'girl', which used only 'child' and 'adult', would still
offer a view of the world in which human beings were divided into those
who were and those who were not possessed of certain age properties. Just
as 'boy', as a young male human being, requires a world in which there are
human beings who are not young or not male, so 'child', as a human being
marked by youth, demands that there are human beings not marked by
youth. Words are always embedded in a cultural system of signification.[17]

Is it a feature of verbal language alone that terms are necessarily locked
into syntactical relations? We regularly talk about 'the language of art',
and much recent art criticism has been built upon the assumption that the
kinds of semiotic analysis developed for language are also applicable to art.[18]
Pictures and statues, as well as words, encode the world, and in the case of
pictures, as of words, it is wrong to create an antithesis between meaning
and interpreter – there is no normative meaning to images or words unless
it is understood by the interpreter.[19] But the elements of a picture are not
exactly like words, and the relationship of the elements of a picture to each
other is structured in a different way to the way in which syntax structures
verbal language. While it is a necessary implication of any pictorial element
that alternative pictorial elements are possible, there are no privileged ways
in which that element might change. A picture of a person may be marked
as female or as of a particular age by a number of different features, more
or less obvious to the glance. Whereas 'adult' is aged but not sexed, and
'girl' both aged and sexed, a figure recognisable as a human being may at

---

[15] Gadamer (1975) 400.   [16] Gadamer (1975) 403.

[17] For a classic Greek exploration of this, see Plato's *Cratylus*, itself a dialogue until recently
misunderstood and neglected; for recent work on *Cratylus* see Sedley (2003).

[18] Cf. Goodman (1969), Bryson and Bal (1991). Cf. Gadamer (1975) 47–8: 'one can see the
advantage of art over natural beauty in the fact that the language of art is a demanding
language which does not offer itself freely and vaguely for interpretation according to one's
mood, but speaks to us in a significant and definite way'.

[19] Cf. Gadamer (1975) 276–7.

first glance display neither definite age nor gender and may yield more or less equivocal signs only on closer inspection. That intimation that we are looking at a particular type of person may come not from the addition of some further discrete sign to a sexless or ageless body, in the way that one might add 'young' to 'woman', but from the way the figure is shown to stand or from other aspects of the general demeanour. Pictures invite labels, but no single set of labels will ever satisfactorily capture all the visual signals that a picture gives.

At the level of syntax, too, the way in which pictorial and sculptural figures relate to each other is not the way that words relate to each other. In particular, because any drawn or sculpted object will possess a whole range of qualities, that drawing or sculpture does not establish its identity by a simple contrast. The salience which the word 'boy' gives to young age can only be produced in a picture or statue of a boy when the image is juxtaposed, actually or through our understanding of a tradition, to other figures.[20] Visual elements can be made to evoke a definitive tradition but do not cease to carry significance in the absence of such a tradition; verbal elements require a definitive (even if continually developing) tradition and are meaningless otherwise.

We might even suggest that the way we understand words and the way we understand visual art invert one another. In verbal language 'the universal concept that is meant by the meaning of the word is enriched by the particular view of an object',[21] that is, context enriches the meaning of words by rendering them particular. But in visual language the object itself is always particular, and what context offers is not particularity but an indication of the place of that object in the world that enables the particularity to be tempered and offers at least some hints towards universal meaning. This is surely one reason why we are happier to think we can understand the art of another culture than we are that we can understand its language (even in translation). Images break down barriers of space and time because they are 'actual apparitions'; texts offer no such sense of epiphany.

In what follows I want to resist the easy subsuming of the visual to the verbal arts. I do so not because I think that the discussion of art as language or text and the application of semiotic methods to visual representations are unrewarding: on the contrary, I regard them as fundamental tools of art history. I do so rather because there are things that words do – not just can do, but always do – that images do not do, or at least do not necessarily

---

[20] For the importance of tradition see R. Osborne (2008c).
[21] Quotation from Gadamer (1975) 388.

do. The visual arts do not offer just another language world that we can compare to our language world, as Gadamer suggests that we compare the world that we enter by learning a foreign language to the world we know in our native language. The visual arts offer us a world which cannot be known in any verbal language.

The language of words not only segregates, it also polarises. 'Logocentrism subjects thought – all concepts, codes and values – to a binary system.'[22] All verbal categories are open to negation: 'not a boy', 'not a youth', 'not a man'; 'not running', 'not young', 'not wrinkled', 'not white'. Words regularly offer us polar opposites – left and right, up and down – and the advantages of polarising encourage treating other differences as polarities – town and country, polarity and analogy. Visual languages can be made to show nega-tion – by crossing out, by signs of erasure – and they can be organised to show polarities (most obviously by juxtaposition). But a visual image does not raise necessarily the question of negation in the way that a sentence raises that question, and elements of imagery do not come paired, as so many words are paired. Consider the application of terms such as 'higher' and 'lower' or 'left' and 'right' as applied to a painting or drawing. Paintings offer us a space and 'left' and 'right', 'higher' and 'lower' are spatial terms. But even these spatial terms turn out to be polarities that are questioned and undermined in the visual arts. The development of a system of per-spective depended upon the viewer's being able to commute 'higher' and 'lower', 'left' and 'right' into 'nearer' and further' – while at the same time continuing to be conscious that the painted or drawn objects were not at different distances at all.

It is not simply an interesting philosophical proposition that the world represented in words is differently structured from the world represented in the visual arts. The existence of these two very different ways of perceiving and describing the world has enormous historical importance. For polarities bring hierarchy:

the movement whereby each opposition is set up to make sense is the movement through which the couple is destroyed. A universal battlefield. Each time, a war is let loose. Death is always at work.

Father/son	Relations of authority, privilege, force.
The Word/Writing	Relations: opposition, conflict, sublation, return.
Master/slave	Violence. Repression.

We see that 'victory' always comes down to the same thing: things get hierarchical.[23]

---

[22] Cixous (1997[1986]) 232.   [23] Cixous (1997[1986]) 232.

These are the terms in which Cixous describes this effect of logocentrism as a prelude to the argument that 'Organization by hierarchy makes all conceptual organization subject to man.' But although male power over women is what is primarily at issue here for the feminist critic, the stakes are yet greater: the very construction of the world as divided between powerful and powerless is in question. Visual arts could do that and have at times done that too, but our language cannot avoid doing that.[24]

Many worlds are indeed divided between the powerful and the powerless. Where almost all interaction is verbal, where decisions are taken by people in power on the basis of documents and where it is by the issuing of verbal commands that decisions are enacted, it may seem reasonable that the history of that world be written exclusively on the basis of all those words. Such an approach is particularly attractive when the history is concerned exclusively with politics, above all politics at a national or international level. This is, after all, a world where, and not least among historians, what counts as knowledge is what can be written down. In the terrifying visions of writers faced with totalitarian regimes it is the issuing of written instructions, obeyed to the letter, that comes to dominate the lives of the powerless. Even in situations where writing is central to the operation of state power, however, the written knowledge on which power claims to be based turns out to be personally mediated, both at the highest level where decisions are made, and at the lowest level where decisions are executed. Think of Oskar Schindler.[25] History based on texts will find even the political decisions and their execution in such a society hard to account for. Take the case of totalitarian societies. Texts will tell us what happened, but not how it happened. Written words have been much less important in those societies than the spoken word; it has been the charisma of the politician delivering the words that has been crucial to delivering popular obedience: in the context of a mass political rally the effects of crowd excitement combine with the oratorical skills of the speaker to condition the audience reaction.

If a logocentric approach cannot do justice to a world permeated by words, consider how it will fare in a world where interaction is primarily face to face. Here people react not simply to what others say but to how they present themselves physically, by clothing, demeanour and facial

---

[24] As the Freudian overtones of Cixous's words indicate, there is an issue here, which I shall not further pursue, for the way in which the structures of textual analysis have become the structures of psychological analysis.

[25] Quoted as saying to Moshe Bejski 'I knew the people who worked for me . . . When you know people, you have to behave toward them like human beings.' On Schindler see Crowe (2004). It is telling that it is through the film that Schindler's list has entered modern memory.

expressions. Recapturing anything like the full history of such a society on the basis of texts alone becomes very clearly impossible.[26] And such worlds of face-to-face interaction between embodied individuals are not merely the preserve of anthropologists, who are, indeed, arguably all too often inclined to think that those they are studying can be understood by quoting what they say. Such worlds are the worlds in which much social interaction takes place: could one imagine an adequate history of either sex that was not marked by bodies in space, seductive voices and the scent of perfume, as well as by love letters? Or imagine an adequate history of gender which did not observe office behaviour and the use of flowers as well as promotion records and language use? Or a history of education which did not examine what happens in the classroom as well as what is written in textbooks or examinations?

Bourdieu has famously argued that in the modern world 'Principles of division, inextricably logical and sociological, function within and for the purposes of the struggle between social groups.'[27] By freezing a certain state of power relations, the classificatory system reproduces social classes. The classifications that Bourdieu is interested in are cultural, to do with the ways in which people position themselves and others in relations to different possible styles of life. Bourdieu was able to show, on the basis of the surveys he carried out among the French in the late 1960s and early 1970s, that reactions to cultural phenomena of all sorts ('the judgement of taste') correlated with education and social class. Individuals effectively put themselves into a social class by the taste they exercised. But although any group is potentially divided by the judgement of taste, the particular classes and divisions of modern France will not be found universally, and the question becomes how can we excavate the fact or nature of such judgements when we cannot carry out a sociological survey.

In everyday interactions we are perfectly used to hearing what people say and measuring it against what we see (and sometimes also smell and feel) them do. But how do we obtain remotely as 'sensual' a perception of the past? Even the most richly descriptive of modern novels – and unsurprisingly it is Proust in particular to whom Bourdieu himself turns – are constrained by the categories of their language. Yet there can be no record of retinal images, let alone of the signals from the nerves. Even, we might think, in the modern world saturated with the images recorded on the artificial retina

---

[26] It would, of course, be equally impossible to recapture anything like the full history of such a society on the basis of images alone.

[27] Bourdieu (1984) 479.

of the camera, the language of the photograph is itself to such an extent governed by conventions, albeit conventions which do not merely replicate the limitations of verbal language, that no adequate history can be written upon the basis of images.[28] Kinsey's archive of images, classified by textual description of the sexual acts shown, gives no better a history of sexual relations in the United States than does his accumulation of statistics.[29]

But the artifice of the photograph, like the artifice of the text, is its strength, not its weakness.[30] What is at issue is not somehow comparing what we hear with what strikes the retina of the eye, or what we say with the images we produce on the retina of an observer. No, what is at issue is the possibility that we might want to tell our story about the world differently when we understand the world by seeing it from the way we want to tell the story of the world when we understand it through spoken or written language. Or rather, the certainty that we will want to tell the story differently because of the impossibility of *not* understanding it differently. The comparison is indeed between two sorts of language, verbal and visual, and with the different ways in which visual and verbal language structure experience. It is not a matter of words always being more or less deliberately economical with the truth, though they necessarily are, while visual images just show the world as it is, for they do not.[31] The comparison is between different ways of selecting from experience to convey that experience to others, between what words make us say and what images make us see.

There is an antiquarian curiosity in this. We might imagine a history of art which illustrated the different ways in which a topic or theme had been shown over a period of time. Such a history of art would constitute a history of how what was seen changed over time, in the same way that histories of ideas or of science or social histories construct a history of how aspects of the world were differently described in different periods.[32]

---

[28] Those conventions are well brought out by Dyer (2005).   [29] Johnson-Roehr (2009).

[30] It is this conviction which most obviously separates my use of images here from the sorts of uses of images explored by Burke (2001). For Burke the various sorts of artifice which separate visual images from retinal images are all obstacles to using pictures for historical purposes. To my mind images do not measure up to the historian's needs for Burke because he is looking for them to supplement, rather than complement, textual histories. For what happens if photographs are made themselves the material of history again see Dyer (2005).

[31] This book will have many occasions to illustrate the ways in which images are economical with the truth as well as many occasions to show that texts are.

[32] This would be a history of seeing in a slightly different sense to Baxandall's famous 'period eye' (Baxandall 1972), for Baxandall's period eye is constructed by looking at what texts say that individuals thought about vision and art, not at what the thoughts of artists actually produced. In fact it would be a history of seeing closer to that offered by Wölfflin in part two of his *Klassische Kunst* of 1899 (see Wölfflin 1953).

Whether or not any explanation of change over time is offered in such histories, such accumulated descriptions offer intrinsic fascination as they reveal something of the past as a foreign country.

But to treat this history of visual images as just another history, to be accumulated alongside existing histories, is to miss the real importance of breaking out of the constraints of verbal or written histories. Making visual images the source of history reveals the partiality of histories based on words. Visual images do not offer insights into different aspects of the past; they offer different insights into those same aspects of the past about which historians already write on the basis of texts.[33]

Few people, even if deprived of sight, live in a world where the only communications they receive are verbal. Most of us negotiate our way through the world using all of our senses, and while many of us give and receive only somewhat basic messages in the languages of texture and smell, we both send and receive complex communications in visual language. Visual messages, themselves reinforced, undermined or otherwise qualified by smells, tactile encounters, non-verbal sounds, and tastes, play a constant counterpoint to verbal messages. Removing the sights from the world of the past does not simply leave that world less colourful; it leaves the words bequeathed by that world at best radically decontextualised, and at worst incomprehensible. To write a history based on texts alone is to write a partial history, a history which treats just *one* of the systems humans have for understanding the world as the *only* way of understanding that world.

This book is an attempt to show, by a detailed discussion of some aspects of the history of classical Greece, and in particular of classical Athens, the nature and extent of the problem of writing history from texts alone. It is also an attempt to show that we can do something about it. As my title, calqued upon Jeanette Winterson's eye-opening novel, itself reveals, this is a somewhat paradoxical thing to do.[34] It is paradoxical because I am committed to using the very means, writing, whose limitations I am so keen to indicate, in order to investigate and to record what is not written. It will not have escaped the reader that my insistence that verbal communications

---

[33] The closest that work on non-classical art has come to exploring the gap between the categories that images use and the categories that texts use has been in work on images of women, where in different ways that gap is signalled in such classic contributions as John Berger's *Ways of Seeing* (1972), with its insistence on the common classification promoted by the high-art nude and the pin-up photograph, or Laura Mulvey's (1973) 'You don't know what is happening Mr Jones', with its insistence on the fetishism lurking behind an individual artist's images. However, both of those works draw attention to the gap by evacuating history (i.e. change over time) from consideration.

[34] Winterson (1992).

polarise, and that the visual and the verbal must be treated as distinct, has been expressed in writing. It is in words that I categorise the problems with verbal categories. If I am right in my contentions, words are indeed the ideal medium through which to expose the limitations of words. But if I am also to demonstrate the alternative experience which images make possible, do I not need to deploy images, rather than texts about images?[35] Indeed I do and I shall. This is a book about what happens if we look rather than read: the images in this book are to be looked at, not just read about. But just as we need visual and other sensory experiences if we are to understand texts, so texts can assist us to observe and to feel. No one who has read Winterson's *Written on the Body* will ever feel a body in the same way again.

'What strikes us first about things in the world is their appearance.'[36] In what follows I try to indicate the profound effect that privileging textual sources has had on our picture of the classical Greek world. In a series of separate studies I compare the structure of the classical Greek world, whether political, social, cultural or religious, as presented by texts with the structure of that world as seen in images. I ask what it would be to put at the centre of our account of the past 'the way we communicate through the senses . . . the art of creating reactions without words, through the look and feel of people, places, and things'.[37] I try to show how what was, and what was not, visibly written on the body was fundamental for the way in which what *was* said and written was understood in the everyday. In the course of doing so I argue that the histories which win approbation as 'good histories', because of how fully they reproduce textual evidence, for exactly that reason, systematically misstate the historical experience as lived.

The words have a Greek for them

But why the classical Greek body? Leaving aside the important practical fact that classical Greece is what I know about, there are three reasons. Classical

---

[35] Compare the photo-essay in Berger (1972).

[36] Nehamas (2007) 19. That does not mean that everyone is struck by the same thing. This is nicely put by the second-century AD author Clement of Alexandria, *Miscellanies* (*Stromateis*) 1.1, 17.1–2: 'All of us who make use of our eyes see what is presented before them. But some look at objects for one reason, others for another. For instance, the cook and the shepherd do not regard the sheep in the same way: for the one examines it if it be fat; the other watches to see if it be of good breed. Let a man milk the sheep's milk if he need sustenance: let him shear the wool if he need clothing. And in this way let me produce the fruit of the Greek erudition.'

[37] Postrel (2003) 6, quoted at Nehamas (2007) 19.

Greece offers a particularly fine example of the way in which concentration on the evidence of texts has caused specifically textual structures to be taken to be the structures of history itself. But classical Greece also offers us a past society about whose visual experiences we are peculiarly well informed. The survival of extremely large numbers of painted pots and substantial numbers of free-standing and relief statues means that we have abundant evidence, outside texts, for classical Greek visual categorisation of the world. On top of that, the status of classical sculpture, in particular, in the western world since the Renaissance means that what was written on the classical body has become written on our bodies. To understand the classical body better is the better to understand our own experience of the world.

Over the past half century, many scholars have argued that the Greeks were peculiarly disposed to see the world in terms of polarities. Important here has been the work of Geoffrey Lloyd, whose *Polarity and Analogy: Two Types of Argumentation in Early Greek Thought* was published in 1966. While acknowledging that 'it is manifestly not the case that all the arguments and explanations that appear in early Greek thought are of the two types', that is arguments from polarity or analogy, Lloyd insisted that 'these two very general modes of reasoning are particularly common in early Greek thought'.[38] He noted particularly the insistence of some pre-Sokratic philosophers that 'a choice must be made between certain pairs of terms', and that 'when we turn to Plato, the recognition of similarities and differences is, one may say, the central problem of the method of dialectic'.[39]

When Paul Cartledge was asked to write a general work on the Greeks for Oxford University Press in the 1990s, he organised the whole work around polarities – Greeks vs. Barbarians, Men vs. Women, Citizens vs. Aliens, Free vs. Slave, Gods vs. Mortals, and so on. As the blurb on the dust jacket puts it,

The book explores in depth how the dominant – adult, male citizen – Greeks sought, with limited success, to define themselves unambiguously in polar opposition to a whole series of 'Others' – non-Greeks, women, non-citizens, slaves, and gods.

In choosing to frame his treatment in this way Cartledge was picking up on a powerful trend in literary criticism during the 1980s that analysed tragedy around the poles of Greek and Barbarian or Athenian and Theban.[40]

---

[38] Lloyd (1966) 431.   [39] Lloyd (1966) 432.

[40] Cartledge (1993), E. M. Hall (1989), Zeitlin (1986). Goldhill (1986) organises his treatment of Greek tragedy around polarities of a different sort, with successive chapters entitled 'Text and tradition', 'Mind and madness', 'Blindness and insight' and ending with 'Genre and transgression' and 'Performance and performability'.

When we look at ancient Greek texts we do indeed find them continually making distinctions and claiming contrasts. Herodotos' description of the world famously compares the various peoples in and around the Persian Empire with the Greeks, and that process of comparing and contrasting inevitably leads him to emphasise the ways in which other peoples are their mirror image. François Hartog famously drew attention to this in 1980 with his *Le miroir d'Hérodote*, showing, with regard to Herodotos' account of the Skythians, that Skythian practices were often presented as Greek practices inverted. This is not a matter of peculiar Herodotean narrow-mindedness – it is hard to think of a less narrow-minded historian than this man who acknowledges that 'custom governs everything'.[41] It is rather a matter of the polarising effect of the distinctions that language encourages when it comes to describing the world and explaining past events. As Hartog points out, the Persians, when fighting Greeks, are presented as anti-hoplites; but when it comes to fighting the Skythians, who refuse to stay in one place and fight, the Persians become a classic hoplite army engaged in classic Greek military strategy.[42]

We might be tempted to take this tendency to portray other peoples as polar opposites of the self to be a particular feature of ethnography. We can trace back the presentation of others as the inverse of self to Homer's *Odyssey*, where agriculture and sacrifice mark out the civilised world, and pastoralism and failure properly to sacrifice mark out the world of lawless monsters such as the Cyclopes.[43] And we can trace the portrayal by contrast on into the classical ethnographic tradition.[44] But not just the classical tradition: it is here that we find the ancestors of 'orientalism', in the sense in which Edward Said has accustomed us to use that term.[45]

Putting Herodotos' practice into this ethnographic tradition has the advantage of showing us that we should hesitate before reckoning what we find in Herodotos peculiar to the Greeks. But it is equally a mistake to see classification by contrast as peculiarly ethnographic. Herodotos does not reserve his method of presentation by contrast for non-Greek peoples. He famously turns his 'ethnographic eye' upon the Greek city of Sparta, and the habit of viewing Sparta as an inversion of other Greek practices came to shape much ancient writing on Sparta, such that scholars have long talked of the 'Spartan mirage'.[46] Sparta became, and has continued in the modern historical imagination to be, a place of egalitarianism, frugality, of

---

[41] Herodotos 3.38.   [42] Hartog (1980) 269.   [43] So Vidal-Naquet (1970).
[44] Rives (1999) 11–21 offers an introduction to that tradition.   [45] Said (1978).
[46] First expounded by Ollier (1933–43).

life lived in public and dominated by communal messes rather than by the family, of the sharing of wives, slaves, hunting dogs and other possessions, marked by absence of interaction with the wider world, absence of manufacturing, absence of trade and absence of money; above all it became a place which, after the imposition of a strict lawcode by a certain Lykourgos, does not change.[47] Sparta is presented as the polar opposite of other Greek city states, and in particular of Athens.

Not all polar oppositions are compatible, however, and conflicts between different ancient texts long ago raised questions about the credibility of this construction and drew attention to its constructedness. Nevertheless this literary picture of Sparta essentially continued to prevail. What has finally not only unmasked the 'mirage' as such but made it possible to create, and impossible to deny, an alternative view has been the realisation of the value of non-textual evidence, in this case the evidence of archaeology.[48]

Archaeology long ago showed, through the pioneering excavations at the sanctuary of Artemis Orthia, close to the banks of the river Eurotas, that although *classical* Sparta has left rather few and modest artefactual remains, *archaic* Sparta was materially extremely rich.[49] Indeed Sparta in the seventh century BC is *so* rich that it bucks the trend that otherwise prevails across the Greek world, where the seventh century is materially less rich than the eighth.[50] It is not simply that archaic Sparta produces elaborate bronzework and sophisticated painted pottery, both of which are exported east and west in significant quantities, but that it developed a lead industry more or less peculiar to it (and responsible for more than 100,000 small lead votives in the sanctuary of Artemis Orthia alone), was one of only two centres of ivory working in the Greek world and developed a unique series of clay masks.[51]

It is not the existence of such luxury items, indicating an unexpected degree of wealth, that makes these finds historically so important, but their deposition in the sanctuary. This makes it clear that that wealth was involved in public and structured competitive display. Take the masks (1.1). Although we do not know the precise cultic purpose to which these were put before they were dedicated in the sanctuary, and although some were unsuitable for wearing, these masks provide good evidence for some kind of performance. What that performance signals is something that we must construct, but although we cannot be certain that the features that most strike us

---

[47] Cf. Hodkinson (2000) 20–6.　　[48] Cf. Cartledge (2001) ch. 12.　　[49] Dawkins (1929).

[50] The best introduction to Spartan material culture remains Fitzhardinge (1980). On Sparta's seventh-century wealth cf. R. Osborne (1997c).

[51] On ivory working see Carter (1984); on the masks see Carter (1987).

1.1 Mask from Artemis Orthia Sanctuary, Sparta.

about the material evidence are the features which most struck the Spartans themselves, these objects do create patterns of similarity and difference through their salient features. Masks in general signal the exploration of difference by modifying the appearance of the body, whether to help to effect a permanent transformation in some rite of passage, or to reaffirm the existing status quo after the exploration of temporary difference. The variety of mask types at Sparta suggests that the differences explored in performance were not of the simplest sort.[52] Whatever we take the performative use to have been, there can be no doubt that the Spartans were advertising differences, not homogeneity, when they wore and dedicated these masks, glorifying the goddess with their offerings.[53] The textual picture of Spartiates as all 'equals' is already shown as too simple. What is more, a potter's burial in the centre of Sparta itself suggests that the craft activities themselves involved Spartan citizens, and not simply helots or the

[52] On masks in general see Napier (1986).   [53] Cf. Hodkinson (2000) ch. 9.

perioikoi ('dwellers-around'), the free inhabitants of other towns in Spartan territory: the act of making as well as the act of wearing these masks may well have divided the citizen body.[54]

The 'Spartan mirage' is in some ways a peculiar and an extreme example of the way in which the encouragement which language gives to polarisation leads to a history built upon texts being built upon polarities. It is also an example where the nature of the polarising claims – of austerity, uniformity and egalitarianism – means that it is unusually easy to relate those claims to the material and visual world. It serves well, however, to alert us to the pressures towards polarisation which texts exert, and to the possibility that visual and material culture may offer a view which does not measure up at all to the terms of texts.

As the example of Sparta shows, what we know about how the Greeks thought about others comes overwhelmingly from texts. This is not because we are short of material evidence for the Greeks, but because deducing what people thought from objects and pictures is always a more complicated business than reading a text. Objects and pictures do not straightforwardly proclaim the opinions either of their makers or of their users: we have to work hard to put those objects and images back into a context where we see not merely the 'actual apparitions' but the whole discourse. We expect historians to advance propositions, and to show that those propositions derive from propositions made by the historical actors themselves. If we are, as Lloyd was, writing the history of philosophy, or at least of argumentation, then we reasonably write the history of the texts in which that argumentation was carried out (though we might be more secure still if we could hear their oral debates). But if we are trying to write a history of how the Greeks saw the world, privileging texts becomes seriously problematic. For while our communications may be dominated by oral or written texts, those texts offer commentary on our being in the world; they are not themselves the means by which we navigate our daily relations to the world.[55] It is important that we do not let their words invent the Greeks.

The way in which distinctions which are easy to make in texts may be difficult or even impossible to make 'on the ground' is well brought out in the earliest prose text of any length written in Athens to survive. The

---

[54] Cartledge (2001) 182.

[55] When Laqueur writes (1990) 19: 'if structuralism has taught us anything it is that humans impose their sense of opposition onto a world of continuous shades of difference and similarity', he seems to me to underestimate the various non-textual ways in which humans relate to the world without imposing such oppositions. Curiously this comment is part of Laqueur himself imposing opposition on the evidence he discusses as he creates his 'one sex, two sex' model.

Constitution of the Athenians, which dates to the last quarter of the fifth century and became included in the writings of Xenophon, although not by him, famously observes that

> It is slaves and metics who lead the most undisciplined life in Athens: there, one is not permitted to strike them, and a slave will not stand out of the way for you. I will explain why this is their local custom. If the law permitted a free man to strike a slave or a metic or a freedman, he would often think that the Athenian was a slave and would have hit him; for, so far as clothing and general appearance are concerned, the common people here are no better than the slaves and metics.[56]

There is no doubt some exaggeration in [Xenophon]'s claim, but it nevertheless highlights the problem.[57] Distinctions between Athenian and non-Athenian, between citizen, metic, freedman and slave are all easy to make in texts. More than that, indeed, it is part of normal parlance to make such distinctions, for individuals not well enough known to be called by their personal name are likely to be called by a name that puts them into a particular group – whether they are called by city name or ethnic or by some other term revealing of status. But how those distinctions operate in society is a quite different matter.

The form that [Xenophon]'s claim takes here is very revealing. The author expects slaves to stand out of the way for him. That is, he expects slaves to acknowledge their subordinate status by their behaviour, to display their status with the way they comport their bodies. But if they do not do that, if they do not behave as slaves, their slave status becomes invisible. A man walking along an Athens street would not, if we believe this fifth-century testimony, be able to ascribe a status to individuals with whom he was not already acquainted.[58] There is no disputing that status distinctions mattered in Athens. Slaves, resident aliens (metics), and citizens all had different positions in law at Athens. But the significance of those differences in daily life must come into question if the differences could not be put into operation at the moment at which they would be of consequence (I discuss these issues further in Chapters 4 and 5). If insubordination cannot

---

[56] [Xenophon], *Constitution of the Athenians* 1.10, trans. R. Osborne (2004a).

[57] See Marr and Rhodes (2008) ad loc. Compare the earlier and equally ideologically determined claim by Theognis that 'it is not the nature of slavery ever to have a straight head, but always crooked, and on a skewed neck; for just as a rose or a hyacinth does not grow from a squill, neither does a free child ever grow from a slave mother' (535–8).

[58] There is confirmation of this in the incident related in [Demosthenes] 53.16, where Apollodoros suggests that a citizen boy (*paidarion aston*) was sent to damage his rose garden, in the expectation that Apollodoros would think him, and treat him as, a slave, so laying himself open to prosecution for *hubris*.

be recognised, it cannot be stopped. We have to allow that even a Greek might be lost for words.

Historians have long been aware that the texts which they employ offer only partial glimpses of life as lived. Scholars repeatedly observe, when it comes to using laws as evidence, that the presence of a law allowing, enjoining or forbidding an action does not indicate that that action was sometimes, always or never engaged in. Not only do repeated laws on a topic suggest that the problem addressed continued despite the earlier legislation, but the practical obstacles in the way of individuals using the resources which law put at their disposal have often been very significant. So, for example, Athenian law denied validity to a will made if the testator was insane, senile, drugged, drunk or under the influence of a woman. Not only is this law unlikely to have been passed as a result of a rash of mad, gaga, stoned, intoxicated or seduced testators, but it was anything but straightforward either for a prosecutor to demonstrate to a jury that any of these conditions had prevailed at the time the will was made, or for a defendant to prove that none of them had.[59] Arguably, the very difficulty of proving the relevant conditions was part, at least, of the attraction and of the strength of the law, since it opened up to public scrutiny all wills made in circumstances where the good sense of the testator could be questioned. The conditions which rendered the will invalid might be entirely invisible – they depended not on observation but upon argument. This law is a text to be commented on by further texts, not a text that could be mapped onto the visible world.

These problems with laws as evidence for how the world was experienced are only a particularly acute form of the problems with all texts. Claims made by texts classify the world under particular descriptions but never show that all, or even most, people at the time saw the world in that way. That we have almost only texts written by high-class men is often presented as a problem for writing the history of women or of 'ordinary' people in antiquity. But in fact not even high-class men can have operated in daily life according to the divisions made in the texts they write.

Persons and objects in the world rarely come with labels on (except in ambitious middle-class households where small children are being taught to read). When we do meet an object telling us what it is, then it is usually attempting to persuade us, is aspirational and is revelatory in no straightforward way. Identification always involves interpretation, and this may be

---

[59] [Demosthenes] 46.14. I discuss the legal implications of laws like this in R. Osborne (1985b). See also R. Osborne (1990b), Christ (1992).

more or less straightforward. Clerical collars pretty certainly identify clergy, and styles of dress enable clergy of different denominations to be more or less securely identified, but identifying a bank manager or distinguishing lecturers from professors on the basis of appearance is almost impossible. Wiles Lecturers form an identifiable class – you can find a list of them on the Queen's University website – but not a class that can be recognised in real life, except at the moment of delivery of the lectures themselves.

As I proceed to draw attention to the consequences of the different ways in which texts, on the one hand, and material bodies (or in their absence images of material bodies), on the other, divide up the world, I shall suggest that we will write a quite different history of classical Greece, and in particular of classical Athens, if we turn not to the history written on stone and papyrus but to the history drawn upon the body. And I will try to show not simply that there are areas of history about which texts are silent, and the material record eloquent, but that in areas of history where texts are loquacious, the history that they offer stands only in oblique relation to the history that those active at the time experienced.

2 | The appearance of the classical Greek body

Greek athletics and the Greek body

When modern scholars look at the male bodies of classical sculpture they see 'broad shoulders, a deep chest, big pectoral muscles, a slim waist, prominent iliac crests, jutting buttocks, and stout thighs and calves'.[1] These first impressions of the sculpted body are then turned into facts about the ancient Athenians. In the fifth century 'Athens was ruled,' Nigel Spivey writes, 'in image terms, by the muscular diktats of the fine male nude.'[2] But this was not just any male nude, this was the nude athlete. Faced with what he regards as 'the first beautiful nude in art' (2.1), Kenneth Clark not only thought he could see 'the eagerness with which the sculptor's eye has followed every muscle, or watched the skin stretch and relax as it passes over a bone' but linked the 'heightened sensuality' which this betrayed to Greek athletics.[3] Clark suggests that, unlike modern athletics, the Greek games were dominated by 'religious dedication and love' and that while they 'competed in almost the same poetical and chivalrous spirit' as medieval knights, 'all the pride and devotion which mediaeval contestants expressed through the flashing symbolism of heraldry was, in the games of antiquity, concentrated in one object, the naked body'.[4]

---

[1] A. Stewart (1990) 75, stressing that this 'approved physique' is a particular Athenian version, achieving more than local Athenian popularity only after 500.

[2] Spivey (1996) 39.

[3] Clark (1956) 29. This conceit is already in Winckelmann (1756) 4: 'Die schönste Körper unter uns ware vielleicht dem schönsten griechischen Körper nicht ähnlicher, als Iphicles dem Hercules, seinem Bruder, war. Der Einfluß eines sanften und reinen Himmels würste bei der ersten Bildung der Griechen, die frühzeitigen Leibesübungen aber gaben dieser Bildung die edle Form.' He goes on a page later to write 'Die Körper erhielten durch diese Uebungen den großen und männlichen Contour, welchen die griechischen Meister ihren Bildsäulen gegeben, ohne Dunst und überflüßigen Ansaß'. (But the suggestion of Charriére (Winckelmann (1991)) that Winckelmann claims a Greek painter to have alleged that his Theseus was 'élevé "au milieu des muscles"' is a fantasy; Winckelmann's expression is 'bei Fleisch erzogen', and Pliny's, from which this derives, 'dixit eundem apud Parrhasium rosa pastum esse, suum vero carne' (*Natural History* 35.129). Winckelmann did indeed share the modern muscular lens, but not here.)

[4] Clark (1956) 29.

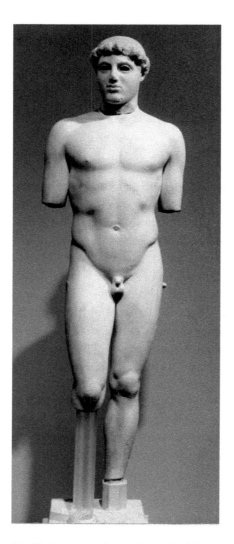

2.1 Votive statue of a youth, ascribed by modern scholars to the hand of the sculptor Kritios (cf. Fig. 4.3).

Clark's vision of the Greeks may now seem quaint, but for recent scholars too the athletic body of classical sculpture supports a much more general fantasy about the Greek world – the fantasy that it was a world obsessed with bodily fitness and mad about going to the gym.[5] 'No city', to quote Spivey again, 'could call itself a city if it lacked a gymnasium. Usually located

---

[5] This fantasy has been fuelled by the use of classical imagery in relation to modern body building: see Wyke (1999).

near the town baths, gymnasia were sociable places regularly visited by many citizens for the purpose of a daily "workout"' (though he goes on to mitigate 'the impression of fanatical attachment to physical culture' by noting that the gymnasium and palaestra doubled as a place of intellectual activity).[6] Rosa Proskynitopoulou, writing a catalogue entry for an exhibition 'Mind and Body: Athletic Contests in Ancient Greece', suggested that 'Every young man in Athens exercised his body and cultivated his mind as part of a daily routine designed to make him into a clean-limbed, virtuous citizen and a credit to his city.'[7]

These scholars are taking the visual evidence and plotting that onto the world classified by texts, the world of muscles, of the cult of bodily fitness, and of the gym. But the 'texts' that support this world are not ancient texts. A fantasy world is conjured up by mixing together elements of textual descriptions of the ancient with the categories promoted in textual description of the modern world. The dangers of assuming that the ancient world, or any world, is adequately described by its texts do not justify describing the world in ways that ignore or contradict the evidence of contemporary texts. And this picture of a universal ancient gym culture is one that the historical evidence provided by ancient texts does not support.

The most recent discussion of athletic participation in Athens concludes that 'athletics remained an exclusive pursuit of the wealthy'.[8] Although the fifth-century pamphlet on *The Constitution of the Athenians* attributed to Xenophon does indeed observe that the Athenian people (the *dēmos*, a word covering the people as a whole and also in particular the lower classes) had built themselves palaestras and undermined elite monopoly of the activities of the gymnasium by giving public support to athletes, the practical obstacles which stood in the way of impoverished Athenians learning athletic skills or accessing regular athletic training were enormous.[9] It is telling that Aischines says that his father Atrometos was an athlete *before the war destroyed his property*.[10] There has to be some truth behind claims in epigrams that fish-porters won Olympic victories and the grumbles that we get in some texts about the success of low-born athletes, but elite domination of the gymnasium was never threatened.[11] Concern to find justification for

---

[6] Spivey and Squire (2004) 27. Young (2004) 83 shows that 'the image of the Greek intellectual athlete proves to be pure myth, and a pernicious one'.

[7] Tzachou-Alexandri (1989) 135.   [8] Pritchard (2003) 332.

[9] [Xenophon] *Constitution of the Athenians* 1.13, 2.10.

[10] Aischines 2.147, and cf. Plato, *Protagoras* 326c.

[11] Fish-porter: Aristotle, *Rhetoric* 1365a26–7 (explicitly exceptional); grumbles: Isokrates 16.33–4. Cf. Kyle (1987) 150 'Although public gymnasia and civic rewards could help reduce the social

modern calls for universal physical education as a way to achieve a cultural distinction to rival that of the ancient Greeks has led to claims about athletics in antiquity that constitute merely wishful thinking.

Alongside this fantasy that every man was an athlete, there is a further suggestion made by these scholars, that the body we see in classical sculpture is a body that has been developed by specific training. Spivey sees the Kritian boy's beauty as specific to the runner: 'With his diaphragm filled, the figure may well be that of a sprinter, whose passing success has been caught forever in marble.'[12] Elsewhere he suggests that 'Greek athletes knew about the muscle-building process which modern weight-trainers term "progressive resistance"', and that sculptors were so fascinated by the muscular developments – 'the reality of a well-muscled torso, complete with six-fold corrugations at the abdomen and that distinctive ridge marking the juncture of thighs and midriff which is known anatomically as the iliac crest' – that they witnessed in the gymnasium that they imagined these developments going well beyond the physically possible.[13]

But were the classical Greeks, in Spivey's terms, 'body fascists'?[14] Did they have an obsession with the particular physical appearance which betokened a particular regime in the gymnasium or palaestra? Literary descriptions of the physical appearance of the male body are remarkably few and far between in any form of classical writing. Revealingly, the fullest descriptions that we get are preserved by the late second-century AD author Athenaios, who in his *Teachers at Table* (*Deipnosophistai*) collected a vast number of quotations relating to food. And it is in a section on gluttony that he comes to discuss athletes and produces a quotation from Achaios of Eretria, a fifth-century BC author of tragedies performed in Athens, which gives us our best literary picture of the male body. Achaios describes athletes in good condition as 'naked-loined, they show off shining arms, swelling with youth, glistening with bloom as to their strong shoulders. They liberally anoint with oil their chests and the hollow of their shields like people brought up in luxury.'[15]

Achaios' description of the athletic body is not a neutral one. There is a definite tone of criticism in the final words of the quotation with their allegation of luxury. This is a reminder that – to the benefit of the

exclusiveness of athletics, prosopography indicates that athletes prior to the rise of patronage [first attested *c.* 300 BC] probably became athletes with the help of familial resources.' Kyle reviews the prosopographic evidence at length at 102–23.

[12] Spivey (2005) 73.   [13] Spivey (1996) 39–40.

[14] Spivey (1996) 39. Compare Fisher (1998) 213 'the all-male atmosphere of the gymnasia and the games, which went with something approaching a cult of the nude male body'.

[15] Athenaios 414d.

historian – every description of the body will be ideologically charged. But it is also an indicator that the gymnasium and what went on there was not universally admired. Further, and still stronger, evidence of that comes in this same section of Athenaios' work, where he records much more critical sentiments about the uselessness of athletes and the inappropriateness of cities rewarding athletic victors.

Athenaios quotes an early fifth-century philosopher, Xenophanes of Kolophon, complaining that athletic victors are looked up to when in fact he, Xenophanes, is more valuable to the community than they, since no athlete can make the city enjoy better government (*eunomia*).[16] More tellingly he also quotes a passage from the *Autolycus*, a satyr play by the Athenian tragedian Euripides, in which the tribe of athletes is declared the worst of all evils in Greece. Athletes, this passage goes on, are slaves to their appetites, unable to endure poverty and addicted to habits that are not admirable.[17] These criticisms are important not because they reflect general beliefs, but because the critics show no sign that they feel the need to counter a belief that the athletic body is a positive asset in its own right. When a classical author identifies the training of the body which makes a person fit for 'those things which belong to a free man', that training is provided not by the gymnasium but by the farm.[18]

The criticisms quoted by Athenaios can be paralleled in texts from the seventh century BC onwards.[19] These texts confirm that offering civic rewards to athletes was a practice standard in Greek cities, but to admire and reward athletic success is a different matter from admiring the athlete for his physical development.[20] Admiring the beauty of those engaged in athletics does not itself show that athletic activity was taken to be the way to produce the admirable body, and particularly when athletics offered the prime context for the display of the body naked.

It is undeniable that ancient Greeks in general, and Athenians among them, admired the beauty of young men in the gymnasium and palaestra, and admired it enough to make it central to their visual culture. Archaic Athenian grave stelai had offered only two sorts of identifying markers for those represented on reliefs. On the one hand there are elements of armour and weapons that pick out the soldier, and on the other there are discuses, oil flasks and the bound hands of boxers. From the end of the sixth century it

[16] Athenaios 413f–414c; Xenophanes fr. 2 Diels–Kranz.   [17] Euripides fr. 282 N; Athenaios 413c–f.
[18] Xenophon, *Household Management* 5.1. The things that belong to a free man turn out to include serving as a soldier, hunting, and running, throwing and jumping.
[19] Cf. Tyrtaios 12.1–14; Diogenes Laertios 1.55; Eupolis 129 Kassel–Austin.
[20] Kurke (1993).

became customary for victors, particularly at Olympia, to dedicate statues of themselves as athletes.[21] These statues were, to judge from surviving bases, mainly of bronze and more or less life-sized. But, as R. R. R. Smith has noted, 'Unlike Hellenistic and later representations, fifth-century victor statues do not have strongly athletic specific body styles – either, for example, as wrestler versus runner, or even as athlete versus hero. They tend to have a monumentally structured body architecture that speaks to the symbolic ideological aspects of the best body.'[22]

But what exactly was the ideologically 'best body'? Smith's own description of the 'best body' as 'hard, disciplined, well-ordered, balanced, strong' reveals already just how these ideological aspects belong to the eye of the modern beholder. A body may show the effects of exercise, but could anything about a body itself show that those who created it and who viewed it at the time of its creation saw 'discipline' there? So too, when Smith goes on to claim that 'the point of reference for "best" was not art or some idea of beauty in the sky but the best real trained and muscle-styled bodies', we may reasonably ask what his evidence is for this.[23]

Smith himself deploys what is by far the best literary evidence we have for the ancient ideology of the athletic body, the evidence from the early fifth-century poetry of Pindar in praise of athletic victors. Contemporary with these early victor statues, we could not ask for a better witness than Pindar to what the Greeks saw in athletic victors and in the athletic body. As Smith is able to show, Pindar repeatedly draws attention to the labour and toil (*ponos* and *mochthos*) required to achieve victory.[24] But when it comes to what that labour does for the body, Pindar is far from explicit. Strepsiadas in *Isthmian* 7 is 'awesome in strength and handsome to behold'; Epharmostos in *Olympian* 9 'in season' (i.e. young) and beautiful (*kalos*) and, like Aristokleidas in *Nemean* 3, his beauty of form matches the beauty of his deeds.[25] But what features of bodily appearance constitute beauty is never made apparent. The most explicit praise relates closely to the achievement of victory – limbs are nimble or bold, and athletes are marked by strength and

---

[21] Rausa (1994) 85–110; Smith (2007) 94–120, 137–9.   [22] Smith (2007) 108.

[23] Smith (2007) 109. The dangers of reading off ancient statues is well seen by comparing surviving bronze athlete statuettes from the early fifth century, such as Smith illustrates in his figures 17, 18 and 23; nothing about their bodies justifies the claim that in the Roman copy known as the Ludovisi diskobolos 'The muscles are an aggressive display of hard athletic training (*ponos*) in the manner of the 470s' (Smith (2007) 122, caption to fig. 24).

[24] Smith (2007) 110, citing Pindar, *Olympian* 6.12, 10.22; *Pythian* 8.73; *Nemean* 5.48; *Isthmian* 3.18, 5.57.

[25] *Isthmian* 7.22, where the word used for body (*phuē*) stresses not looks or the effects of training but natural endowment; *Olympian* 9.94; *Nemean* 3.19.

daring.[26] Of the various qualities Smith attributes to the bodies of athletic statues, Pindar justifies 'strong' and 'trained' (the trainer appears in *Nemean* 5 as the craftsman of the athlete),[27] but 'hard' and 'disciplined' are modern projections from the talk of labour, and there is no Pindaric justification at all for 'well-ordered', for 'balanced' or for 'muscle-styled'.[28]

If the terms in which Pindar describes athletes offer no support for the view that the body most admired was the body developed through athletic activity, do the terms in which classical writers describe the sculpted body support that view? One of the stories of Sokrates' visits to craftsmen told by Xenophon in *Memoirs of Socrates* (*Memorabilia*) concerns precisely a visit to a sculptor of athletic statues.[29] Sokrates compliments Kleitias on how lifelike (*zōtikos*) his figures are, and suggests to him that he achieves this by imitating the form (*eidos*) of living persons. In particular, he suggests, the statues become persuasive in as far as something very like the true likeness is captured of the way in which poses struck (*schēmata*) cause parts of the body to be pulled this way and that, stretched, and relaxed or made tense (*enteinomena, aniemena*). Modern translators sometimes feel compelled to make explicit where this tension lies. So E. C. Marchant in the Loeb Classical Library translates the passage as: 'Then is it not by accurately representing the different parts of the body as they are affected by the pose – the flesh wrinkled or tense, the limbs compressed or outstretched, the muscles taut or loose – that you make them look more like real members and more convincing?' But Xenophon does not specify which parts of the body are subject to what sort of pulling or compression, and he offers no reason for going beneath the surface of taut or relaxed skin. That a sculptor shows awareness of the way in which the body changes its shape under the influence of athletic activity does not demand that the physiological processes at work are identified.

It is time to return to the palaestra and look closely at the bodies that are admired there. Plato provides two memorable scenes of admiration for the beautiful body in the palaestra in his dialogues *Charmides* and *Lysis*. In *Charmides* Sokrates is imagined just back from serving with the Athenian

---

[26] *Olympian* 9.96, 111; *Pythian* 2.56, 5.110, 8.37; *Nemean* 1.25, 5.39, 7.59; *Isthmian* 4.4.

[27] But not, despite Smith's claim, explicitly of the athlete's body. The word I translate as 'craftsman', *tekton*, is the word for a joiner or carpenter.

[28] Smith (2007) 133 similarly attributes to the Motya Charioteer 'discipline, poise, hard work, good breeding'; his attempt to find 'muscle development' and description of the 'prominent backside' as 'hard' (p. 132; cf. 'expensively trained muscle-development', p. 135) seems to me particularly fantastic.

[29] Xenophon, *Memoirs of Socrates* 3.10.

army at Poteidaia. He goes along to the palaestra of Taureas, is greeted enthusiastically and, having told of his own adventures, asks about news at Athens, news about philosophy and news about the young men. An answer to the last question is pre-empted by the arrival of young men known to hang around the most beautiful of them all, who then himself duly enters. Sokrates claims to find all young men beautiful, but when Charmides comes in view he is duly amazed by his stature and beauty, and notices that Charmides turns the heads of young boys as well as of men 'as if they had seen a statue (*agalma*)'. An opportunity is shortly manufactured for Sokrates to sit beside Charmides, and at that point he is set alight by seeing inside Charmides' cloak (*himation*) and experiences wild desire for him.[30]

In *Lysis*, set in a newly built palaestra, at issue is not Sokrates' passions but those of Hippothales for Lysis. Hippothales' companions complain that Hippothales wearies them by always talking about Lysis, by the poems and prose he writes about him, and by the songs that he sings, badly, about him. Sokrates has not heard of Lysis, although Hippothales assures him that Lysis' father is well known, but Hippothales expects that Sokrates will know Lysis' appearance (*eidos*): 'he can be recognised by that alone'.[31] Sokrates does not want to hear Hippothales' poems and songs but wants to know what their substance is. They turn out to be praise of Lysis' family and their wealth. Sokrates objects that it is silly to praise like this someone whose love one is still trying to win, since such praises will only make them more vain, and harder to catch. When Sokrates catches sight of Lysis himself he describes him as worth talking about not only for being beautiful (*kalos*) but for being noble (*kaloskagathos*).[32]

The descriptions in these dialogues are as remarkable for what they do not say as for what they do. We are given the impression of stunning beauty not so much through description of the beautiful body as through description of the effect that it has on others.[33] What is more, the descriptions of beauty show no interest in connecting beauty with the activities of the palaestra or gymnasium. The palaestra provides the setting for these dialogues, as a place in which young men who are desirable and desired are to be found, but at no point is there any suggestion that athletic activities have had any role in making these bodies beautiful. Charmides had 'no bad appearance' even as a child, and Hippothales' love of Lysis turns as much upon who he is, his family and noble demeanour, as it does upon his physique. When a model of beauty is required, it is not some legendary athletic hero who is

---

[30] *Charmides* 153a–155b.   [31] *Lysis* 204e6.
[32] *Lysis* 207a2–3.   [33] I return to this question in Chapter 7, below (p. 188).

invoked, but rather a statue – perhaps particularly, given that the term used is *agalma*, 'thing of delight', a statue of a god.[34] Not only is this welcome confirmation that the bodies of men and the bodies of statues were treated by classical Greek viewers as to be assessed in parallel terms, it emphasises that it is a particular appearance that is aimed at, not the inscribing onto the body of the evidence of athletic endeavours.

Greeks were not ignorant that the activities of the gymnasium changed the body not just temporarily but over the medium to long term. Athletic activity is often represented either as a way for the body to become able to do things it could not normally do, or associated with general 'good condition' (*euexia*). But athletics is not presented as a way to make the body beautiful.[35] It becomes commonplace to link athletics and medicine. In *Gorgias* Plato suggests that athletic trainers and doctors are the best at knowing whether a body is in good condition.[36] In the *Republic* Plato distinguishes the sort of athletic activity which the musician will engage in, with a view to keeping fit and promoting the spirited element of his soul, from the sort of athletic labours and diet which aim to produce strength, before proceeding to suggest that the main effect of athletic activity, as of music, is on the soul – music softens and the gymnasium hardens the soul.[37] When the author of *On Ancient Medicine* notes that those in charge of athletic activities and training are constantly making discoveries, it turns out that their discoveries are about cause rather than effect. The discoveries concern 'what food and drink are best digested and make a man stronger', not the development of a particular physical appearance.[38] Elsewhere in the Hippokratic writings it is striking to find that what doctors think brings

---

[34] On *agalma* in the archaic period see R. Osborne (1994) 90; for classical use of *agalma* see Stroud and Lewis (1979) 193 and nn. 23 and 24. For the idea that if you want real beauty you should look not at a real body but at a statue, compare Alkidamas, *On the Sophists* 28.

[35] If banishing ugliness were tantamount to creating beauty then one passage which might suggest an association between athletics and beauty would be Plato, *Sophist* 229a1, where *gumnastikē* is said to deal with ugliness (*aischos*) in the body, medicine with illness. Plato is here attempting to make the problems and treatments of the body parallel to the problems and treatments of the soul, and modern commentators have had some difficulty in deciding what he means by ugliness, which is the equivalent of ignorance in the soul, which is further glossed, presumably in an attempt to make the parallel work, as *ametria* (*Sophist* 228a–c).

[36] *Gorgias* 464a3–6. Cf. *Protagoras* 313d4.

[37] Plato, *Republic* 410b–d; cf. 403c–404c. In the *Republic* 410b Plato uses two words for the strength that the athlete aims at, *ischus* and *rōmē*, neither of which have particular reference to any part of the body, but older translators could not resist translating one or both terms as 'muscles' (Jowett, Shorey) or 'muscular strength' (Cornford). More recent translators (Grube, Waterfield) go for 'physical strength' or 'physical fitness'. The body fascists arrive with Griffith, who talks of 'improving their physique'.

[38] *On Ancient Medicine* 4.2.

athletic bodies into good condition is barley gruel – hardly the food of body-builders.[39]

Classical writers not only show no very clear understanding of how athletics affects the body but are often straightforwardly critical of the condition which athletics and athletic trainers promote. The 'good condition' (*euexia*) which is a recognised product of the gymnasium is nevertheless, taken to extremes, a treacherous condition. According to the author of *Aphorisms* 1

Such conditions cannot remain the same or be at rest, and, change for the better being impossible, the only possible change is for the worse. For this reason it is an advantage to reduce the fine condition quickly, in order that the body may make a fresh beginning of growth. But reduction of flesh must not be carried to extremes, as such action is treacherous; it should be carried to a point compatible with the constitution of the patient.[40]

Aristotle in the *Nicomachean Ethics* talks of due measure both in medicine and in athletic training, and he suggests that extremes of bodily condition are regarded as something that both should properly avoid.[41]

The closest we come to anything that might be called 'body fascism' is in a passage of Plato's *Gorgias*. Sokrates here contrasts cooking to medicine and bodily adornment to athletics. Bodily adornment (*kommōtikē*) is declared deceitful and ignoble and slavish, misleading by shapes and colours and smoothness and clothing 'so as to make people neglect their proper (*oikeios*) beauty, the beauty through athletics, as they seek out an alien beauty'.[42] There is a clear implication here that athletic activity is the proper way to produce the body beautiful. But it is notable that the body beautiful that is produced is marked by colour, shape and smoothness. Cosmetics can produce results that look like the results of athletics only because we are not dealing here with body-building, but with getting a body into good condition. The point is not to develop any particular body type, but rather to make one's body look to be in top condition.

The association between youthful beauty and athletics in Aristotle's *Rhetoric* is even more telling. Starting from the position that excellence of the body is health, Aristotle maintains that 'beauty varies with time of life' and then explains that 'In a young man beauty is the possession of a body fit to endure the exertion of running and of contests of strength; which

---

[39] *Acute Diseases* 9, 39.21–40.1.
[40] *Aphorisms* 1.3. Compare Xenophon, *Memoirs of Socrates* 3.5.13, where the athlete who has lost top condition is likened to Athenians who have similarly neglected themselves and become worse.
[41] *Nicomachean Ethics* 1096a31–4, 1106b1–5, 1138a29–31.   [42] Plato, *Gorgias* 465b3–6.

means that he is pleasant to look at; and therefore all-round athletes are the most beautiful, being naturally adapted both for contests of strength and for speed also.'[43] The telling point here is that it is beauty that makes a man suitable for athletics, and athletic success that is proof of beauty, not athletics that makes him beautiful.[44]

The medical writers' body

The more general discussions of the male body in the medical writers show that medical conceptions of bodily good condition make no contact with the activities of the gymnasium. Most of the copious Hippokratic writings of various dates from the fifth to the third century BC, collected under the name of Hippokrates of Kos, himself a fifth-century figure, are much more concerned with the interior make-up of the human body than with the exterior. Typical is the claim made in *On the Nature of Man*:

The body of man has in itself blood, phlegm, yellow bile and black bile; these make up the nature of his body, and through these he feels pain or enjoys health. Now he enjoys the most perfect health when these elements are duly proportioned to one another in respect of compounding, power and bulk, and when they are perfectly mingled. Pain is felt when one of these elements is in defect or excess, or is isolated in the body without being compounded with all the others.[45]

Such a claim about human physiology could not be translated directly or straightforwardly into recommendations for how to live and has no obvious implications for the appearance of the body.

Even when writers address themselves directly to issues of appearance or physique, they limit their interest to flesh colour and whether the body is hard or soft, linking this to 'dry' or 'moist' constitutions.[46] The key terms here concern flesh, colour and consistency – ruddy, dark, soft, fleshy, lean,

---

[43] Aristotle, *Rhetoric* 1361b3–12 (trans. Rhys Roberts).

[44] Similarly Aristotle goes on to observe that 'athletic excellence of the body consists in size, strength and swiftness; swiftness implying strength' (1361b21–2), where strength and size are preconditions for athletic success, not athletic activity a way of developing strength or size.

[45] *On the Nature of Man* 4.

[46] Cf. *On Regimen in Health* 2 (trans. W. H. S. Jones, adapted) 'Those with appearances (*eidos*, that which is seen) that are fleshy, soft and red, find it beneficial to adopt a rather dry regimen for the greater part of the year. For the nature of these physiques is moist. Those that are lean and harsh, whether ruddy or dark, should adopt a moister regimen for the greater part of the time, for the bodies of such are constitutionally dry. Young people also do well to adopt a softer and moister regimen, for this age is dry, and young bodies are firm. Older people should have a drier kind of diet for the greater part of the time, for bodies at this age are moist and soft and cold.'

harsh.[47] Even when the effect of running on the body is discussed, it is in terms of moistness and dryness producing softness and hardness:

This kind of running [i.e. running in a cloak] is beneficial to those who have a dry body, to those who have excess of flesh which they wish to reduce, and, because of the coldness of their bodies, to those who are getting on in years. The double course, with the body exposed to the air, dissolves the flesh less, but reduces the body more, because the exercises, being concerned with the inner parts of the soul, draw by revulsion the moisture out of the flesh, and render the body thin and dry.[48]

It is not easy to translate this abstract discussion into visible physical consequences. But we are helped here by the treatise on *Airs, Waters, Places.* This treatise is concerned with the effects of the environment on the human constitution, and it accounts for the different appearance of the peoples of different lands by the prevailing climatic conditions. In the course of this we find descriptions of the effect of wetness and dryness on physical appearance, and it turns out that they manifest themselves primarily in the nature of the flesh. This is particularly clear in the description of the Skythians:

Their appearances (*eidea*) are gross, fleshy, showing no joints, moist and flabby, and the lower bowels are as moist as bowels can be. For the belly cannot possibly dry up in a land like this, with such a nature and such a climate, but because of their fat and the smoothness of their flesh their appearances (*eidea*) are similar, men's to men's and women's to women's.[49]

Moistness is here seen as responsible for making the body swell, become fat and smooth. And one observation here is particularly significant: the fleshy body, the author notes, shows no joints, it is visibly inarticulate.

Articulation was something with which both medical and other writings were much concerned. There is a very long (87-chapter) Hippocratic treatise entirely on joints, concerned with possible dislocations and methods of putting them right. Once more there turns out to be a link between fleshiness and bodily articulation. The author observes that when joints become dislocated they can be relocated more quickly in fleshless people than in those who are well-fleshed. Similarly, inflammation happens less in moist and fleshless than in hard and enfleshed, but in that case the joint is less tight subsequently.[50] Modern translators have sometimes translated 'well-fleshed' as 'well-muscled', but in fact muscles play little part in the story

---

[47] The term I have translated as 'harsh' is translated by Jones as 'sinewy', but there is no allusion to sinews in the Greek.

[48] *On Regimen* 2.63.   [49] *Airs, Waters, Places* 19.   [50] *On Joints* 8.

in this treatise. The author knows that there are such things as muscles and can refer, for example, to the part of the upper arm where the muscles are attached, but he gives muscles no active part in his story.[51] This is consistent with the generally small part which muscles have in Hippokratic medicine.

There was one Greek word used to differentiate muscles from all other body parts, the word *mus*. *Mus* is also the word for a mouse and a mussel, and it is applied to muscles because of their shape (at least the shape of the biceps). This word for muscles is used only twenty times in the whole corpus of Hippokratic writings.[52] The absence of use goes together with a lack of interest in what muscles do. At one point the Hippokratic treatise *On the Art* refers to 'such limbs as have rounded flesh, which they call muscle'.[53]

The lack of interest in the function of muscles is even more clearly revealed by the second word which is used to refer to them. This is the term *neura*. *Neura* is a term used not only to refer to muscles but also to refer to nerves, sinews, tendons, ligaments and cords.[54] That is, it is a term which identifies those elements of the body which are stringy in appearance. To use *neura* of a part of the body is to show no interest in its physiological role, and to name it simply for its stringy appearance.

Only once does a Hippokratic writer show any recognition that exercise affects muscles. This is in the treatise on nutrition, where it is noted that muscles are harder and less inclined to be flabby than other parts, except for bone and sinew, and that parts that are exercised are harder to change, becoming stronger than their own kind and so less inclined to flabbiness than their own kind would otherwise be.[55] The absence of more precise association between exercise and muscle development should be seen in part as consequential on the absence of understanding of the circulation of the blood. Although Greeks know, as the passage cited on running in a cloak shows, that running heats the body up, the connection between heartbeat, blood circulation and muscle use is quite unknown.

Since doctors are concerned primarily with the body of the patient who is at rest, it might seem unsurprising that they are more concerned with organs and with joints than they are with muscles. But when Aristotle gives

---

[51] *On Joints* 1.
[52] *In the Surgery* 11, 15; *On Fractures* 22, 35; *On Joints* 1, 30, 31, 45, 52, 57; *Instruments of Reduction* 1, 4, 23; *Aphorisms* 7.36; *Koan Prognosis* 26.471, 29.498; *On Diseases* 1.3; *On the Art* 10; *On Nutriment* 51; *On the Nature of Bones* 16; compared with 460 mentions of muscles in the plural in Galen; see Kuriyama (1999) 129. Galen suggests that serious study of muscles began in the first century AD with Marinus. The development of dissection clearly played a part in this.
[53] *On the Art* 10.   [54] Cf. Craik (1998) 116–18.
[55] *On Nutriment* 51. The term that I have translated 'less inclined to flabbiness' is a term meaning literally 'harder to melt' (*dustēktōteros*) used only here in the Hippokratic writings.

an account of how animals move he too manages to do so without involving muscles at all: in his treatise *On the Movement of Animals* he compares animals to puppets and identifies the bones of animals as like the wooden levers in puppets, and the sinews as like the strings.[56]

When a body displays what we might describe as soft or weak muscles, Greek texts generally describe it as jointless. So in Sophokles' *Women of Trachis* when Herakles is consumed by the poisoned robe he contrasts his previous prowess and achievements to his current state of being jointless.[57] Similarly, at the beginning of Euripides' *Orestes* when Orestes is lying sick he describes himself as 'jointless and weak in limbs'.[58] This notion of the inarticulate body was a particularly resonant one, for the term *arthron* was applied not simply to what we would call joints but to any distinct part of the body, including the eyes, mouth, genitals and internal organs.[59] It was also applied beyond the body to the structure and articulation of language. Xenophon has Sokrates discuss the way in which the tongue 'gives joints to' sounds, and connecting words, particularly the article, came to be known as 'joints'.[60] Aristotle compares infants' inability to control their limbs generally with their inability to control their tongue, and he goes on to talk about the distinct sounds made by different animals as a matter of articulated voice ('the voice in joints').[61]

The sculpted body

Modern scholars who look at classical sculpture and see well-developed musculature are not imagining things.[62] The bodily forms which modern

---

[56] Aristotle, *On the Movement of Animals* 7 701b2–10. Compare discussion of sinews at *History of Animals* 3.5 515a27–b26.

[57] Sophokles, *Women of Trachis* 1103.

[58] Euripides, *Orestes* 228. West's decision to translate the line as 'I am limbless, I have no strength in my body' (where 'body' translates *melē*), is incomprehensible to me.

[59] Eyes: Sophokles, *Oedipus the King* 1270; mouth: Euripides, *Cyclops* 625; genitals: Herodotos 3.87, Aristotle, *History of Animals* 504b23; internal organs: Mnesitheus at Oribasios 8.38.7.

[60] Xenophon, *Memoirs of Socrates* 1.4.12; connecting words: Aristotle, *Poetics* 1457a6: an *arthron* 'is a non-significant sound which makes clear the beginning of an utterance, its end or its dividing-point, and which by nature is placed both at the extremities and in the middle, e.g. "or", "because", "but"' (trans. Janko); article: *Rhetoric to Alexander* 1435a35.

[61] *History of Animals* 536b5–8 for infants; 536b10–12 for animals.

[62] Nor are those who look at classical sculpture and see veins. But I am sceptical whether this implies interest in medical discussions of veins and arteries such as appear in *On the Nature of Man* 11 (note the absence of any indication of veins on painted pottery). For claims that there is a link between medical and philosophical discussions of blood, and indeed medical and philosophical discussions of respiration, about which I am even more sceptical, and the appearance of fifth-century sculpture, see Métraux (1995) 43–68.

scholars identify as muscles are indeed represented in classical sculpture. But the presence of contours on the sculpted body that correspond to muscles in the body of a man does not mean that the sculptor thought in terms of muscles. Even when a sculptor shows muscles in a state of development unlikely to have been achieved other than by those engaging in the artificial exercise of the gymnasium, it does not mean that such bodily forms were identified as what athletic activity was supposed to produce.

All our ancient literary evidence suggests that classical Greek viewers did not see *muscular* development either on the bodies in the gymnasium or on the sculpted body. They saw something quite different. They saw some bodies that were glistening, others not; some that looked hard, some soft; some that were well articulated, with joints easy to distinguish, and some that lacked joints. They saw flesh that was soft or hard, more like the flesh they associated with women or more like that they associated with men. If they had some acquaintance with medical writings they might translate these sights into views about whether the body was moist or dry. Colour, consistency of flesh and clarity of joints, these are what for classical Greeks was written on the body, whether the living body in the gymnasium or palaestra or the sculpted body in sanctuary or cemetery.

For all the stress that modern scholars have laid upon the musculature of the sculpted body of the classical period, it is not in the emphasis given to the muscular structure that classical sculpture differs from archaic sculpture. As Ridgway has observed, Attic kouroi of the archaic period, though not those of other regional traditions, already articulate the body according to the scheme of human musculature.[63] What is different about early classical sculpture is that the representation of the body in new and markedly asymmetrical poses draws attention to the way in which the body shape responds to stance by representing asymmetrical stretching.[64] Those trained in modern anatomy can examine, for example, the later copies of the *Doryphoros* of Polykleitos (2.2) and find there a representation of individual muscles, accurate for the position adopted.[65] This says much for Polykleitos' observation of the human physique, but it does not mean that either Polykleitos himself or a contemporary Greek viewer would describe the *Doryphoros'*

---

[63] Ridgway (1977) 54: 'In fact, Attic kouroi alone display structural coherence and definite interest in musculature. All other kouroi present abstract renderings of anatomical forms which may pass for natural but are rather simplifications of more or less convincing stylizations of the human body.'

[64] Whether this observation is dependent upon the philosophical theories of Anaxagoras, as Métraux (1995) ch. 4, esp. 74–5, suggests, I doubt.

[65] So above all Leftwich (1995). On Polykleitos' work more generally see Borbein (1999). I shall return to the *Doryphoros* in Chapter 3.

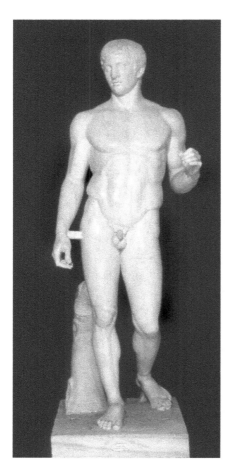

2.2 Roman copy identified as of the *Doryphoros* ('Spear-carrier') of the classical Greek sculptor Polykleitos. From Pompeii.

body, any more than they would have described the body of a kouros, in terms of muscles.

We do not know whom, specifically, Polykleitos' *Doryphoros* represented, though it has sometimes been suggested that it was taken in antiquity to be Achilles.[66] The name 'spear-carrier' implies that the figure is a warrior, but if the spear is a javelin he becomes an athlete. To create a specifically athletic body required evoking the particular attributes or actions of the athlete.[67] In the case of Polykleitos' *Diadoumenos* it is the binding of the ribbon round

---

[66] Achilles is an inference from Pliny, *Natural History* 34.18, see Stewart (1990) 160; on the question of the relation of the *Doryphoros* to Polykleitos' *Kanon*, see Pucci (2005).

[67] Cf. Ridgway (1977) 53–4; Smith (2007) 107.

2.3 Copy identified as of the *Diadoumenos* ('Athlete crowning himself') of the classical Greek sculptor Polykleitos. From Delos.

his head and the slightly down-turned gaze, not his muscles, that mark him as an athlete. Bodily forms were not enough to identify the athlete – because there was no obsession with the gym-fit body – and the distinctly different bodies of *Doryphoros* and *Diadoumenos* (2.3), already remarked upon by Pliny, reinforce this point.[68] The forms with which the sculpted body was endowed, whether in the fifth century or in the fourth, did not invoke the gymnasium through displaying some particular development of the body. Not for nothing has it been not the lean body but the 'nervous energy' of the Lysippan 'Agias' that, together with his pose, has caused viewers to see there 'the fighter keyed-up and tense'.[69] The classical sculpted body offers a rich mixture of surface features (including traces of what we would

---

[68] Pliny, *Natural History* 34.55, quoted below, p. 116 (Ch. 4).
[69] The phrases are from Stewart (1990) 187. For Lysippos' leaner ('sicciora') bodies see Pliny, *Natural History* 34.65.

identify as veins as well as of what we would identify as muscles)[70] which
will have impressed viewers variously according to the wealth or poverty of
the viewers' own experiences.

The impression which the sculptors sought to give emerges most clearly,
perhaps, where modern scholars register failure. So while Polykleitos'
anatomical observations of the different parts of the body of the *Doryphoros*
seem to be accurate for a body standing in that position, scholars have noted
that the pose adopted by the statue is not one naturally assumed by human
bodies in real life: 'the pose is . . . not . . . strictly natural for either walking
or repose. In the tradition of a fifth-century natural philosopher or physi-
cian, Polykleitos has broken down the motor capabilities of the body into
a series of opposites for the purposes of schematic and clear exposition.'[71]
Particular observations of the male body are put together by Polykleitos into
an artificial construct; this is just one more piece of evidence that what mattered to him was getting the parts right, enabling individual observations to
be checked off by viewers against their general experience, not invoking the
precise circumstances. Temptations to see the Kritian boy as a sprinter are
as much to be resisted as are temptations to see in him a chivalrous spirit.
The classical sculpted body was indeed ideological, but the ideology was no
more that of current-day critics than it was that of Kenneth Clark.

Drawing on the body

Scholars' determination to find the muscular body is in many ways still
more marked in the case of the graphic art of painted pottery than in that
of sculpture. The rich reference that classical sculpture makes to the form
of the human body will always make it hard to know whether the features
represented held the significance for sculptor or viewer in antiquity that they
have for us today. We can dissect neither the smooth solidity of the marble
nor the tense surface of the bronze. And our own vision is irredeemably
clouded by the investment in the perfection of the classical body which
our own tradition has made for us. Classical sculpture certainly evokes the

---

[70] Cf. Ridgway (1997) 341 of the Antikythera youth: 'An anatomical study of the statue's veins and
tendons would be welcome, given our uncertainty about such renderings on the basis of
Roman copies.'

[71] Leftwich (1995) 47; cf. Ridgway (1981) 203–4: 'It is thus superfluous to ask whether the
Doryphoros is walking or standing: his pose is thoroughly artificial and only made to look
plausible; it is actually slightly uncomfortable, with the trailing leg too far displaced for proper
poise, yet elegant and convincing from an aesthetic point of view.'

experience of observing real bodies, but we need to juxtapose what we see to the categorisation drawn and written on the body in antiquity if we are to make claims about how the Greeks themselves might describe the nature of that experience. The drawings on painted pottery are in this respect a much richer source for how classical Greeks saw the body than are classical sculptures. For, rather than reproducing the body, drawings always select features to represent in order to give in just two dimensions the appearance of the body. That selective reference reveals not just what the eye observes, but what the brain has been culturally conditioned to see as crucial in making a human appear human or a Greek appear Greek.

As it happens, a great deal of attention has been devoted to the way in which pot painters render the human body because of its importance for the identification of artists' hands. One of the basic assumptions made by those identifying individual painters has been that they adopt a scheme for displaying the body which they then apply more or less without thinking: 'a peculiar system of renderings through which a certain conception of the human form found expression'.[72] That is, they adopt a formula for ears or clavicles or ankles and use that formula on any suitable occasion. So it is that the scholar most responsible for the classification of Athenian pottery according to painters' hands, (Sir) John Beazley, identified the painter whom we now call 'the Berlin Painter' (2.4, 2.5, 2.6) from the following features of his drawing of the human body:

I would draw attention to the bounding lines of the breasts, with the curvilinear triangle at the pit of the stomach; to the omission of the off clavicle; to the line of the hither clavicle, recurving at the pit of the neck without touching the median line of the breast; to the curved line which runs down from about half-way along the line of the clavicle, separating the shoulder and breast; to the smaller arc in the middle of the deltoid; to the indication of the trapezius between neck and shoulder; to the pair of curved lines on the upper right arm; to the projection of the wrist when the position of the hand requires it; to the two brown lines on the neck, indicating the sterno-mastoid; to the marking of the body between the lower boundary of the breast and the himation; to the form of the black lines indicating the ankle; to the pair of brown lines running from each ankle up the leg; to the forward contour of left leg and knee showing through the himation; in the himation, to the peaked folds on the left upper arm, the loose fold in the region of the navel, and the triangle where the inside of the garment shows at the shoulder.[73]

Two things are to be noted in this long description. The first is that Beazley finds very few occasions to refer to the musculature of the human

---

[72] Beazley (1922) 90.   [73] Beazley (1922) 76; compare Beazley (1911) 286–8.

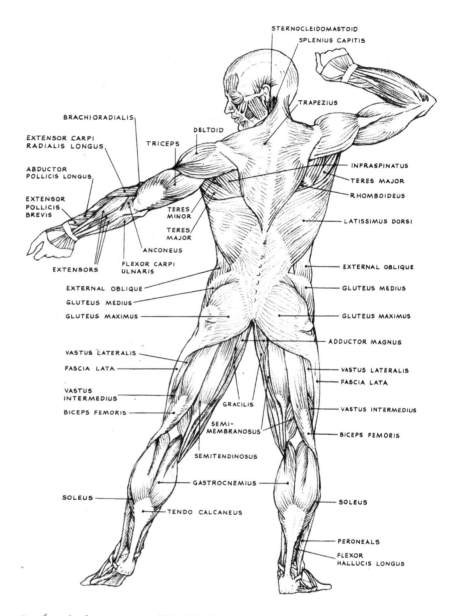

STERNOCLEIDOMASTOID
SPLENIUS CAPITIS

BRACHIORADIALIS
EXTENSOR CARPI
RADIALIS LONGUS
ABDUCTOR
POLLICIS LONGUS
EXTENSOR
POLLICIS
BREVIS
EXTENSORS
FLEXOR CARPI
ULNARIS
EXTERNAL OBLIQUE
GLUTEUS MEDIUS
GLUTEUS MAXIMUS
VASTUS LATERALIS
FASCIA LATA
VASTUS
INTERMEDIUS
BICEPS FEMORIS
SOLEUS

DELTOID
TRICEPS
TERES
MINOR
TERES
MAJOR
ANCONEUS

TRAPEZIUS

INFRASPINATUS
TERES MAJOR
RHOMBOIDEUS

LATISSIMUS DORSI

EXTERNAL OBLIQUE
GLUTEUS MEDIUS

GLUTEUS MAXIMUS

ADDUCTOR MAGNUS

VASTUS LATERALIS
FASCIA LATA

VASTUS INTERMEDIUS

BICEPS FEMORIS

GRACILIS
SEMI-
MEMBRANOSUS
SEMITENDINOSUS
GASTROCNEMIUS
TENDO CALCANEUS

SOLEUS

PERONEALS
FLEXOR
HALLUCIS LONGUS

2.4 Écorche figure in pose of Herakles from the Athenian red-figure amphora in Havana ascribed to the Berlin Painter.

body. The second is that the muscles involved are not the muscles of the muscular man. Of the three muscles referred to, one is merely a locator ('smaller arc in the middle of the deltoid'). The other two are muscles of the neck, the trapezius, the long muscle at the back of the neck, and the

2.5 Herakles from an Athenian red-figure hydria from Vulci, ascribed to the Berlin Painter, *c.* 480 BC. Colección Museo Nacional de Bellas Artes, Havana.

sterno-mastoid, the muscle at the front of the neck. So Kurtz, in developing Beazley's description, writes:

Two brown lines are standard in the neck of unbearded males (often omitted from bearded men on modest and late vases) for the surface reliefs of *TRAPEZIUS* posteriorly and *STERNOCLEIDOMASTOID* anteriorly. When the painter is careful, he varies the lines according to the position of the head, but usually he adds them mechanically.[74]

So was the Berlin Painter trying to conjure up the underlying musculature when he made the marks with which he articulates the body? Juxtaposition of figures drawn by the painter to images of bodies in the same position showing the muscles reveals no straightforward relationship. The major

[74] Kurtz (1983) 22.

2.6 Satyr from the Athenian red-figure amphora from Vulci after whom the Berlin Painter is named, *c.* 480 BC.

lines drawn by the painter do not correspond to muscles at all.[75] Take the back view of Herakles on an amphora in Havana (2.4, 2.5). Here lines indicate the outline of the shoulder blades and the top and bottom of the buttocks, but although the outline of the body might be held to reveal biceps and triceps (their contours much gentler than would be seen in a real-life arm in this position) and the muscles of lower and upper leg, no internal graphic indications of swelling muscles is offered. Where graphic

[75] Note that Kurtz, who thinks that we see in the Berlin Painter's figures the 'features visible to the sensitive eye of an artist watching active people who are both lean and muscularly well developed' (1983: 19), accounts for the lines that do not correspond to 'natural' features as follows: 'He is capable of observing natural forms closely and of reproducing them accurately, but he often chooses to distort them for artistic effect, in much the same way as he contrives drapery-folds to enliven contours', going on to observe (p. 33) that 'An ambitious design, carefully executed, tends to display the human body in unusual poses with anatomical features which are considerably more stylized than the standard renderings.'

indications of divisions of the body are very much greater (as with the
Satyr on the Berlin Painter's name-vase (2.6) or Herakles with the tripod
on an amphora in Würzburg), there is certainly some relationship between
the graphic traces and muscular contours. However, such correspondences
remain anything but systematic. The painter is not concerned to show
observed muscular contours but is attempting to make visual sense of the
structure of the body. Thus it is that on upper arm, forearm and shin, lines
are drawn that broadly correspond to the underlying bone structure. Across
the breast a line is drawn that marks off the hard breast from the soft belly;
that line corresponds to no anatomical feature at all but provides a means of
joining up lines which may reasonably be thought to mark the lower edges
of the two deltoid muscles of the shoulder in order to separate off the whole
upper body as a unit. The contouring supplied by muscles is one of the ways
of giving some three-dimensionality to the body, but it is not the defining
principle of what it is, in the Berlin Painter's view, to be a man.

One further indication that the Berlin Painter was not thinking in muscular terms is provided by what happens to some of the traits over time.
Kurtz notes that the 'pectoral triangle' at the base of the sternum, which
'reflects the surface reliefs of the well-developed male chest' is 'sacrificed
to expediency' in later pots. By contrast the 'pectoral fullness lines' parallel
to the sternum which 'indicate the fullness of the muscle' become straight
in late figures so that they are 'unintelligible to the eye which has not been
made familiar with the earlier rendering'.[76] Were such lines as these seen,
by either the painter or the contemporary viewers on whose satisfaction he
relied to sell his pots, as bearers of meaning with regard to the muscularity
of the body, it is hard to conceive that he could come to render these lines in
an unintelligible way without being thought to reduce his bodies to meaningless incoherence. Rather we should think of the Berlin Painter as having
developed a system of articulation of the body which mixes observation of
body surface and knowledge of the underlying bone structure. This is a system intended to produce recognition, not to reproduce the visible surface,
and accordingly the painter employs this system with scant regard for any
relationship to real bodies in particular positions.

I have taken the Berlin Painter as an example both because it is his
graphic work that has been most closely compared to anatomical drawings

---

[76] Kurtz (1983) 23. Note Kurtz here also on the line that demarcates chest from shoulder: 'this
DELTOID-EOPECTORAL LINE follows the furrow between *PECTORALIS MAJOR* and
DELTOID. Early it arises from the point of medial curvature in the *CLAVICLE*; later, as the
collar bone loses its curvature, the line drifts, as [the Zurich Apollo] where its original purpose
could not be imagined.'

by past scholars and because the detailed articulation of the body surface which he offers in some of his work provides the best chance to observe the relationship between this articulation and human musculature. But what I have observed of the Berlin Painter could be observed of any other Athenian pot painter: however detailed the articulation of the body that they offer, that articulation does not depict the muscular body.[77]

This point can be reinforced by looking at the representation of the body by artists in late Renaissance Italy. Sixteenth-century Italian drawings belong to an age when athletics and the naked athletic body had no part in contemporary society but when artists had been educated, ultimately by Galen, to gaze upon antique sculptures with eyes conscious of muscles. If we compare the legs of the satyr on the Berlin Painter's name-vase (2.6) with the legs of the Apollo Belvedere as drawn by Bandinelli in *c.* 1516–17 (2.7) the difference is striking.[78] By contrast to the satyr, Bandinelli's Apollo displays the clear outline, as well as the contours, of the various thigh muscles, the vastus medialis, sartorius, and rectus femoris, along with the muscles of the lower leg, the gastrocnemius and soleus. This difference is particularly striking given that Bandinelli is supposedly drawing a statue and that the statue in question, the Apollo Belvedere, is not itself one that puts any great emphasis on musculature. Like the Berlin Painter, Bandinelli has applied a scheme to the body that he is depicting. But for Bandinelli, as not for the Berlin Painter, anatomy has become a way of looking and his scheme is dominated by the muscular body.[79]

If we are wrong to think that what the Berlin Painter was seeing and depicting was the *muscular* body, we would be equally wrong to think that what he was seeing and depicting was either arbitrary or meaningless. The lines which he draws interpret the body in two ways. They give the body depth and they articulate it: this becomes a body with substance that can move. Some lines, such as the great curves of the shoulder-blades seen in the Herakles in Havana (2.5), both delimit the mobile unit of the upper arm and suggest something of the rounded contour of the shoulder. Similarly, on the same body, the outline of the right buttock is not at all in accordance with nature but ensures both that the hip is seen to be articulated and, as with the delineation of the left buttock also, that the roundedness of the flesh is conveyed. The line at the top of both buttocks corresponds neither to a line at which the body flexes nor to a contour but serves in the case of

[77] Compare Buitron-Oliver (1995) 89–98.
[78] Bandinelli, Milan Bibl. Ambr. F.269, inf. 108; see Bober and Rubinstein (1986) 71–2.
[79] Cf. J. Hall (2005).

2.7 Drawing of the so-called Apollo Belvedere by Bandinelli, *c.* 1516–17.

the right side to define the limit of the upper leg, and on the left it maintains consistency of articulation. The dark relief lines are particularly employed for crucial contours (the line of the shin) and for crucial articulations (the kneecap). The fainter lines serve frequently not just to suggest the third dimension (as with the curve of shin or thigh of the satyr) but to show the limits of a part of the body (as with lines extending the length of shin or of upper or lower arm, or with the central line of the torso or the outline of the divisions of the belly or the complex of lines that mark the ribcage). The painter is concerned to set his figures in action, to give the impression of movement, and this requires that we see the parts of the body at work and come to believe that this body could indeed sustain the action shown.

The painter engages the eye and the mind of the viewer in multiple ways. The lines with which painters articulate the bodies they draw are at the same time mimetic of the body, and of the way in which the body is conceptualised, and a means of rendering an impression of action and of character. For these lines contribute much to the power and energy, potential or being actualised, of the figures. Those curves of thigh and shin offer visual springs; the lines which extend along the lower or upper leg, or along the lower or upper arm, add tensile strength. Depiction of the muscles which we associate with energy is not required to energise these figures. The conceptualisation of the fit body as articulated, rather than as muscular, was not arbitrary, and the more the body shown by the artist offers clear visual divisions between its parts, the greater the impression that this body can be deployed in vigorous action.

As Beazley's catalogue of the graphic peculiarities which make up the Berlin Painter presupposes, the detailed way in which different artists drew the human body varied. But even regardless of the technical change from the flat silhouettes of black-figure to the heavy suggestion of a third dimension in the twisting figures of red-figure, the essentials of the depiction of the body do not vary. Regardless of exactly what lines artists choose to draw, it is articulation and contour that they offer, with knee caps and elbows rarely neglected and lines regularly extending the length of upper and lower arm, of thigh and shin. Shoulders attract curved lines, even at the cost of severing shoulder from arm, and long curving lines divide breast from belly and ribs. The top of the thigh is never allowed to fade into the torso without the intervention of a solid more or less horizontal line. And, when we have seen this, we can see that sculptors are doing exactly the same thing: their exaggerated iliac crests point not to obsessive athleticism but to conveying the impression of a well-articulated body, even at the expense of reproducing something not written on even the most athletic male body.

Bodies of thought

In the first half of this chapter I tried to show how the culture which some modern scholars have read off classical statues of the male nude was not a culture which could be read out of ancient texts. The well-articulated male bodies seen by the authors of ancient texts may make modern scholars think of young men training in the gym, of body builders and a cult of muscularity, but no ancient writer shows any inclination to think of the gym as a place for developing muscles, nor do they associate athletic activity with 'body-building'. Classical sculpture is indeed so richly referential to the contours of the body that we, the heirs of Renaissance artists, can find our gym-trained muscular bodies depicted there, but this does not mean that ancient viewers interpreted those contours in that way.

In the second half of the chapter I have tried to show that the more selective reference to bodily form conveyed by the lines which pot painters draw upon the naked male body cannot be understood in terms of desire to emphasise the musculature over and above any other physical attribute. Rather, those lines give both a structure to the body, picking up on features such as arm and leg bones which are known but not seen, and an impression of motion, and potential for motion, that makes sense of the story to which the figure is made to contribute.

These regularities within an individual painter's oeuvre and across the oeuvres of different painters show that we are not dealing with arbitrary marks, individually devised for the particular pose shown, but rather with a way of making sense of the body which is no less systematic for being ultimately based on the artist's personal choice. This systematic conception written by painters upon the classical Greek body warns us to be aware of what we are doing when we impose our own conceptualisations of the body upon the classical body. It also alerts us to the relationship between the theoretical understandings of the body found in medical writings and more popular conceptions of the body. To the soft and hard flesh described by the classical medical writers we can juxtapose the suggestions of more or less rounded contours. Against the medical writers' concern with joints we can place the emphasis on extent, and separation, of parts of the body. This does not make texts descriptions of the body as drawn on pots, nor pots the translation into line of the words of the doctors, but it alerts us to the role of cultural understandings of the body in shaping the way in which the visible body is seen and represented in both words and visual arts. What Bandinelli sees and draws on the body of the Apollo Belvedere is closely related to what the scholars with whom we started this chapter see and describe in their verbal accounts, but in neither case are they seeing what fifth-century viewers saw.

For all that writers and visual artists share a cultural understanding of the body, the seen body does not convey the same information as the body that is described in words. Even when writers and artists share a classificatory framework, the writer's classifications work differently from those of the artist. When writers talk of articulated or unarticulated bodies, of hard bodies and soft, dry bodies and moist, they are always slotting the body into a polar position in a table of opposites. But when the Berlin Painter, or any other artist, chooses to reveal a body as more or less articulated, or offer more or less rounded contours, the body depicted is neither absolutely 'articulated' nor absolutely 'inarticulate', neither absolutely 'hard' nor absolutely 'soft', but a body which offers itself to be read in dynamic relationship to the body imagined by this language in which hardness and softness, articulation and inarticulacy figure. What is more, not only is the body of the artist never simply soft or hard, articulated or inarticulated, it is always a body in action, doing something, engaged with other bodies or with a world of human activities. The artist works with conceptualisations which relate to the conceptualisations revealed in texts, but because the artist shows particular bodies in particular circumstances he or she never works with only one concept at a time, always with conceptualisations in context, in dialogue with one another. Texts may offer ideal types, placed in relationship to a grand classificatory grid, but visual arts must always respond with the particular body situated in a local action.

But if artists work with a situated body, the choice of situation is theirs. Just as the schemes which painters adopted for showing the physical body were themselves selected from a potentially limitless variety of ways of conveying the body's presence and action, so the situations which painters and sculptors chose to depict were also selected. And just as aspects of their schemes of depiction relate to the conceptual schemes deployed by writers, so too aspects of their choice of situation relate to the selection of categories into which writers choose to slot individuals. It is with how those visual and verbal selections relate to each other that the rest of this book is concerned, and I begin with the question of how artists chose to situate the body.

3 | The distinguished body

A figure approaches along the street. Do I know them? Can I pick out distinctive items of clothing, a familiar bag, a distinctive gait? No luck. But it is clearly a man. Middle-aged. Professional. Is that a face I know? Does he look as if he recognises me? Yes. We smile and pass.

Dozens of times a day we play out this drama, as we negotiate our daily routines. Some individuals we recognise easily, because they are familiar, because we expect them to be in a particular place at a particular time. Others we end up uncertain about, even when we have passed them by. Some confound us by giving a cheery greeting when we had assumed that we did not know them. Often because they are out of context. The former student now carrying the rolled umbrella. The colleague in tennis gear. Better not to reveal that we recognise that friend, given what he is up to now.

We divide our world between those we do know and those we do not. On the way to deciding whom we can put into which group we sort those we meet by gender, age, dress sense, race, the sort of occupation we think they must do, how fit they are, sexual orientation. All the forms of discrimination the law disapproves of are constantly in play, alongside those which the law itself flirts with, as we try to make sense of the world in which we live. Although in any particular case we may limit ourselves to placing a person in only some of these categories, the closer the dealings we find ourselves having, the more interested we become in locating people on all these sorts of axis.

Are such discriminations natural or cultural? Do all people everywhere ask the same questions of those they meet, seek to place them in the same sorts of categories? Or do some individuals or some societies concern themselves with some distinctions and others with quite different distinctions? My discussion of the way in which the human body was described and depicted in classical Greece, whether by writers or artists, already suggests that we should expect cultural distinctions to figure large. Classification by lifestyle does not depend upon the language of the muscular. But having muscular language surely affects predispositions to identify particular lifestyles.

My concern in subsequent chapters will be with those distinctions made in texts which are not visible, or not visible in the same way, on the seen or represented body. In that discussion I take my cues and my agenda from texts, with serious consequences for the nature and range of visual representation discussed.[1] But the importance of the distinctions made by language, but not in art, can be fully understood only if we are aware of the range and selection of representations that were offered by the visual arts, and of the ways in which painting and sculpture make their own distinctions. In this chapter I therefore begin by reversing the direction of my enquiry, starting by looking at those aspects of personal and group presentation which are signalled in painting and sculpture and then turning to texts to ask whether those visual priorities are also to be traced in texts. In doing so I reveal the limitations of my own enquiry: however much my analysis focuses on the visual, I can only express what I see there in words. The verbal categories not signalled visually are easy to point out in a text; the visual categories that cannot be expressed in words will always escape my text.

If my question is 'what distinguishes the visible body, any visible body?', my evidence is the only body visible to us, the sculpted and particularly the painted body. Understanding statues and pictures is not the same as understanding people, but the two are certainly related.[2] It is only by locating the figures they depict against the categories we employ to negotiate our way through life that images offer us illumination or guidance with regard to life. Even if a work of art enriches only our appreciation of the visual patterning of the world, it presupposes that visual patterning matters to us on a day-to-day basis – even if only as a source of pleasure. Of course individual sculptures or pictures may invite us to make particular discriminations, to class according to peculiar criteria, which may be in tension with prevailing ideologies. But my question here is: are there classifications which all or most images lay themselves open to, classifications which they can be reckoned to derive from the visual classifications of their flesh and blood referent? Which clues do artists expect invariably to provide about the human figures they represent, and which only variably?

[1] One only needs think about gender or class to see the limitations of the discussions that follow.

[2] In the early twenty-first century think only of the 'size zero' debate. For the particular issue of the relationship between female clothing as shown by pot painters and female clothing in real life, see Llewellyn-Jones (2002).

3.1 Athenian red-figure amphora found at Vulci ascribed to the Andokides Painter, *c.* 520 BC.

Distinguishing bodies in red-figure pottery

One of the earliest surviving pots painted in the red-figure technique is an amphora found at Vulci in Etruria and now in Berlin (3.1), which has been ascribed to the hand of the Andokides Painter.[3] On one side it shows Apollo

---

[3] *ARV* 3.1, Berlin Staatliche Museen 2159. The eventual deposit of this and the other pots discussed here in Etruria raises the question of whether the artist painted to communicate with a non-Greek society and whether the prime viewers should be thought of as sharing in a culture different to that which we know from classical Greek texts. Although there are certainly some pots and some potters who tried especially to attract Etruscan buyers, the evidence which I and Reusser have both assembled elsewhere suggests that these were exceptional cases, and that most Athenian pottery which ended up in Etruria was not distinct from pottery that ended up in Athens itself (R. Osborne 2001b, Reusser 2002).

3.2 Scene of athletes on the exterior of an Athenian red-figure cup signed by Pheidippos as painter and Hischylos as potter.

and Herakles struggling for the tripod, on the other a scene in a palaestra. Two pairs of figures are engaged in wrestling, while another looks on. The spectator encourages us to stand and gaze, and the frontal gaze of one of the wrestlers challenges us not merely to gaze but to respond. But what constitutes a suitable response? What does the painter tell us about these figures? Positive identifiers of sex are offered in the form of beards, nudity and male genitals; positive and negative indicators of age are offered in the size of the figures and in their beards or beardlessness.

If this image readily confirms the expectation that the palaestra is a place for men, the figures otherwise give little away. Just as we cannot deduce anything special about the amphora shown in the scene – it is just a default amphora – so we cannot readily deduce whether these bodies, which are more or less uniform in build, are offered as images of those who are distinctly fit, and we are seeing the palaestra as a place where serious athletic competitors prepare, or whether they are simply default male bodies, and we are seeing the palaestra as a place to which men of all sorts occasionally resort. Comparison with other pots, however, suggests that the physically fit male body is unmarked in red-figure painting, given significance only when in the company of the corpulent or emaciated (3.2). How fit he was, was, it seems, not the first question an Athenian wanted to answer when he saw a man, even in the palaestra.

The figure in this image who is hardest of all to classify is the spectator on the left. This figure is distinguished from the others by long hair, by fluff on the cheeks, by the wearing of a highly decorated himation and by holding not merely a stick but also a flower. The wearing of himation without chiton, as well as the palaestra context, firmly gender the figure as male, but the fancy clothing, the hair and the marked emphasis on an aesthetic rather than a physical activity separate the figure out from the others shown. This is not simply another potential participant in the wrestling; this is a figure different in kind. Whatever we make of this figure, the painter seems to be inviting us to divide young men into more categories than one, to wonder whether different young men might not have different interests and priorities.[4] And the frontal gaze of the bearded wrestler on the right challenges us with the question of where *we* fit in. When we turn the pot round to view the parallel wrestling activity of Apollo and Herakles, the aesthetic young man finds his match in the long-haired and clean-shaven Apollo in his short but fancy chiton.

Some twenty years later a painter who has become known as the Kleophrades Painter painted another amphora which also ended up at Vulci (3.3).[5] On one side we see a ritual scene. A warrior departing for battle examines the liver of a sacrificial victim (*hieroskopia*) in order to determine whether his departure is well omened. This is a scene that has been quite common in late sixth-century black-figure pottery but which is about to go out of fashion completely.[6] On the other side (3.4) is a scene of a quite different sort, showing three revellers with containers for wine and musical instruments. In the *hieroskopia* scene there are four human figures and a dog. The figure on the left is identified as Skythian by his bonnet, axe, striped garment and shoes, and perhaps by a rather slight and straggly beard. In front of him is a naked boy holding out the liver for inspection: his size might in itself be an indication of youth, servility, or both, but the pendant dog, which leads us to hear his master's voice, suggests we are here dealing with a slave. The departing warrior in the middle is shown as a hoplite by his helmet, cuirass, spear and greaves, and as young by his beardlessness and the hair on his cheek. The figure to the right is marked as female by her chiton and himation and by her hair. In the absence of other female figures she remains of uncertain age, though from the context we might imagine her to be the youthful hoplite's mother.

[4] Those persuaded by Davidson (2006, 2007) that Athenian society was marked by age classes may be attracted to seeing the spectator as distinct in age from the participating youths.
[5] *ARV* 181.1, Würzburg, Martin von Wagner Museum 507.
[6] On these scenes see Lissarrague (1990).

3.3 Scene of hieroscopy from an Athenian red-figure amphora from Vulci ascribed to the Kleophrades Painter, *c.* 500 BC.

3.4 Scene of revelling from the other side of the amphora shown in Fig. 3.3.

In the scene of revelling there are three figures, all naked. The figure on the left is identified as revelling by the amphora and kylix he carries and the garland in his hair, as male by his genitals and beard and by the detailed articulation of his body, and as of a certain age by that beard. Similarly the central figure, who carries both a large skyphos and the sort of lyre known as the barbitos. This central figure differs from the figure to the left both in the colour of his beard and because he has his genitals tied up – both a sign and an enforcement of sexual control. The nudity of the figure on the right suggests, at first glance, that this is another male figure; but breasts and genitals confound this expectation and identify this figure as female, while the pipes she holds in each hand show her to be an aulos-player, and the necklace she wears suggests she is engaged in sexual attraction.

Age, occupation and ethnicity separate the men on the two sides of this pot, with servant, light and heavily armed soldiers, and revellers all distinct. No clear division of age separates the two women, but one is identified by dress and context as part of a family unit in a world of duty; the other is identified by undress, jewellery and pipes as operating in a world of pleasure that refuses ordinary conventions. Our classification of these individuals depends on what they do, what bodies they have, and how they present their bodies. As with the Andokides Painter's amphora, our sense of what is at stake in each image is heightened by the contrast between the two images: what is a man's life about? What is a woman's place?

Ten or twenty years later and an artist who has been dubbed the Harrow Painter paints scenes on the shoulder and front of a hydria (jug).[7] In the main scene (3.5) we see a woman seated on a stool under a portico with Ionic columns. She wears a sakkos, chiton and himation, with the himation well wrapped round her, and she holds a mirror: appearance matters to her. In front of her stands a boy, marked as young by his size, wearing a himation, similarly wrapped. Outside the portico stands a man carrying something in a bag, leaning on a knobbly stick and wearing a himation in the standard style of the free man, *epidexia*, so that his right shoulder, chest and back are exposed; he is marked as of a certain age by his beard.[8] Behind him, and of the same size, but youthful since beardless, is a fourth figure, male and again well wrapped in himation.

What is going on here involves youth, age and clothes. The language of clothes operates here not, as in the two pots already discussed, in what

---

[7] *ARV* 276.70. Tampa, Florida. This too is from Vulci.
[8] For this style of wearing the himation see Plato, *Theaetetus* 175e; Aristophanes, *Birds* 1568; and Diggle (2004) 210–11. See further below, pp. 66–7.

3.5 Scene of confrontation between women and male figures on a hydria attributed to the Harrow Painter from Vulci.

is worn, but in how it is worn. Here we see the display of modesty (the well-wrapped himation) and of manhood (the mature man's himation that leaves much of the upper body bare). And in both cases this is a display of leisure too: neither the well-wrapped figure nor the man who has only his right arm free can expect to engage in serious physical labour. Accessories are relatively few but negotiate attraction (the mirror) and exchange (the bag). Space is differentiated, and the play of inside and outside the house raises the issue of the public and the private. Exactly what story we tell depends on what we think is in that bag – money to buy sexual services? Knuckle-bones for gaming?[9]

---

[9] G. P. Ferrari (1986), (2002) 14–16; Meyer (1988).

The categorisations offered by these three pots are representative of the categories offered by much red-figure pottery. Painters mark gender systematically – it would be hard to find a single well-preserved pot on which there could be serious doubt about whether a figure should be identified as male or female. But this does not prevent painters sending initially conflicting signals and playing with our gender expectations, as both the Andokides and the Kleophrades Painters do in these pots. Women's age is rarely marked, but length of hair, whether it is covered and what jewellery is worn in it, all offer means of suggesting distinct self-presentations, the significance of which is often obscure to us and may not always have been immediately clear to the painters' contemporaries. Men's age is indicated at least roughly, by height and beard, and sometimes, in the case of youths reaching maturity, quite precisely, by sideburns and hair length.[10] Beyond that, painters' primary interest is in exploring relations between the figures that they represent, relations that are played out in part by the very self-presentation that is managed by dress and demeanour.[11]

Definitive activities are used to distinguish men, but these are often more or less temporary activities (revelling, athletics, some aspect of military performance) and only occasionally more permanent occupations (as with those engaged in workshops). Cobblers, potters, foundry workers, doctors, farmers, shepherds, carriers, fishermen, various salesmen, and so on, can all be found on individual pots, but the proportion of pots showing occupations of these sorts is small. Pots may show women engaged in some activities (fetching water at a fountain, picking fruit, spinning, making music, washing, involved with religious ritual) but those activities rarely seem to be chosen to capture characteristic employment or to highlight the contribution of female labour to the economy, either of the household or more generally (3.6). Rather these activities involve or suggest relationships, both with other figures in the painted scene and with figures, human and divine alike, outside the scene. The scenes on painted pottery are dynamic, not static, full of narrative potential, not merely descriptive: it is to the relationships that the viewer's attention is directed.

Features that we might expect to be absolute turn out to be primarily instrumental. So in both men and women ethnicity may be indicated but

---

[10] If Davidson (2007) (cf. 2006) is right in his construction of Athenian age terminology into a system which closely linked age and appropriate sexual role, then knowing a youth's precise age would have been extremely important. But I am sceptical about Davidson's system.

[11] For a particular sort of exploration of relationships see Neer (2002) ch. 3 on the way in which the 'Pioneers' of red-figure painted pottery insert themselves into the company of the symposia they depict.

3.6 Athenian red-figure cup attributed to the Euaion Painter, showing a woman spinning, *c.* 470 BC. The frontal gaze of the woman and the transactions to left and right of her between young men and women encourage the viewer also to enter into an imagined transaction with this woman.

is rarely flagged up. The servant in the scene of hieroscopy is not physically distinct from the adults except in size and we cannot definitively make him either family member or non-Greek. For both men and women clothing and behaviour, rather than bodily form, are the main indicators of status, so that status, as well as gender, becomes something performed.[12] Clothes may mark out occupation, as in the short cloak or the hat of the rustic, and they may mark out wealth and pretensions.[13] But the distinctions signalled by the way in which the body and its clothing or lack of clothing are displayed primarily indicate how the men and women shown are interacting with one another. The viewer has to engage in the scene and may be invited to do so by such frontal faces as that of the wrestler in the Andokides Painter's palaestra scene. The engagement must be interrogative, for the scene does not tell us how reality is but asks us how we construe a scene such as this.

[12] Awareness of the importance of performance of gender begins with Butler (1990); see also Pellegrini (1997).
[13] See below, Ch. 4, p. 107.

Pots were themselves part of an interaction. The scenes shown on the pots employed at a party, or in the cemetery, both set an agenda for conversation and invited certain sorts of interaction. So too the interactions with which the viewer is invited to engage are frequently a matter of impressing the other by style, where style is captured not just in elaboration but in the way in which a garment is worn. But just as the thoughts of participants turn to love at the symposia described by both Plato and Xenophon in their works entitled *Symposium*, so the most frequent reference point for the relationships explored in the scenes on pots is sexual. Figures are made to signal modesty or its absence, that they are urbane and know the ways of the world or that they have no wish to enter into the complicated play of exchanging gifts and favours which the very context of the symposium itself, at which the pots were mainly used, surely encouraged. For some pots we can write narratives about military or athletic prowess for the figures shown; for far more pots it is narratives of personal relations that are most obviously called for.

Given the sympotic context of these and the vast majority of pots painted in archaic and classical Athens, the priorities that they display in their differentiation of figures are hardly surprising. For these pots were made for men to drink from on an occasion when the only women present are those offering musical and sexual services. In such a context the activities that made a man a man figured more prominently in the discourse than activities engaged in by women, and the issue of how to classify a person's sexual intentions was high on the agenda. But does this mean that pots reveal only the sorts of visual distinctions on display at the symposium? To discover the degree to which the classificatory priorities of red-figure pottery were indeed context-specific it is necessary to look at a body of imagery made for quite different viewing circumstances.

Distinguished men and distinguished women on gravestones

From about 430 it became regular in Athens for those of sufficient resources to commemorate the dead by erecting a stele bearing a sculpted scene.[14]

---

[14] For the question of just how wealthy one needed to be to acquire a sculpted stele see Bergemann (1997) 131–6; Oliver (2000). Note Bergemann's conclusion (1997: 142): 'Fast jeder, Bürger oder Metöke, reich oder arm, konnte sich eine Grabstätte leisten und in mehr oder weniger aufwendiger Form ausstatten. Überdies scheinen sich die Bezirke reicher Bürger und reicher Metöken in dem zur Schau gestellten Aufwand, wie in ihrer Anlage einander im wesentlichen entsprochen zu haben.' On the smaller corpus of reliefs certainly for slaves see below, p. 153 n. 82.

3.7 Grave stele of Ktesileos of Erythrai and Theano from Athens, *c.* 400 BC.

Initially most stelai represent one or two figures in relatively low relief. In the course of the fourth century a much wider range of stele types came to be employed, ranging from pedimented architectural frames containing four or more virtually free-standing and life-sized figures (so-called *naiskoi*) to stelai with a small recessed panel with low-relief scenes (so-called 'Bildfeldstelai'). But the iconographic repertoire of the various types of stelai is closely related.[15]

Many figures on grave stelai are distinguished not by being shown engaged in some particular specific action or occupation but only by their bodies, their clothing and the implications of the tableau they create. So a stele from around 400 BC shows, as the inscription on the frieze of its gable declares, Ktesileos of Erythrai and Theano (3.7).[16] Ktesileos is a mature bearded man, wearing a himation that is draped over both shoulders but leaves his upper torso exposed. He stands in a relaxed posture with his weight resting on his right leg and his left crossed in front of it, and his hands are limply linked

---

[15] Compare Bergemann (1997) 69–96, 117–30.   [16] *CAT* 2.206, Athens NM 3472.

in front of him. He looks down upon Theano, who is seated on a stool and wears a sleeved chiton with himation over it; she wears a headband, rests her feet on a footstool, and with her right hand extends her himation in a veiling gesture that draws attention to her sexual desirability and to her devotion to Ktesileos in marriage.

What is represented in this relief is primarily the relationship between Ktesileos and Theano. We look upon a married couple, now severed by death, enjoying each other's company and the public advertisement of their intimacy. We can deduce something of their wealth – these are the clothes of the well-off. But beyond identifying both figures as mature, rather than youthful, the stele does little further to help us classify them or give them a particular place in a social, economic or political world. In particular we might note that nothing at all marks out Ktesileos and Theano as foreigners or metics, rather than citizens. But for the identification in the inscription of Ktesileos as from Erythrai, a city on the eastern coast of the Aegean, opposite the island of Chios, we would assume that we were looking upon two Athenians.

Not all stelai are quite so intimate, or quite so reticent. In particular, stelai with but a single figure, where the only interaction is with the viewer, frequently offer some sort of indication of that figure's place in the world. Men on these single-figure stelai are further distinguished by posture and attributes.[17] Sometimes posture and attributes give little away: Tynnias is simply shown as a mature bearded man, sitting on a chair, wearing a himation and carrying a stick; another man in a himation sits on a stool and uses his stick to tease a small dog; a third bearded man in a himation simply leans on his stick.[18] More often single male figures offer more definite indications of occupation.

Many of the occupations in which young men are shown are leisure occupations. Naked youths, or youths in himatia, carry strigils that associate them with the gymnasium; exceptionally a figure may adopt a posture which marks him as engaged in a particular athletic activity, as when Agakles is shown as a naked man with raised arms, apparently engaged in the pankration (3.8).[19] Beardless men in himatia with aryballoi hanging from their wrists, and dogs beside them, associate themselves with both the

---

[17] Cf. Bergemann (1997) 76–83.   [18] *CAT* 1.251 (Tynnias), 343, 384 (leaning on stick).

[19] Naked with strigil: *CAT* 1.221, 1.348 (with dog and bird); in himation with strigil, 1.392: *CAT* 1.081, 1.191, 1.201 (with dog), cf. 1.436 (in himation with aryballos); engaged in pankration: 1.100 (Agakles is, exceptionally, both naked and bearded, a condition which his active engagement in athletic activity serves to justify). Cf. *CAT* 1.302 where a young man, with himation draped over his shoulders, plays with knuckle-bones.

3.8 Grave stele of Agakles son of Phrynichos from Khasani (Argyropolis), *c.* 400 BC.

gymnasium and the hunt, those with dogs, birds or rabbits and perhaps a hunting stick, with the hunt alone (3.9).[20]

Other stelai celebrate men of various ages in public-service occupations. Naked young men and bearded men carry shields or may be helmeted and adopt an aggressive stance indicative of their role as soldiers.[21] Men wearing the chlamys (short cloak) and short chiton lead or stand beside horses, marked by dress and animal as cavalry men.[22] More unusually a beardless young man in a helmet and military dress gallops by on a lively horse; another young man in a short chiton with helmet and shield behind him sits on the prow of a ship or a bearded warrior kneels and raises his shield on the prow of another ship; and a bearded man in chlamys and chiton,

---

[20] Aryballos and dog: *CAT* 1.154, 214 (essentially naked); aryballos, strigil, bird and dog: *CAT* 1.227, 1.278; hunting stick, dog and rabbit: 1.289, cf. 1.200; bird, rabbit and dog, 1.330a, cf. 331 (fragmentary).

[21] Naked with shield: *CAT* 1.215, 1.361; bearded, clothed with shield and spear and carrying helmet: *CAT* 1.153; bearded with shield: *CAT* 1.378; bearded, clothed, helmeted and in aggressive stance with shield: *CAT* 1.194, cf. 1.277, 1.460. See further R. Osborne (2010b).

[22] *CAT* 1.434, 472.

3.9 Grave stele of Stephanos from Tanagra, *c.* 400 BC.

wearing a travelling hat (*petasos*) and carrying a spear, is accompanied by an epigram referring to his *aretē* (virtue/courage) and his good deeds (*erga agatha*).[23]

Some bearded figures have indications of particular institutional or economic roles. Bearded men in long ungirt chitons and carrying a knife in one hand declare an identity as priests involved with sacrifice.[24] When a similar

---

[23] Young cavalry man: *CAT* 1.209, cf. 1.429; on prow of ship: 1.330 (Demokleides), 1.458 (Demetrios); older man with *petasos* and spear: 1.193 (Athenokles).

[24] *CAT* 1.186, 1.250; 1.390, without attributes but with ungirt chiton, may also be a priest.

figure appears with long ungirt chiton but with a kantharos rather than a knife in hand we may be supposed to identify him as a priest of Dionysos, the god with whom cups of that shape are particularly associated in painted pottery.[25] Some images are unique in their attributes: a bearded man with aging body, wearing a himation that leaves his chest exposed, sits with one hand on a staff and in the other keeps upright a round object with slightly hollow surface, the precise identity of which scholars dispute (bellows? copper ingot? bowl?); the inscription identifies him as Sosinous of Gortyn, copper-smelter, and refers to his 'justice, moderation and excellence'.[26] A beardless man wearing a serious expression and a himation sits staring at the comic mask he holds facing him in his hand (with another mask in the background).[27]

Women's posture and attributes on these single-figure stelai are less varied.[28] Regularly wearing both (sleeved) chiton and himation or chiton and peplos, they may stand holding in one hand a small box, a bird, a piece of jewellery, a mirror, a doll – or occasionally some other object, such as a water jug (3.10).[29] Or they may sit holding a spindle, with a wool basket beside them, or holding a lekythos.[30] Such attributes both point variously to domesticity and invoke a sense of the ephemerality of the pleasures of life. Closer to representations of men are female figures who stand holding a temple key and so identify themselves more definitely – as priestesses.[31] Unusually, viewers may be invited to associate a female figure with a divinity or figure from mythology and so interrogate her role and relationship. One female figure stands in a pose borrowed from Aphrodite, her elbow on a loutrophoros (a pot shape associated with being unmarried), her chiton slipped from her right shoulder and her himation wrapped only round her waist (3.11). Another stands in the pose of Eurydike, the wife whom Orpheus fails to rescue from Hades – her himation is pulled as a veil over her head and her gaze is downcast in sorrow. A third figure takes her elaborated drapery and pose from Kephisodotos' *Eirene* (*Peace*).[32]

---

[25] *CAT* 1.377.   [26] *CAT* 1.202.   [27] *CAT* 1.400.

[28] For a survey of the representation of women on grave stelai see Bergemann (1997) 83–6.

[29] Box: *CAT* 1.050, perhaps 1.080, 1.264; bird: 1.082, 1.187 (duck), 1.210a, 1.224 (an unusual figure, named Myttion, in a *kandus*, see below, p. 149), 1.254, 1.276, perhaps 1.291, 1.321a, 1.327, 1.332, 1.356, 1.428, 1.431 (a particularly fine piece in which a loutrophoros with a scene of parting is shown in front of the main figure); jewellery: 1.281, 1.284; mirror: 1.152, 1.170, 1.188, 1.283, 1.471; doll: 1.247, 1.311 (with heron in front of her), 1.312, 1.328, 1.329, 1.367; hydria: 1.334.

[30] Spindle: *CAT* 1.176, 1.220 (cf. 1.246, no spindle but wool basket), 1.309; lekythos 1.181.

[31] These are collected by Connelly (2007); *CAT* 1.248 (standing), 1.350a.

[32] *CAT* 1.182 (Aphrodite) cf. 1.267, 1.189 (Eurydike), 1.315 (Eirene).

3.10 Grave stele of Pausimache from Paiania, first half of the fourth century BC. There is a grave epigram which names her parents as Phainippe and Pausanias and celebrates her virtue (*aretē*) and modesty (*sōphrosunē*).

Women appear in very much the same restricted range of poses as men – indeed, given the absence of any equivalent to the military poses in which some men are shown, the female range is more restricted still – but they appear in a much greater variety of costume so that the discrimination between female figures is far richer. This is not just a matter of the number of different items – one or two chitons, a peplos, a himation, a back mantle, various forms of covering or adornment for the hair – but of the ways in which these items may be worn. That there is an elaborate discourse of

3.11 Grave stele said to have been found in Athens or Attica, *c.* 400 BC.

modesty going on here is undoubted, even if the subtleties of that language largely escape us.[33] It is easy enough to see that the covering or revealing of the chiton serves as an indicator of the degree of intimacy being offered to the viewer, but who should we take the viewer to be? In particular, once more than one figure is represented on a stele it becomes a real and pressing question whether the privileged viewer is internal, one of the servants, friends or relations shown gathered round, or external, the mourner or the passer-by who views the relief in the cemetery. The difficulty is actually highlighted when gestures of veiling are shown. Gestures of veiling serve to indicate a consciousness of being looked at, so they draw attention to the performance which is involved in these choices of clothing.[34] The external

---

[33] This is partly because of a lack of scholarly consideration of the topic. It is notable that the only work devoted to body language in the ancient world (Cairns 2005) is dominated by discussion of texts, and it discusses no images relating to ordinary life (as opposed to the stage) between geometric art and the Hellenistic period. The variations in dress are brilliantly illustrated by Kunisch's analysis of the figures of the painter Makron (Kunisch 1997: 41–52).

[34] On veiling and its indication that a woman is 'to-be-looked-at' see, in a rather different context, Naficy (1999).

viewer is made conscious that they have entered into a direct relationship with the veiled or veiling woman, that they have stepped into the position of the husband, whether or not that woman is herself looking out of the picture plane.[35]

To discuss grave reliefs with more than one figure, and most grave reliefs do have more than one figure, would enormously increase the number of figures found in the sorts of attitudes and activities described, but it would add surprisingly few new attitudes, activities or attributes. Figures of men indicate age: children are distinguished by size, youths or young men by beardlessness, or bearded figures divide between the simply 'mature' and those who show in their bodies or faces some positive signs of age. There is no female equivalent of the beardless youth, and mature women rarely show positive signs of age, though they display a great deal of variety in the clothes and jewellery they wear and how they wear them. Sculptors use additional figures to suggest emotional attachments and to explore relationships, rather than to illuminate participation in a new range of communal activities.

There are some activities that demand that more than one figure be shown, and notably one of the few activities added to the repertoire of grave stelai when additional figures are shown is women giving birth (6.2, see pp. 159–60).[36] This is particularly notable both because it is not a scene easy to make aesthetically attractive, and because it is not otherwise customary to show on stelai the crisis which results in death.[37] Classical texts variously emphasise the parallelism between men going to war and women giving birth, and these stelai seem to represent a desire to make women's most risky civic role apparent, just as scenes of men as soldiers showed off their most risky civic contribution.[38]

Grave stelai have the advantage that some of the accompanying inscriptions give not just the name but tell us something about the individual commemorated.[39] Such identifications sometimes correspond to items in the stele – as the mysterious round object on Sosinous' stele may represent

---

[35] On viewing on grave stelai see Turner (2009). I am indebted to Susanne Turner for making me think about the complexities of the (gendered) gaze on grave stelai.

[36] These scenes are collected by Demand (1994) 123–6.

[37] See further below, Ch. 5, pp. 127–8.

[38] The most famous instance of the parallel is Euripides, *Medea* 248–51; the Spartans are said to have named on tombstones only men who fell in war and women who died in childbirth: Plutarch, *Lycurgus* 27.2–3; see Low (2006). See generally Loraux (1981c). Demand (1994) 128–30 rightly insists that the equation of military service and childbirth is only at the level of commemorating the circumstances of death on a stele, insisting that women dying in childbirth are depicted as passive rather than active.

[39] For an elaborate example see below, Ch. 5.

something connected to his occupation as a copper-smelter. But on other occasions nothing in the image classifies the individual commemorated: the figure of the seated woman in chiton and himation who commemorates the aptly named Paideusis ('Childcare') has no attributes which point to her being the wet-nurse referred to in the accompanying inscription, and nothing that indicates her social status.[40] Status and origin are indeed notable for not being indicated, as we have already seen in the case of the Erythraian Ktesileos (3.7). So nothing about the image of an athlete scraping himself with a strigil or about the bearded man seated in a chair enables ancient or modern viewers to identify Agetor son of Apollodoros or Menekles as men from Megara, as the inscriptions reveal that they were.[41]

The gap to which the occasional reference to occupation or to which reference to non-Athenian origin draws attention, between how a figure would have been identified in life and how a figure is identified in the relief of the stele, serves only to emphasise the very restricted visual repertoire which these stelai employ. Men are classified by the presence or absence of a himation, a beard, and of a small range of attributes (strigil, aryballos, bird, dog, stick, spear or shield, horse). Women are classified by their particular clothing – chiton combined with peplos or himation, presence or absence of the 'mantlet' or 'back-mantle' – and by the way in which it is worn – whether it is shown to veil the head or some other allusion to veiling is made, whether the mantlet is secured by crossed straps.[42] They are also classified by what they hold – birds, mirrors, spindles, boxes. Women's hair varies in length, in style, and in whether it is adorned or covered.

What are we to make of these visual classifications? There can be little doubt that some of them are basic. It is hardly an accident that only beardless youths appear on stelai naked.[43] Nudity is not here simply the mark of the athlete, for men continued to exercise naked in the gymnasium when maturely bearded (cf. 3.8 the grave monument of Agakles), it is also a mark of sexual status, of being the desirable object rather than the desiring subject. These naked young men frequently look out from the stele, engaging the gaze of the viewer, inviting the viewer not merely to write their narrative but to be part of it, to feel the loss by feeling the desire that others felt for them

[40] *CAT* 1.249 (*IG* ii² 12387); cf. 1.354 (*IG* ii² 12813) where Tithe ('Wet-nurse') has been taken to be a proper name. Another wet-nurse, Pyraichme, holds a skyphos and has a chous at her feet, and these have been thought linked to the Choes festival with which small children were particularly associated: *CAT* 1.376, *SEG* 21.1064.
[41] *CAT* 1.221 (*IG* ii² 9301); *CAT* 1.272 (not in *IG*).
[42] Clairmont discusses the costumes on stelai in *CAT* Introductory volume pp. 30–5. On veiling see Llewellyn-Jones (2003). On the back-mantle see Roccos (2000).
[43] R. Osborne (1997b), Daehner (2005).

when alive. The birds and rabbits that these young men carry are both the proof of their prowess in hunting and suggestions that they were themselves objects of desire, to be caught whether by gift or by other kindnesses. By contrast, bearded men present themselves in a role, as soldiers or priests, or they carry some object suggesting an end in view. When shown sitting they display themselves as those who have served and now resume their past life, and they invite the viewer to resume that life with them. Direct engagement with the viewer is rare, for we are to celebrate what has been, not enter imaginatively into the future of which they have been deprived.

The limited range of occupations to which allusions are made in the case of these male figures is striking. In real life young men won glory in a wide range of ways, by participating in musical as well as athletic competitions, by taking part with others of their tribe in the dithyramb, for instance, or by performing in a dramatic chorus. Yet the literary and musical activities which figure quite prominently on pots are conspicuous only by their absence from grave stelai. The range of occupations of mature men was even wider, since Athenians were prone to identify individuals by the particular job or work that marked them out, whether or not that occupied all their time.[44] In the face of this, the reticence of both the images and indeed the texts on stelai becomes itself eloquent: in death we are not invited to identify individuals in the way we have identified them in life. But that the discourse of occupation is so limited does not mean that there is no discourse.

Their context in the cemetery affects what grave stelai show quite as much as the context of the symposium affects the iconographic choices of painted pottery. If what one needs to know about a person in life is that he is the person who sells sesame seed, that identification becomes irrelevant after his death. Grave stelai are bound to privilege aspects that are exemplary, ways in which the deceased was the person we would all like to be (physically admired; doing our duty by our friends and our city; a conduit between the community and its gods), and aspects of our behaviour that continue to be important (fidelity to spouse; bond of a family group).

Social distinction?

Neither the grave stelai nor the images painted on sympotic pottery offer a neutral window on the world: neither gives us the view of the 'man in the street'. There is, and can be, no such view. All views are occasioned,

---

[44] Harris (2002).

and it is the advantage of stelai and pots that they offer insights into the view of the world on two very particular occasions, insights into how the world was viewed at two particularly intense moments. Although both party interactions and mourning are moments when participants seek in some sense to escape from the world, they are also moments at which those involved demand security. In their different ways grave stones and sympotic pots ought to reflect images of a world in which one can feel secure because the familiar landmarks are all there.

These sets of images reveal that both at the party and in coping with death the landmark distinctions which artists thought it necessary to offer were distinctions between men and women, distinctions between young men and older men, and distinctions of modesty. Neither in painted pottery nor in grave stelai does the run of imagery suggest that daily occupation was something that those interacting with an individual wanted to know. This was not, on this evidence, a society where the first social question was 'What do you do?' It was not a society in which it was important to be able to detect every nuance of social position. The images certainly create an imaginary society, but that society is utopian; it is moral, rather than political, and not tied to the particular categories and divisions of the Greek *polis*.[45] Nor is it easy to see divisions here by social class or education, or the sort so manifest in Bourdieu's France.[46] The way in which pot painters infiltrate characters bearing their own names into what scholars have sometimes been tempted to see as the elite world of the symposium is one indication that a taste for fancy parties did not act as a class indicator.[47] So too the repetition on much cheaper *Bildfeldstelai* of the compositions found on high-relief tomb monuments denies that different social classes marked their difference by the taste they displayed in the cemetery. That scholars have been able to suggest that the iconography of cheap ceramics exactly copied that of expensive vessels of silver and gold further emphasises the apparent coherence of the judgement of taste across the spectrum of wealth.[48] Wealth was certainly something that could be shown off, but showing it off appears as something of a matter of personal choice, not of common social expectation.[49]

[45] The claims about a supposed 'Bürgerideal' made by Bergemann (1997: 155–6 and index s.v.) seem to me either to be false or to use the notion of 'citizen' in a very loose way. See further below, pp. 105–8.

[46] Bourdieu (1984).   [47] Neer (2002) ch. 3.

[48] Vickers (1985), Vickers and Gill (1994); against the extreme view that they offer see Neer (2002) 206–15 with further references.

[49] The Roman world offers us a quite different situation, as seen graphically in Petronius' *Satyrica*, in the distinct self-presentation of freedmen, and in many other ways: Veyne (1961), Bianchi Bandinelli (1967), Kampen (1981), with reservations from Petersen (2006). Cf. R. Osborne (2006).

The distinctions that men at the symposium and men and women visiting, or passing through, cemeteries most want to make, on this evidence, are distinctions between character traits: how are we to imagine this person interacting socially? To turn drawn or sculpted images of men and women into a scene whose dynamics can be reconstructed, the viewer demands clues to the sort of social performance each participant might be expected to engage in.

How do the expectations of those viewing scenes on pots and on stelai relate to the expectations of those viewing life unfolding before them in the Athenian street? Painted and sculpted images are much impoverished as sources of information by comparison with live bodies. Not only are they silent and without smell, but they do not move.[50] In the street there is always going to be so much more going on that allows an assessment to be made of the people we meet.[51] But for all that we have much more information we can tap into in the street, it is not obvious that the information is such as to allow different sorts of questions to be asked or different sorts of distinctions to be made. Sound, smell and movement enrich our experiences of others and may allow speedier, more confident and more nuanced discriminations to be made, but they do not change the agenda of what we want to know about people. Painted pots and sculpted stelai concentrate on the distinctions people want to make in two particular circumstances, but it is the circumstances of viewing, rather than the limitations of the representational medium, that separate art from life.

On the evidence of painted pottery and sculpted grave stelai the discriminations Athenian viewers wanted to make had much in common with the discriminations we make ourselves. In public contexts we are not surprised to find military uniforms being worn, past military service being paraded, and those ordained as priests displaying that fact. Nor does it cause us surprise if such signs are suppressed in private contexts. Symposia were essentially private affairs, and it is part of the fiction that governs representations on grave reliefs that, despite the fact that these monuments by the side of major roads stood to be seen by allcomers, they follow the presentational rules that applied inside the household, in particular revealing and naming women.

Athenians, on this evidence, concern themselves less with assessments of occupation or age than we do. Patterns of working life, we might speculate, were more variable in this world without a nine-to-five day and without weekends, while ages of life-change were more predictable: more or less all

[50] For the significance attached to movements by classical authors see Bremmer (1991).
[51] This is something which photographs can sometimes catch; cf. Dyer (2005).

women married in their middle teenage years and men formally became soldiers when they reached sexual maturity (later than in today's world) and married at around thirty. We want most to know what sort of lifestyle those we meet lead, so as to judge what to talk about (and whether we want to see more of them or not). The Athenian version of this was not concern with occupation but with how (modestly, brazenly) a person performs their gender.

In these images gender is performed by men and women alike by what they do and by how they do it. In the case of men, there are a variety of occupations outside the home in which masculinity might be displayed. Pots from time to time show all these roles, grave stelai show a much more restricted range. But the same is not true of images of women (3.6). When T. B. L. Webster surveyed images of women on Athenian pottery he concluded that 'The most common subject is women at home', and went on, 'Home is indicated by alabastra or mirrors hanging on the wall and by tame birds or animals among the figures. The common occupations are spinning and working at wool, washing, dressing.'[52] Women at home dominate grave stelai also, and home on those stelai is marked by mirrors and spindles and by the presence of tame birds, but not by washing or dressing. In what the two sets of images share we see the extremely limited range of women's life that was publicly acknowledged, the limited range of history that is written on women's bodies. In what separates the two sets of imagery we see the areas where male fantasy might wander in a party, but not in a cemetery.

The images of women's lives are not merely marked by limited range, however, but also by the way in which the subject matter of scenes involving women is hard to label with any precision. When a group of Francophone scholars assembled the photographic exhibition and accompanying text that was *La cité des images* they explored men's lives in the city in the context of warfare (ch. 3) and sacrificial ritual (ch. 4), in the educational and courtship possibilities of the hunt (chs. 4 and 5), and in the activities of the symposium itself (ch. 8).[53] Images in which women play a predominant part they collected in a chapter entitled 'L'ordre des femmes' (ch. 6). Images of women do, of course, appear in other chapters, and particularly in the chapter on religious festivals (ch. 7), but that these scholars, like Webster, could find no useful subdivisions for women's scenes is extremely revealing. In devoting a whole book to the iconography of women on Athenian pots, Sian Lewis divides the images between 'Domestic labour' (ch. 2), 'Working women' (ch. 3), 'The women's room' (ch. 4), as well as 'Women and men'

---

[52] Webster (1972) 242.   [53] Bérard, Bron and Durand *et al.* (1984).

(ch. 5).[54] That women with wool baskets figure in all five of these chapters, and women and men in chapters 3 and 4, as well as 5, serves to confirm the difficulties that Webster and Bérard and his colleagues experienced.

That images involving men can be more or less neatly divided into categories (war, the gymnasium, the symposium, the revel, the hunt), whereas images of women do not divide by subject in the same way, no doubt reflects a social fact. Men had available to them, and were expected to perform, a range of roles outside the house, whether to serve their city or to enhance the standing of their household. Women had opportunities for religious service, but otherwise their major public roles were as household representatives at funerals and other public family rituals. So when sculptors and painters approach the representation of the performance of gender differently for the two sexes they are reflecting social reality. The subject of scenes, whether on pots or on grave stelai, in which women are significantly involved is primarily the women themselves and their relationships within the household.

Because much of men's performance of their masculinity took place outside the household and involved relationships with more or less unknown others that needed to be regulated by law or by political decisions, our texts about men are very interested in dividing men into groups. These groups are defined politically, in terms of social status, and in terms of economic capacity. Women's lives impinged, by contrast, hardly at all on those outside the household, and in areas where there was potentially a role (property ownership, exchanging goods made in the household), Athens, notoriously, chose to restrict or forbid such activities by law. Athenian women could not own more than a trivial amount of property, and all their economic transactions had to be done by means of a male 'sovereign' (*kurios*).[55] The organisation of the Athenian state and the documents that it generated have little interest in classifying women, beyond the interest that develops in the fifth century in controlling whom an Athenian man might marry. By contrast, the state repeatedly put men into classes, by family home, by age, by wealth, by more or less temporary public service.

Athenian texts are not, of course, silent about women, nor do they treat women as an undifferentiated group. But texts invariably present women in relation to men. This is nowhere seen more clearly than in Aristophanes' three 'women' plays. All three plays turn upon women's relations to men. In *Lysistrata* the famous sex-strike is an attempt to make men run the war against Sparta more sensibly. In *Women at the Thesmophoria* the women

[54] S. Lewis (2002).   [55] Schaps (1979).

are ganging up on Euripides because of his unflattering presentation of women on the stage. In *Assembly Women* women take over the political assembly from the men so as to run the state more effectively. The literary presentation of women in literature, whether in comedy, tragedy, their extremely restricted role in history, or in the orators, turns always to their relationship to men and tends always towards polarities and essentialised views, towards a world of virtuous mothers and scheming prostitutes.

The visual evidence surveyed in this chapter does not give us the material to assert alternative groupings of women in the face of the literature's caricatures. What I have argued above, however, is that it does suggest the lines upon which the Athenians themselves differentiated women's behaviour. The differences that we find signalled on pots and on grave stelai are the differences that Athenians looked for and interpreted in those they saw around them. In the case of women, the textual material that we have available to test this reading of the imagery is both limited and hard to handle.[56] In the case of men, however, there are a small number of texts which are concerned much more with how men negotiate their way through daily life than they are with how men interact with the institutions of the state. This is true of some lawcourt speeches, and it is true of much of old comedy and of new comedy. Plays such as Aristophanes' *Clouds* are full of explicit and implicit claims about how men should behave, what they should wear and how they should wear it. Dikaios Logos insists that the proper man must neither shuffle nor hurry, neither murmur nor giggle, and when he is defeated it is his himation that he hands over.[57]

The most concentrated textual descriptions of personal and interpersonal conduct, however, come from a work by Aristotle's most famous pupil, and his successor in charge of the philosophical school at the Lyceum, Theophrastos. In his *Characters*, written around 310 BC or a little earlier, Theophrastos chose the pen portrait as a way of pursuing the sorts of ethical questions Aristotle himself had raised in the *Nicomachean Ethics*.[58]

Theophrastos adumbrates some thirty characters. We find 'The Dissembler', 'The Toady', 'The Country Bumpkin', 'The Rumour Monger', 'The

---

[56] For the classic discussion of the problem of reading off real women's lives from the different sorts of textual material available see Gould (1980).

[57] Aristophanes, *Clouds* 963–4, 983, 1104. Note too the handing over of the himation on entry to Sokrates' *phrontistērion: Clouds* 497, which is surely a heavily symbolic gesture (cf. 179). I am grateful to Ashley Clements for pointing out to me the wealth of play with clothing and other behavioural proprieties in *Clouds*.

[58] For the historical background to Theophrastos' *Characters* see Lane Fox (1996), Millett (2007a). The most recent edition of the *Characters* is Diggle (2004).

Penny-Pincher', 'The Shameless Man', 'The Tactless Man', 'The Superstitious Man', 'The Man of Petty Ambition', 'The Arrogant Man', 'The Coward', 'The Shabby Profiteer', as well as various men who talk too much, praise themselves, run down others, and men who are just unpleasant. Theophrastos' choice of titles gives a good idea of what one might want to know about the people one meets: one wants to know whether one can trust them, and what one should make of what they say. But how did Athenians recognise such people? On Theophrastos' evidence they recognised them by what they did, but above all by what they said.[59] It is the actions and the turns of phrase of these people that betray their character, and the *Characters* are accordingly full of snippets of conversation; 'The Toady is the sort of man who says to a person walking with him "Are you aware of the admiring looks you are getting?"'[60]

If appearances were something of which Athenians were very conscious, it is nevertheless much more rare for Theophrastos' character sketches to give us any idea of a distinctive physical appearance or way with clothes. Such physical traits as there are, offer small chance of being conveyed in painting or sculpture. The Arrogant Man keeps his head down when he walks down the street.[61] The Country Bumpkin sits with his knees showing in the Assembly, and the Illiberal Man turns up his tunic when he sits down, presumably to the same effect.[62] The Oligarchic Man, out in his himation in the middle of the day, is marked out by his trimmed hair and pared nails.[63] Part of the description included under the heading 'The Obsequious Man' describes someone who keeps having his hair cut, changing his clothes and anointing himself with perfumed oil.[64] The most extensive description is of the 'Offensive Man' who 'parades about with scaly and blanched skin and black nails... His armpits are infested with lice and their hair extends over much of his sides, and his teeth are black and rotten... He goes out to the market wearing a thick chitoniskos and a thin himation full of stains.'[65]

All Theophrastos' characters are male. On his showing, the ways in which character was physically displayed by men were subtle – not a matter simply of what a man wore, but of how a man wore it and of the signs of grooming, or lack of grooming, that might accompany it. If an Athenian hoped for admiring glances he needed, on this evidence, to look to the bearing of his head, to the neatness of his grooming, to the turn of his garment. It was from such clues that others would decide upon his honesty, his taste, his politics and his intelligence.

[59] For the Superstitious Man and his doings see below, pp. 166–7.   [60] *Characters* 2.2.
[61] *Characters* 24.8.   [62] *Characters* 4.4, 22.13.   [63] *Characters* 26.4.   [64] *Characters* 5.6.
[65] *Characters* 19.2, 4, 6 (trans. after Diggle).

When we look at a pot or a grave relief we find there body language among men and women which relates above all to personal relations, to what sort of engagement one could expect to have with this individual. The way bodies are presented offers cues for conversational gambits, but on these pots and sculptures the cues do not suggest questions, even to men, of the 'So what do you do?', or even 'Where did you grow up?' sort. Rather the cues point to questions to men such as 'How did you enjoy the Panathenaic games?' or even 'I've just been talking to someone who thinks Euripides' Phaedra deserves our sympathy – don't you think that's amazing?' They point to questions to women such as 'Aren't you proud of your son?' or 'Isn't it amazing how pet birds seem to detect one's mood?' Rather than guessing about a man's line of work, or a man or woman's social background, images on pots and on grave reliefs encourage us to guess about their attitudes, about how they relate to other people and how they get on in life.

Juxtaposing the characters presented in painting or sculpture to the characters presented by Theophrastos reveals both much that is common between the two, and much that is very different. What is common is the ethical interest, that is the interest in assessing a person's ways. What is most strikingly different is that Theophrastos is not interested in *people*'s ways, but in *men*'s ways. His *Characters* inverts the bias of the famous seventh-century BC poem by Semonides of Amorgos on the characters of women.[66] Women have only walk-on parts in Theophrastos, whose world is a man's world. And a man's world which expects to be consumed, as indeed Semonides expected his women's world to be consumed, by male readers. These acts of classification in and by words – by Theophrastos' own words and by the words which Theophrastos attributes to his individual characters – show no interest in the classifications with which I will be dealing in the next two chapters, the classifications on which the structures of Athenian society were based. Theophrastos is interested in traits which cut across political groupings, and his whole philosophical project depends upon the assumption that all his classes of man can be found in the various groups into which society at Athens was formally divided – in the metics, to whom Theophrastos himself, from the city of Eresos on Lesbos, belonged, or in the citizens. Because Theophrastos' characters reveal themselves by what they do, only those who have agency, and of whom agency is expected, can figure in his world. In a world where men have, and are expected to have, more agency than women, female versions of Theophrastos'

---

[66] On Semonides 7 see R. Osborne (2001a), Morgan (2005). Semonides' decision to use animal imagery for the women complicates any useful comparison between text and art.

characters would be like the male ones, but with a much more restricted range of exemplary actions.

Neither for pot painters nor for sculptors of stelai is agency a primary issue. Even when sculptors of grave stelai show only a single figure there is always a relationship set up between sculpted figure and viewer. By contrast, the presence of the authorial voice destroys the possibility of the same sort of relationship between one of Theophrastos' characters and the reader. Drawn and sculpted figures reveal their ways less by what they do and the initiatives that they take, and more by how they present themselves to view. Theophrastos makes his characters reveal themselves by the ways in which they act and react; sculptors and painters concentrate on *dispositions* to act. Painters and sculptors put us in the position of someone spotting another in the street and needing to come to an instant assessment; Theophrastos puts us into the position of leisurely observers who can develop a view over time. The pot in the symposium offers a starting point for a story, as one of the drinkers lifts a cup and tells a tale about the mythical or ordinary life characters that he identifies, about how they got themselves into the situation they are now in, and about what happens next. The visitor to the cemetery tells what the man or woman commemorated was like in life, picking up clues from the characteristic scene into which they have been frozen on the stone.

On Athenian grave stelai neither image nor epigram, even in those cases where there is a more substantial inscription, focuses on the past achievements of the dead – by contrast to images in other cultures. The emphasis is much more upon the sort of person than upon the catalogue of what they have achieved. There is no attempt to establish an authorial voice offering a verdict on deeds done; the emphasis is on the sort of person who lived. Grave stelai in this way offer the past tense of the street-side encounter. What matters when we meet is not what the person met has achieved or will achieve but the sort of person we will find if we engage with him or her now. In what follows I explore the consequences of the contrast between those concerns and the concerns which the *polis* community expresses in its laws and conventions, concerns which cause it to focus not upon the nature of the encounter now but to insist on writing an ongoing history onto the human body.

In the rest of this book I shall be looking at the labelling of bodies that occurred in political and religious contexts, and considering the significance of the failure of those labels to manifest themselves in figural representations in either graphic or sculpted form. But, as Theophrastos' *Characters* makes very clear, the political designations of in-groups and out-groups (citizen, foreigner, slave) and the religious concern with standing in relation to the gods (is this person a god, a hero, or a man? is this person polluted?), were neither the only nor the primary ways in which Athenians were concerned to classify individuals. This is apparent in an official form from the terms in which Athenians choose to honour both their own citizens and men from elsewhere for services, praising them for their excellence or 'manly goodness', justice, piety, good intentions, love of honour, and moderation.[67] In daily life the judgements Athenians made about others included such judgements of character alongside and often rather than judgements of status. Those judgements of character observed appearance, actions and, perhaps above all, interactions. Understanding interactions is crucial to understanding Athenian social history, and the historian who ignores the evidence of the visual arts can only produce an impoverished, and indeed misleading, history.

---

[67] Whitehead (1993); cf. R. Osborne (1999) on the politics of this practice.

4 | The citizen body

The citizenship debate

The question of what it is to be a citizen has entered UK politics only recently. There were no British citizens until 1981; until then there were, technically, only British subjects.[1] That technical change impinged rather little upon the lives of most UK residents, though it significantly changed the relationship of Britain to Commonwealth and colonial British subjects. What has impinged upon UK residents is the move in the last decade to have 'Citizenship' become a subject in schools. In 1998 the Qualifications and Curriculum Authority (QCA) published a document entitled *Education for Citizenship and the Teaching of Democracy in Schools*, explicitly announcing the intention of changing the political culture of the United Kingdom.

The question of what it was to be a citizen attracts a lot of attention from Aristotle in his *Politics*. The question of who was a citizen was important enough to Athenians for them to change the rules in the fifth century about who qualified and for them to hear a number of court cases in the fourth century brought against men alleged to have illegitimately infiltrated the citizen body.[2] But what is a citizen? And what in classical Athens was a citizen? How do we identify the citizen body either now or in the past? If we line up side by side, identity-parade fashion, the great sculptural portrayals of mature men, can we identify which is a citizen? Could Athenians actually recognise an Athenian citizen?

The narrowly legal approach identifies citizens by descent and residence. So under the British Nationality Act 1981, British citizens are those whose parents had been born, adopted or naturalised or registered as citizens of the United Kingdom, whether themselves born in the United Kingdom or not, or those who were born and then lived ten years continuously in the United Kingdom.[3] In this formal sense, as Thomas Janoski has noted, modern

---

[1] Layton-Henry (2001) 117.
[2] Aristotle discusses the citizen in book 3 of *Politics*; the Aristotelian *Constitution of the Athenians* 26 gives an account of Perikles' citizenship law; Demosthenes 57 and Isaios 12 are cases arising from challenges to citizenship.
[3] Layton-Henry (2001) 123.

'citizenship begins with determining *membership* in a nation-state. Internally this means establishing "personhood" within a defined geographical territory. Out of the totality of denizens, natives, and subjects of a territory, "the citizen" is given specific rights.'[4] Crucial in this definition of citizenship is that it defines 'bounded populations with a specific set of rights and duties, and excludes others on the grounds of nationality'.[5]

Those who were behind *Education for Citizenship* have undoubtedly exploited the close relationship between the exclusionary definition of the citizen and nationalism, but they have done so in support of a way of looking at citizenship which stresses not the binary divide between the citizen and the non-citizen, but rather the difference between the citizen and the good citizen.[6] Fundamental here is what Michael Ignatieff has called 'the myth of citizenship'.

'The myth of citizenship holds that political life is the means by which men realize the human good.'[7] In seeking 'to create active and responsible citizens' the 1998 report and subsequent curricular reforms have taken for granted 'the values to individuals and society of community activity'.[8] To assume such values is to ignore that 'from its inception . . . citizenship was an exclusionary category, justifying the coercive rule of the included over the excluded'.[9] It is also to ignore the strong trend in liberal political theory that sees such a 'civic republican' notion as fanciful, holding that man 'is a bundle of passions and interests which he satisfies chiefly in market relations and private sociability: the political or public realm is a necessary evil – the institutional arrangements necessary to protect and enhance private freedom'.[10]

But the wishful thinking extends beyond selective historical blindness and a cavalier attitude to philosophers. The 1998 report and subsequent educational reforms also defy the pressures of 'economic processes ceaselessly generating inequality' at a time when the attempt of the welfare state 'to undergird formal legal rights with entitlements to social and economic security so that citizenship could become a real as opposed to a purely formal experience' is being systematically disassembled.[11] Most remarkably, but most fundamentally, the moves attempt to harness the 'myth of citizenship'

[4] Janoski (1998) 9.   [5] Ichilov (1998) 14.
[6] Cf. Crick (2000) 116: 'surveys show that parents favour the idea of citizenship education (Institute for Citizenship, 1998) but perhaps not always "political education"'.
[7] Ignatieff (1995) 53.
[8] I quote from Bernard Crick, who chaired the advisory group responsible for the 1998 report: Crick (2000) 120, 115 (a quotation from the terms of reference of the advisory group).
[9] Ignatieff (1995) 56.   [10] Ignatieff (1995) 54.   [11] Ignatieff (1995) 66.

to an agenda of multicultural pluralism. To quote Bernard Crick once more, 'Pupils must be encouraged (indeed each one of us – never too late to learn) to find and formulate their own values and group identities, but to recognize that in the United Kingdom (let alone Europe and the wide world beyond) there is a diversity of values – national, religious, regional and ethnic.'[12]

The way in which these educational initiatives in the United Kingdom have exploited a concept which has heavy overtones of exclusion in order to promote a policy of inclusion was neither ignorant nor innocent.[13] Whatever the political incentives driving it, it built upon a long history of equivocation over what citizenship is and should be. Scholarly discussion has maintained that there are simply various different 'traditions' on the question of what it is to be a citizen. For Michael Ignatieff, for example, it is a matter of a 'civic' or 'republican' discourse and 'liberal political theory' or 'modern western political tradition'.[14] For John Pocock, on the other hand, the opposition is between the 'classical ideal' and the 'Roman legal conception of citizen':

What is the difference between a classical 'citizen' and an imperial or modern 'subject'? The former ruled and was ruled, which meant among other things that he was a participant in determining the laws by which he was to be bound. The latter could appeal to Caesar; that is, he could go into court and invoke a law that granted him rights, immunities, privileges, and even authority, and that could not ordinarily be denied him once he had established his right to invoke it. But he might have no hand whatever in making that law or in determining what it was to be.[15]

Skinner and Stråth, on the other hand, find a conflict between 'the classical figure of the citizen', which 'implied that a human being achieved morality only within the *civitas*', and the language of rights which 'arose in the context of articulating the moral claims of human beings independently of the positive order of the *civitas*'.[16] And this is very far from exhausting the suggestions made by scholars as to the nature and origins of the inconsistencies and incoherencies involved in contemporary discussions of citizenship.[17]

---

[12] Crick (2000) 120.
[13] It was certainly not an ignorant or innocent move; note Crick's use of 'legal citizen' and 'subject' in the following statement (2000: 117): 'we are a democracy, however imperfect, and its legal citizens should know how it works and how it could be improved if we could change our collective mentality from being subjects of the Crown to being good and active citizens'.
[14] Ignatieff (1995) e.g. 53, 56, 57.   [15] Pocock (1995) 39.   [16] Skinner and Stråth (2003) 5.
[17] Janoski (1998) 8 sees the differences as reflecting 'legal, normative, and social scientific perspectives'; Layton-Henry (2001) 116 detects variation not only between the republican and the English non-republican tradition, in which 'various privileges, duties and obligations ... define one's place as a fully participant member of society', but between the latter and the Common Law tradition from which the notion of citizens' rights is absent and the duty of passive obedience is due from subjects and resident aliens alike.

The assumption, implicit if not explicit, in many of these modern discussions of different ways of thinking about citizens is that the variety of conceptions not only has a history but is itself a product of history: as if, were we able to get behind that history, we would find a simple and coherent notion of the citizen. In particular the implication is that before the Romans came along with their juristic notions of citizenship, or before the development of notions of rights in the sixteenth century or of the modern western political tradition inaugurated by Hobbes and Locke in the seventeenth century, there was simply 'the classical ideal of citizenship'. This ideal is often defined with more or less direct reference to Aristotle and his notion of the citizen ruling and being ruled in turn. But to turn to Aristotle is to discover that the answer to the question 'what is a citizen?' was already a major puzzle to him.

In this chapter I want to take a long hard look at the citizen in classical Greece, and in particular the citizen in classical Athens. I shall try to show that there never has been a simple and coherent idea of citizenship, and that this is because neither the genetic nor the moral qualities expected of a citizen, then and now, were written on the body. The difficulty of defining the citizen body in other than arbitrary or pragmatic ways is closely related to citizenship not being visible on the body. Citizenship was then, as it is now, a category invented and manipulated in an attempt variously to include or exclude individuals and to encourage or cajole them into particular types of behaviour that do not relate to their immediate interests. I begin with a discussion of Greek theorising about citizenship, move on to look at how terms that we translate as 'citizen' were actually used in Greece, and particularly in classical Athens, and at how far there was a sense of citizens as a corporate group, and then turn to the visual record to show how citizenship is not a category that painters or sculptors are interested in signalling.

Aristotle and the classical concept of the citizens

Aristotle devotes considerable space to the question of 'who should be called a citizen (his Greek term being *politēs*), and who the citizen is'.[18] He starts by dismissing residence as the source of citizenship, since residence is not a sufficient qualification, and he dismisses possession of legal rights on the same grounds. He identifies as sufficient 'having a share in giving

---

[18] *Politics* 1275a1. Translations follow R. Robinson (1962).

judgement and exercising office', treating attending the assembly and serving on a jury as counting for this purpose,[19] but he then observes that this is only really applicable to democracies since in other constitutions it may be only a subset of those who exercise office who give judgement.[20] In practice, Aristotle notes, the citizen is defined as one whose parents are both citizens, though this gives problems both for the first inhabitants of a city[21] and for the question of what happens when the constitution changes, since 'when the constitution takes another form and differs, the city also cannot be the same'.[22]

By this point in the discussion Aristotle seems already to have used the term 'citizen' in a number of senses. When he notes that for practical purposes citizens are those both of whose parents are citizens, he requires that women can be citizens, and indeed himself uses the feminine form of the word *politēs, politis*.[23] But in no Greek constitution known to us did women have rights to give judgement and exercise office; not only did they not attend the assembly or serve as jurors, they could not even appear in their own right in courts.[24] Unlike the boys, not yet enrolled, and old men, exempted from service, whom Aristotle agrees to reckon to be qualified citizens, women appear not to meet Aristotle's citizen definition at all.[25]

Aristotle's suggestion that being a citizen involves sharing in office involved him in two puzzles. One is that it means that what it is to be a good citizen will depend on what offices are available to be shared in, that is, what the constitution is. So whereas what it is to be a good man is absolute, what it is to be a good citizen is relative to the constitution.[26] Aristotle insists that 'While good ruling is distinct from good obeying, the good citizen must possess the knowledge and the ability both to obey and to rule; and the goodness of a citizen consists in understanding the government of free men in both directions.'[27]

The second puzzle is whether one can really take simply going along to a democratic assembly to be sharing in office. Aristotle now changes his ground somewhat, his discussion of the good citizen having led him to take a stronger line on what counts as 'ruling'. As a result he proposes that 'there are several kinds of citizen, but the citizen most properly so called is

---

[19] *Politics* 1275a23, 30–2.

[20] *Politics* 1275b5–12. For discussion of why Aristotle needs a broad definition of citizen see Cooper (1990) 228–9; for the question of whether Aristotle ends up with first-class and second-class citizens see Keyt (2005 [1993]) 210–11; Rosler (2005) 180.

[21] *Politics* 1275b22, 33.   [22] *Politics* 1276b2–4.   [23] *Politics* 1275b33. So again at 1278a26–8.

[24] On women and the courts at Athens see Goldhill (1994).

[25] *Politics* 1275a16 (cf. 1278a5–6) for qualified citizens.   [26] *Politics* 1276b16–34.

[27] *Politics* 1277b13–16.

he who has a right to honours'.[28] So can those who qualify for citizenship in the practical sense, being the children of citizens, but do not share in office be citizens?[29] Working men have no rights to honours in aristocratic constitutions and the propertyless no rights to honours in oligarchic ones.[30]

I have dwelt on Aristotle's argument in part because of the ways in which it offers a parallel to the equivocation over 'citizen' which is to be seen in the contemporary citizenship debate, and in part because it reveals very clearly the practical complexities of what are on the face of it relatively straightforward and legalistic exercises in classification. Whatever language one uses, whether it is Aristotle's own language of the 'somehow citizen' (*politēs pōs*) and the 'citizen absolutely' (*politēs haplōs*), or talk of 'broader' and 'narrower' senses of citizen or 'first-class' and 'second-class' citizens, there is no hiding the fact that Aristotle finds himself torn between quite different ways of conceptualising the citizen.[31] Here again there is a tension between citizenship as an exclusionary category, for which one either qualifies or one does not, and citizenship as an activity which may be well done or less well done, and without which human good cannot be achieved.[32] Aristotle both inadvertently and advertently employs 'citizen' in a number of different senses, even as he proposes particular definitions. However successful Aristotle has been in giving the impression to those who read him that there was a single classical ideal of the citizen, as a man who ruled and was ruled in turn, his own text shows that the concept of the citizen was already a contested one.

Modern discussions of classical Athens, however, often regard citizenship as a straightforward matter.[33] 'At Athens, in the fourth century at any rate, a citizen could be defined as someone whose parents were Athenian citizens', writes Mogens Hansen in his standard textbook, citing the Aristotelian *Constitution of the Athenians* 42.1, which reads: 'They share in the

---

[28] *Politics* 1278a34–6, where 'properly so-called' translates *legetai malista politēs*. Newman (1887–1902) vol. III, 173–4: 'Aristotle's inquiry into the nature of citizen-virtue results, in fact, in a change in his standard of citizenship.'

[29] *Politics* 1277b34–5.   [30] *Politics* 1278a18–32.

[31] See above n. 2 for scholars' descriptions of Aristotle's categories. In view of the discussion to follow, I should observe here that Aristotle makes almost no use of the word *astos*. It occurs once in the *Rhetoric* in a quotation from Euripides' *Medea*, and twice in *Politics*, once at 1278a34 when he remarks, surely with Athens in mind, that populous cities end up restricting *politai* to those born *ex amphoin astoin*, and once at 1300b31 in remarking on separate courts being set up, one 'for *xenoi* against *xenoi*', one 'for *xenoi* against *astoi*'.

[32] *Politics* 1253a1–4, 1278b 17—24; cf. *Nicomachean Ethics* 1142a10 'and yet perhaps individual well-being cannot exist without management of a household (*oikonomia*) and without a political system (*politeia*)'.

[33] For consciousness of some of the problems see Connor (1994).

politeia who have been born from *astoi* on both sides.'[34] Hansen then goes on in successive sections to discuss 'Rights of citizenship' and 'Duties of citizenship'. 'The population of Athens', Hansen has already told us,

like that of every city-state, was divided into three clearly differentiated groups: citizens; resident foreigners, called metics (*metoikos*); and slaves. The division shows that Athens was a society based on 'orders' rather than 'classes', for the tripartition was by legal status, i.e. it was based on privileges, or otherwise, protected by law. Membership of a group was typically inherited, and the groups were ordered hierarchically . . . [35]

The exclusionary nature of citizenship at Athens is still more strongly stressed by Josiah Ober, who writes that 'Foreigners and slaves, who were excluded from citizenship, could be looked down upon by even the poorest and least well-educated citizen. The citizen "in-group" was, therefore, a hereditary aristocracy when compared to non-citizen "out-groups".'[36]

Aristotle has exercised a great deal of influence over the ways in which modern scholars, and Hansen in particular, have conceptualised the classical Greek *polis*.[37] But Aristotle's concern with citizenship as a capacity that needs to be actualised, in ruling and being ruled, and with what makes a 'good' citizen has left no mark on the way in which Hansen and others write of Athenian citizenship. Even so, however, Hansen finds himself unable to maintain a consistent view of what it was to be a citizen at Athens. His definition is gender neutral and allows for women as well as men to be citizens. He is initially scrupulous in identifying the differences between male and female citizen rights – 'Metics and slaves lived alongside the citizens in a city-state, but the state itself was a community of citizens only, and of male citizens at that',[38] 'Female citizens were not registered at all'[39] – but he soon lets his guard down: 'The principal privilege of an Athenian citizen was his political rights; in fact they were more than just a "privilege": they constituted the essence of citizenship.'[40] Women, it appears, were citizens but did not have 'the essence of citizenship'. Even when scholars adopt a legalistic mode of describing citizenship at Athens that employs notions (such as rights) not employed by classical Athenian writers, they nevertheless, it appears, find Athenian citizenship impossible consistently to encapsulate.[41] Why is this?

---

[34] Hansen (1991) 94.   [35] Hansen (1991) 86.   [36] Ober (1989) 261.
[37] See Schofield (1999) 100.   [38] Hansen (1991) 88.   [39] Hansen (1991) 96.
[40] Hansen (1991) 97.
[41] On whether the language of rights is appropriate and whether it is employed by Aristotle see Schofield (1999) ch. 8.

Citizenship terminology in classical Greece

To answer the question of why Athenian citizenship is impossible consistently to encapsulate it is necessary to delve more deeply into the discourse of citizenship in the Greek world and in Athens in particular.[42] Those who are content to accept the conclusion may prefer to pass over this detailed discussion and resume reading at page 102.

There are two terms which scholars translate as 'citizen', *politēs* derived from *polis*, and *astos* derived from *astu* (standardly translated 'town'). *Polis* gives us the adjective *politikos*, with its 'political' overtones; *astu* gives the adjective *asteios*, the equivalent of 'urbane'.[43] It has been easy therefore to assume *politēs* to have primarily a political sense, *astos* a primarily local sense.[44] More recently Mogens Hansen has insisted that '*astos* is never used in the sense of "townsman" but invariably used about citizens and almost synonymously with *politēs*. The only difference is that *astos* tends to denote a man of citizen birth, whereas *politēs* is used when the emphasis is on a citizen's exercise of his political rights'.[45]

Both *astos* and *politēs* are found already in the Homeric poems.[46] Although literary commentators sometimes happily translate them there as 'fellow-citizens',[47] the term carries no implications of any political involvement, and Scully must be correct when he observes that 'In Homer, *politai* are not "citizens" but more simply "inhabitants of a *polis*".'[48] The regular Homeric term, used 229 times in the *Iliad* alone, for those subject to the rule of a king is *laos*, 'people'; the leader has responsibility to and for the people, but the people do not themselves have a political role.[49] This is precisely the

---

[42] It is remarkable that until recently there has been so little informed discussion of the discourse of citizenship in ancient Greece – to such an extent that the position adopted by E. E. Cohen (2000) (see below n. 44) could seem initially plausible. Now, as well as Lévy (1985), see Blok (2005), Brock (2009).

[43] On urbanity and rusticity see Ramage (1973).

[44] This tendency is taken to an extreme by E. E. Cohen (2000) ch. 2, 49–63, which begins (49): 'In the fourth century, the residents of Attika shared a fundamental identification not as *politai* (citizens), but as *astoi* (locals). As *astoi*, they stood in complementary polarity to *xenoi* (foreigners).' See R. Osborne 2003. That it is a mistake to take *politikos* as having 'political' overtones emerges clearly from the social use of the term by Aristotle, *History of Animals* 488a8, who remarks that '*politika* creatures are such as have some one common object in view; and this property is not common to all creatures that are gregarious. Such *politika* creatures are man, the bee, the wasp, the ant, and the crane', where *politika* is best translated 'social'.

[45] Hansen (1997) 11; cf. Hansen and Nielsen (2006) 48.   [46] Lévy (1985).

[47] So Hainsworth (1993) on *astoi* at *Iliad* 11.242; Kirk (1985) on *polietai* at *Iliad* 2.806. Heubeck and Hoekstra (1989) on *Odyssey* 13.192 recognise that *astoi* there may mean 'fellow-countrymen' or just 'people'.

[48] Scully (1990) 1, cf. index p. 222.   [49] See especially Haubold (2000).

structure imagined also by Hesiod, who writes in *Works and Days*: 'But for those who give straight judgements to visitors and locals and do not deviate from what is just, their city (*polis*) flourishes and the people (*laoi*) bloom in it.'[50]

Throughout archaic texts, living in a particular *polis* or *astu* is enough to qualify one as a *politēs* or *astos*. *Politai* (and it is the plural form that is most commonly found) is certainly used by archaic authors in political contexts, but never in contexts which demand that political power rests with the *politai* or where *politai* are contrasted with some other group of (politically disempowered) residents in a *polis*. Alkaios of Lesbos talks of 'longing to hear the assembly summoned and council' after he had been driven away from his father's property 'among the mutually destructive *politai*', but when he comes to express what defends the *polis* it is striking that he he employs simply the term 'men', not *politai*.[51]

Similarly, *astoi* is used by archaic poets to refer to the whole population of the city, and may variously be equated with the *politai* or the *dēmos*. So Solon writes that 'the *astoi* themselves want to destroy a great city through folly, persuaded by money, and the intentions of the leaders of the *dēmos* are wicked'.[52] Theognis both tells Kyrnos not to be cut up when the *politai* are distressed and not to trust any of the *astoi*.[53] *Politai* and *astoi* alike here are political subjects and refer to a community who do things together, but they are not a demarcated subset of the city residents. The terms are happily used by poets who have no political interest, so that Xenophanes can talk of someone becoming 'more glorious for the *astoi* to look upon', and Anakreon can write of a boy with a lovely face: 'many of the *politai* found their hearts fluttering'.[54]

This continues to be the pattern of usage into the fifth century. Pindar uses *politēs* only five times, and in all cases it is best taken as referring to city residents – in one instance explicitly contrasted with foreigners (*xenoi*).[55] He uses *astoi* rather more frequently and in five cases makes the contrast between *astoi* and *xenoi*; in one case he opposes *astoi* to kings (*basileis*).[56] Neither term is used to distinguish one section of the population of the city from another, or to flag up those who have political capacity. *Politēs* and *astos* alike seem only to have a residence requirement.

[50] *Works and Days* 225–7; I quote Haubold's translation.　[51] Alkaios frs. 130, 112, cf. 426.
[52] Solon 4.5–7.　[53] Theognis 219, 283.　[54] Xenophanes 2.6; Anakreon 1.12 (*PMG* 346).
[55] Pindar uses *politai* at *Olympian* 5.16; *Pythian* 4.117, 296, 9.28; *Nemean* 2.24; *Isthmian* 1.51. It is in this last case that the contrast is with *xenoi*.
[56] *Astoi: xenoi Olympian* 7.90, 13.2; *Pythian* 3.71, 4.78; *Isthmian* 2.37. *Astoi: basileis Pythian* 1.68.

The earliest author who uses *politai* to mean those able to engage in political life is Herodotos, writing in the last third of the fifth century, and in his text too the vast majority of uses of the word do not carry that connotation. Enoch Powell, in his famous *Lexicon to Herodotus*, divides use of *politēs* into three categories: he lists eight passages in which the word means 'citizens', seven in which it means 'fellow-citizens' or 'fellow-countrymen' and eleven passages in which it means 'subjects of a king or tyrant'. In some of these cases the point is actually obscured if *politēs* is burdened with political content. So at 2.160.2 the Egyptians ask the Eleans whether their own *politai* take part in the Olympic games, and hearing that they do, they comment that there is no way they will not favour their own *astos* and so wrong the foreigner (*xenos*). Here the crucial distinction is between the local and the foreign, and the question of whether or not the local has political capacities is not merely irrelevant but would distract from the point at issue.

Closer examination reveals that in two, or possibly three cases, where Powell classifies the meaning as 'citizens' 'fellow-countrymen' is in fact a better translation,[57] but in five passages, at least, being given political capacities is indeed more or less explicitly what is at issue.[58] The clearest case of all concerns Teisamenos of Elis, the seer. Herodotos recounts that 'Teisamenos saw that the Spartiates thought it very important to make him their friend, and learning this he raised his price, indicating to them that he would do what they wanted if they made him their *poliētēs* and *gave him a share of everything*, but not on any other condition.'[59] Teisamenos' request for a share of everything here makes it clear that he is not merely asking to live at Sparta. Herodotos goes on to say that he reckons Teisamenos to have imitated Melampous in asking for both kingship and *politeia* – in the earliest occurrence of the abstract noun *politeia* to mean 'citizenship'.[60]

---

[57] So at 2.167.1 when those who learn craft skills are said to be held in less esteem than the rest of the *politai* there is no reason to think the comparison is only with those residents with political capacities. Even less probable is it that at 5.16.2 the Paionian *politai* who worked together to build platforms were only the politically empowered. At 1.150.2 it seems to me ambiguous whether the Smyrnaeans divided between other Ionian cities are being identified as given political powers or simply accepted as residents.

[58] Herodotos 5.57.2, 7.156.2, 8.75.1, 9.33.4 and 9.35.1.   [59] 9.33.4, cf. also 35.1.

[60] 9.34.1. On the invention of the abstract noun *politeia* at this period and its various uses see Meier (1990) 171, n. 63. Dawson (1992) 8 suggests that the 'basic meaning' of *politeia* 'is best conveyed by a phrase like "the condition of the citizen body"', and notes that 'we should bear in mind that *Politeia* did not have the formal legalistic connotations of "constitution". It did include the political system, but it included also the whole social system.' In the light of this latter observation Dawson's 'basic meaning' might be better rephrased as 'the condition of those who live in the city'. Cf. also Schofield (1999) 59–60.

Powell offers three meanings for *astos* in Herodotos: 'native', 'fellow-countryman' and 'the people', used of both Greek and non-Greek communities. The most interesting and revealing passages are those in which *astos* is used alongside other terms denoting civic status. In book 1 Herodotos discusses the Lycian practice of taking their names from their mothers rather than their fathers, and goes on: 'If a woman who is an *astē* cohabits with a slave, the children are considered noble; but if a man who is an *astos*, even if he is the most prominent of them, has a *xeinē* wife or concubine, the children have no honour (*atima*)'.[61] Here *astos* status is contrasted both with slave status and with foreign status, making it clear that it involves freedom and being a city resident, but the terms used for the status of the children in this passage, *gennaia* and *atima*, point to social standing, not merely to political capacities. In book 7 Xerxes is made to claim it as a universal fact that

if one *poliētēs* prosper another *poliētēs* is jealous of him and shows his enmity by silence, and no *poliētēs* (unless he has attained to the height of excellence; and such are seldom seen), if his own *astos* asks for counsel, will give him what he deems the best advice. But if one *xeinos* prosper, another *xeinos* is beyond all men his well-wisher, and will if he be asked impart to him the best counsel he has.[62]

Not only does Herodotos move easily here between *politēs* and *astos*, but, as in the passage about Eleans at the Olympic games quoted above, which also uses both *politēs* and *astos*, the point is one about how fellow-members of a community regard each other, not about those who have or lack political capacities.

How does Herodotos' use of *astos* and *politēs* compare with contemporary Athenian usage? Athenian inscriptions and the Xenophontic *Constitution of the Athenians* use both terms rarely but in similar ways. In the *Constitution of the Athenians*, *politēs* is used twice. At the beginning of the work the author observes that it is fair that any *politēs* can speak given that the *dēmos* rows the ships and so empowers the city.[63] Later he observes that the *dēmos* can observe which *politai* are *chrēstoi* and which *ponēroi*, but it chooses to be friendly to those who can be most advantageous to it, even if they are *ponēroi*.[64] *Astos* is used just once, and that is when legal status is explicitly at issue: 'we allowed slaves equality of speech (*isēgoria*) with free men, and metics equality of speech with *astoi* because the city needs metics'.[65] *Astos*

---

[61] Herodotos 1.173.5.   [62] Herodotos 7.237.2.
[63] [Xenophon], *Constitution of the Athenians* 1.2.
[64] [Xenophon], *Constitution of the Athenians* 2.19.
[65] [Xenophon], *Constitution of the Athenians* 1.12.

occurs in two Athenian fifth-century inscriptions, and *politēs* in three. One instance of *politēs* is too fragmentary to be comprehensible, one occurs in a proxeny inscription of 416/15, promising that harm to Proxenides will be treated like harm to a *politēs*, and the third case is in the Standards Decree, where anyone, *xenos* or *politēs*, who holds office in the cities and does not act according to the decree is threatened with confiscation of property. In this last case it is clear that *politai* and *xenoi* between them are meant to cover all eventualities.[66] *Astos* occurs in the decree from the 430s about tribute to Apollo, where both *astoi* and *xenoi* who are archers are promised the same pay, and in the list of sailors of uncertain late fifth-century date. Here on four occasions there is a heading '*astoi* sailors', distinguishing the names that follow both from specific officers (the helmsman, the ship's carpenter, etc.) but also from *xenoi* and *therapontes*.[67] Again, in as far as these few cases provide a picture, it is the Herodotean picture of *astos* being used as the narrow term for legal status, *politēs* as a more general term for free inhabitants of the *polis*.

Rather more evidence comes from Thucydides. Thucydides uses *astos* on six occasions, on five of them in explicit contrast with *xenos*. Twice this is in the context of who attended the public funeral of the war dead and heard the funeral oration, once it is about the Athenians sending out all their troops, and once about encouraging everyone to inform on the mutilation of the Herms – *astoi*, *xenoi* and *douloi*.[68] In the fifth occurrence Alcibiades is made to express sentiments that chime with those of Xerxes in Herodotos and contrast the grudging attitude of *astoi* to choregic and other glory to the positive impression that such things make on *xenoi*.[69] The sixth use of *astos* is particularly interesting. In telling the story of the murder of Hipparchos, Thucydides describes his assassin Aristogeiton as 'a man of the *astoi*, a middling *politēs*'.[70] Here *astos* appears as something one is or is not, *politēs* as something that admits of further qualification.

If we turn to Thucydides' use of *politēs*, which he employs twenty-seven times, we find no explicit comparison with *xenoi*. The closest to such a contrast is in Perikles' speech in response to the Spartan ultimatum, where Perikles discusses the possibility that the Peloponnesians might try to buy off

---

[66] *IG* i³ 94.6 (fragmentary), 91.19 (Proxenides), 1453 clause 3 (Standards Decree).

[67] *IG* i³ 138.3 (tribute of Apollo), 1032.3, 50, 172, 305 (*xenoi* is restored at 71 and 417, *therapontes* at 227).

[68] Thucydides 2.34.4, 2.36.4, 4.94, 6.27.2.

[69] Thucydides 6.16.3. This is remarkably close to the sentiment expressed by Xerxes at Herodotos 7.237.2.

[70] Thucydides 6.54.2.

Athens' *xenoi* sailors, leaving Athens with inadequate forces, just themselves and their metics, and then remarks that the most important thing is that the Athenians have helmsmen (*kubernētai*) who are *politai*.[71] The contrast here, however, seems to be not between those who have and those who do not have political capacities at Athens, but between those who, whether as citizen or as metic, have a long-term link to the Athenian community, and those who do not. Such a reference to all the residents of the city seems to be general in Thucydides' use of *politēs*, whether in relation to Athens (as when he talks of the Four Hundred harming the *polis* and the *politai*)[72] or elsewhere (in the stasis at Kerkyra 'the middle sort of *politai* (*ta mesa tōn politōn*) were destroyed'.[73] Particularly revealing are Perikles' insistence that it is 'best for the whole city to flourish, not for individual *politai* to do well but the whole to slip', and Thucydides' description of the crowd seeing off the Sicilian expedition consisting of 'the *politai* and if anyone else well-intentioned (*eunous*) was there'.[74]

We can follow this tendency to use *astos* if issues of legal status are in question, and to use *politēs* only rarely to refer to those residents of the city who are politically capacitated, throughout Athenian authors of the later fifth and fourth centuries. This is the case with Lysias who uses *politēs* some 112 times, but in fewer than half a dozen of these when possession of political capacities is at issue.[75] When, for instance, Lysias says that Alcibiades was 'such a *politēs*' from the beginning that everyone should treat him as an enemy (*echthros*), it is his behaviour as a member of the community that is at issue.[76]

Two Lysias passages are particularly interesting from our point of view. In the speech *Against Philon* Lysias is trying to persuade the Athenians to reject Philon at his scrutiny and not allow him to be a member of the Council. He maintains that it is proper (*dikaios*) for no others to give counsel than those who, in addition to actually being *politai*, also desire this (i.e. to be a *politēs*), and he goes on to distinguish these from those who 'although *politai* by nature treat every land in which they have what they need as their

---

71 Thucydides 1.143.1.   72 Thucydides 8.72.1.   73 Thucydides 3.82.8.

74 Thucydides 2.60.2, 6.32.2.

75 The most plausible cases are 30.27, where *politēs* is contrasted with *doulos* (but here *politēs* effectively means 'highest status of free man'), 31.9 where *politēs* is contrasted with *metoikos* (but it is submitting to paying the metic tax and having an official patron (*prostatēs*) that is stressed), and 23.7 where the speaker asks Plataians if they know a *politēs* of theirs called Pankleon, and is told that they know no *politēs* of that name but do know a slave (see further below, pp. 218–19). In all these cases community membership is certainly at issue, but political capacities are never flagged up.

76 Lysias 14.1.

fatherland'; such people, he claims, 'would let go of the common good of their city for the sake of private gain, since they regard not the city but their property as their fatherland'.[77] Although possessing political capacity was obviously a prerequisite for serving on the Council, Lysias' concern here is not with 'being a *politēs*' in that sense but with being a devoted member of the community, with economic behaviour flagged up as the crucial indicator.

The second peculiarly revealing passage comes in Lysias' prosecution of Eratosthenes, where he compares his own family's behaviour as metics with the behaviour of the Thirty. Such a comparison might seem to put the political capacities of the citizen at centre stage, but in fact Lysias immediately goes on with a passage which reveals that he is thinking of those political capacities as additional to being a *politēs*, rather than the central matter. For in describing the way the Thirty acted as *politai* (*epoliteuonto*) he says: 'These men drove many of the *politai* into the hands of the enemy, many they killed unjustly and left unburied, many who were possessed of rights (*epitimoi*) they deprived of rights (made *atimoi*), and they prevented the marriage of the daughters of many who were about to be married.'[78] The very fact of contrasting *politai* with political capacities to *politai* without capacities flags up that the central concern here is with permanent membership of the community, not possession or absence of political capacities.

Lysias uses the term *astos* only once, and does so in a context where he contrasts *astos* with *xenos* and then immediately glosses *astoi* as being *politai*. He is claiming that according to what the court decides *astoi* will learn either that wrongdoing will be punished or that if they do what they desire they will become tyrants of the city. Although political action is in question here, the focus is not on the possession of political capacities but on behaviour within the city community, and the point of discussing the interests of both *astoi* and *xenoi* in the result of the case is to stress that what the court decides sends a message both to permanent and to temporary residents, that is to all free agents.[79]

Isokrates offers a similar picture. There are some 135 passages in which he employs the term *politai*. But in only three of these are those possessed of political capacities at issue. In the *Panegyric* he talks of men who are by nature *politai* but deprived of their *politeia* and reduced to being metics.[80] In *On the Peace* he contrasts the fifth century, in which *politai* put *xenoi* and slaves on triremes but themselves fought as hoplites, with the present in which *politai* row and it is *xenoi* who serve as hoplites.[81] And in the

---

[77] Lysias 31.5–6.   [78] Lysias 12.21.   [79] Lysias 12.35.   [80] Isokrates 4.105.   [81] Isokrates 8.48.

Aeginetan Speech he talks of *politai* who were in Troizen.[82] But use of the term *politai* in the sense simply of 'residents of the *polis*' is not only possible in the other passages, it is actually necessary in a number of cases that the restriction of *politai* to those with political capacities is not strongly felt. So in the *Panegyric* he makes a point about the Athenians having the smallest land in proportion to the number of *politai*, where it must be the total number of residents that is at issue not how many residents have political capacities. A little later in the same speech he talks of men who lament the fate of the Melians but dare to wrong their own *politai*, where the contrast must be between residents of one, foreign, place, Melos, and residents of home territory, not between those politically capacitated in the two places.[83] In *On the Peace* he extols the city which preserves those whose ancestry lies in its territory, over the city which gathers *politai* from all men at random; again this is not a matter of who is politically empowered but of who the city's residents are.[84] In the *Evagoras* when Evagoras is praised for making the *politai* Greeks rather than barbarians, it is all the residents who are in question.[85] Finally, in two passages of the *Antidosis* when Isokrates praises Athens for having been a cause of good things to many Greeks and not just to its own *politai*, and when he says that it is the greatest thing for a *sophistēs* that his pupils have good repute among the *politai*, it is all in Athens who are in mind, not only those who could attend the Assembly.[86]

Isokrates uses the term *astos* only once, and he does so to contrast those who use 'the most reckless of *astoi* as advisers', with others who 'choose the wisest from all men'.[87] Here Isokrates wants to emphasise the narrowness of the circle from which advisers are drawn in the first case, and the breadth in the second: *astos* is the term which spells restriction. Isokrates also uses once the term *politis*, the feminine form of *politēs*. The *politis* had no political capacities, of course.[88]

The contrast between *astos* and *politēs* emerges still more clearly from the speeches of Isaios. Isaios uses the term *politēs* some sixteen times, but never in a way that requires political capacities and occasionally, as when he uses the phrase *metrios politēs*, it is essential that political capacities are not in view. In fact political capacity is much closer to the surface when he uses, once, the term *politis*, noting an opponent's claim that 'our mother was not a *politis*, and nor were we'.[89] By contrast *astos* is used by Isaios six times, and always with possession of political rights at issue, either directly (as

[82] Isokrates 19.31.   [83] Isokrates 4.107, 110.   [84] Isokrates 8.89.   [85] Isokrates 9.66.
[86] Isokrates 15.171, 220.   [87] Isokrates 3.21.   [88] Isokrates 14.51.
[89] Isaios 8.43. The occurrence of *metrios politēs* is at 7.40.

when he talks of 'making a child an *astos*') or indirectly, as when he stresses the *astos* status of parents in order to stress the consequent status of the child.[90]

Isaios' range of subject matter is highly restrictive since he specialised in arguing inheritance cases, but his linguistic usage is only corroborated by authors whose interests in the life of the *polis* range more widely. None ranges more widely, or is more highly sensitive to verbal nuance, than Plato. Plato's dialogues both serve to confirm the picture which has begun to emerge from other authors and enable us to enrich our sense of the semantic reach of the terms involved.

Plato's use of *astos* offers straightforward confirmation of the way in which that term became the term of choice for political status. He uses the word in just over twenty places, more than half of them in *Laws*, and he consistently uses the word to mark legal status, using it in opposition to other status terms, and particularly to *xenos* and *metoikos*. When describing how too great a desire for freedom destroys democracy, in *Republic* 8 Plato draws attention to the anarchy that results when sons expect to be like their fathers and have no fear of their parents, and when *metoikoi* are put on a par with *astoi* and *astoi* with *metoikoi*, and *xenoi* likewise.[91] In *Laws* legal status matters both for the nature of the offence and for the nature of the punishment. With regard to punishments, in cases of misrepresentation in the courts 'if the motive appears to be love of money', a *xenos* must leave the country and never return on pain of death, but an *astos* must die for letting love of money become the obsession of his life.[92] Or again in the case of theft of public property, a *xenos* or *doulos* is to be fined, on grounds of probably being curable, but an *astos* must be punished by death, since in his case the crime shows that he is impervious to education.[93] With regard to crimes, the regulations for killing in self-defence show a series of subtle discriminations of legal status, with no pollution incurred if an *astos* kills a *xenos* or a *xenos* an *astos*, and if a *doulos* kills a *doulos*, but not if a *doulos* kills an *eleutheros*.[94] This is particularly interesting since *astos* is used as the status term when killing across status groups is involved, but when killing within status groups is mentioned then Plato talks of *politēs* killing *politēs* (and *xenos* killing *xenos*). In similar fashion Plato explicitly rules out status distinction between free victims of slave violence, laying down the same

---

[90] Isaios 4.10 for making a *paidion* an *astos*; the other references are 6.25, 7.16, 8.19, and 12.7 and 9.

[91] *Republic* 563a1.   [92] *Laws* 938c2.   [93] *Laws* 941d4–942a4.

[94] *Laws* 869d2–7. For the implications of this for our understanding of pollution see below, Chapter 6.

procedure for all cases where a *doulos* strikes an *eleutheros* whether *xenos* or *astos*.[95]

Politēs is sometimes used by Plato to refer to legal status, but unlike *astos* it is also used in many other ways. Even with regard to status, *politēs* seems to be used often where reference needs to be comparatively wide, where women are involved, or where it is the *polis* as a religious community rather than just a political community that is in question. So, in *Laws* the woman in charge of supervising marriage is given powers to order the punishment of slaves, *xenoi* and *politai* who do not dispute her judgement, while handing over to the *astunomoi* those *politai* who do question the judgement.[96] When fake goods are denounced, *douloi* and *metoikoi* get to keep the object in question, but *politai* are obliged to dedicate it to the gods.[97] In cases of temple robbery, slaves and *xenoi* are to be branded, *politai* are to be put to death.[98] When prosecution for murder is concerned, the same procedure is laid down for *xenoi* prosecuting *xenoi*, *astoi* prosecuting *xenoi*, and *xenoi*, *astoi* and slaves prosecuting slaves; but when someone kills an innocent slave, fearing he might become an informer, he is to be treated as if he had killed a *politēs*.[99]

The potential breadth of *politēs* even as a term denoting political status, is nicely revealed by one further passage of *Laws*. Plato has it laid down that 'No resident (*epichōrios*) should be among those who labour at craft activities (*demoiourgika*), nor should the servant (*oiketēs*) of a resident man. For a *politēs* man has got enough skilled work (*technē*), needing practice and many lessons, preserving the common good order of the *polis*.'[100] Here the logic of the sentence demands that *politēs* cover both of the instances signalled in the first clause, that is both the resident and the resident's servant. More straightforwardly, '*politai* and *xenoi*' is the phrase used in *Meno* when the reference is simply to 'all free men'.[101]

Frequently Plato uses *politēs* in a way which simply conjures up a member of the *polis* community. Characters regularly refer to others as 'my *politēs* and yours' or '*politai* of your comrade'.[102] It is often co-ordinate with comrades, or kin, or those belonging to the same household.[103] It is the term used when

[95] *Laws* 882a2.   [96] *Laws* 794b4–c2.
[97] *Laws* 917d4; this follows immediately on from a passage where taking action against an offence is required specifically of 'the passer-by who is an *astos*, not less than thirty years old', 917c5.
[98] *Laws* 854d1–e7.   [99] *Laws* 872a7–c6.   [100] *Laws* 846d1–6.   [101] *Meno* 91a5.
[102] *Hipparchus* 228b4, *Meno* 70b2 for these cases. See also *Protagoras* 315c4, 324c3, 6, 339e6, *Hipparchus* 228e2, *Minos* 321b7, *Laws* 629a5, 630a4, 753a2, *Apologia* 37c8, *Parmenides* 126b8.
[103] *Republic* 494b9–10, 568a5, *Laws* 627b3, *Protagoras* 337c8.

the whole community needs to be referred to, for instance when speaking of the common joy or trouble of a community.[104]

Striking, and most important for our understanding of the complexity of the notion of the citizen, is the way in which being a *politēs* is something which admits of being performed well or badly. Although the evaluative language of the Xenophontic *Constitution of the Athenians* is also the language of social class, Thucydides already talks of the good *politēs*, referring not to social class but to personal virtue and participation in the community.[105] The issues of who has been a good *politēs*, and of how *politai* might be made better, recur constantly through Plato's discussions.[106] This qualification of *politēs* is a feature common to many classical texts. Even Isaios variously refers to the good *politēs*, the middling (*metrios*) *politēs*, the useful (*chrēsimos*) *politēs*.[107] As we have already seen, the issue of what exactly being a good *politēs* is, and how it relates to being a good man, is a major preoccupation of Aristotle in *Politics* book 3.

Citizen discourse and the citizen body

We have, I suggest, now seen enough of citizen discourse in classical Athens to understand why Aristotle and modern scholars find Athenian citizenship so hard to deal with consistently. If we imagine the 'natural history of a *polis*', rather as Aristotle does in *Politics* 1, it is easy to see that who belongs to a household admits of little dispute, and when households are put together to constitute a *polis* relatively little further ambiguity is generated. But when the 'natural' rule of the senior within the households comes into question, and new conventions arise as to who is empowered or obliged to do what in the *polis*, belonging to the community can come to mean various different things in different contexts. Both *politēs* and *astos* are words that start by meaning members of communities, the community of the *polis* and of the *astu*. They go on with those meanings, but while, in Athens at least, *astos* comes to be used precisely for those given political capacities, and so to indicate a particular legal and political status, *politēs* remains widely used to cover a whole range of ways of belonging to the community, of which having political capacities is only one. *Politēs* is the term which comes naturally to the lips and pens of Athenians when they look around and need to refer to

---

[104] *Republic* 462b5, 464a4, *Menexenus* 243e5, cf. *Protagoras* 324d8, *Euthydemus* 292b6.

[105] On the *Constitution of the Athenians* see R. Osborne (2004a) 11–12; Thucydides' good *politai*, 3.42.5, 6.9.2, 6.19.1, 6.53.2.

[106] *Protagoras* 319a5, *Gorgias* 502e4, 513e7, 515c1, 515c7, 515d10, 517b7, 517c2, 518b1, *Meno* 90a6, *Theages* 127d7, *Laws* 822e5, 823a2.

[107] Isaios 6.9, 7.40, Budé fr. 3.1.1.

those they see, or those from whom they expect a certain sort of action, but it never becomes a narrow technical term. While Hansen's negative strictures about the absence of association between *astos* and residing in a town are well made, both his claim that *astos* refers particularly to those of citizen birth and his claim that *politēs* is used to emphasise a citizen's exercise of his rights are mistaken.

Establishing what exactly an Athenian had in mind when using the word *politēs* is fundamental to my enquiry because it reveals how social classification worked in Athens (and indeed, though we do not have the same density of information, for all we can see in the rest of the classical Greek world too). The question which an Athenian implicitly answered when deciding to talk about his *politai* was not the question of who could vote in the Assembly or stand for office; it was the question of who was a member of the Athenian community and who was an outsider. Membership of the community extended easily to cover women, children and even in some circumstances metics. Belonging to the community brought about expectations of behaviour, not thoughts of rights, and if one asked an Athenian man to subdivide the class of *politai* the first thought he would have would be to differentiate between good or useful *politai* and bad *politai*.

Modern scholars have, at least since its publication in 1891, been influenced by the way in which the Aristotelian *Constitution of the Athenians* begins its description of that constitution by isolating who 'share in the *politeia*', that is who it is who rules and is ruled in turn.[108] When that is the question, the answer has to be 'those born from two citizen parents who have been inscribed into the demes at the age of 18'. But for Athenians that is a different question from 'who is a *politēs*?' If we are to understand the Athenian citizen body, we must start not from the question of who ruled and was ruled in turn but from the way Athenians classified those around them into *politai* and others.

I have noted that *politēs* is a term found first in the plural, to refer to a group doing things together. But to what extent were the *politai* conceived of as a body? That is a question with two parts, one of which concerns the extent to which and circumstances in which *politai* were classed together

---

[108] [Aristotle] *Constitution of the Athenians* 42.1. The Aristotelian resonance of this phrase is rightly picked out by Sandys (1893) ad loc. but obscured by Rhodes (1981) ad loc. Even Sandys fails to note the most relevant Aristotelian passage, *Politics* 1275a22–33. Lysias 30.15, cited by Rhodes on *Constitution of the Athenians* 9.5, shows that 'sharing in the *politeia*' might be understood as *exercising* political capacities, not merely potentially possessing them, for it describes citizens who have gone into exile, but not been stripped of citizenship, as not sharing in the *politeia*.

and separated from others. The other is a narrower question about the use of the image of the body. That latter question can be relatively quickly answered.

Greek authors find that body analogies come readily to hand. Plato in the *Republic* investigates justice in the state by investigating the relationships of parts of the soul.[109] Five hundred years later, Lucian in *Anacharsis* develops the thought of the city as a human organism in a slightly different way, suggesting that walls and buildings are the body of a city, and citizens themselves are the soul, which is why cities take particular care of the souls and bodies of their citizens.[110] When in book 1 Aristotle thinks about the relationship between household and *polis* he employs the analogy of the body to demonstrate that the *polis* is prior: 'for the *polis* is by nature prior to the household and each of us. For the whole must be prior to the part. For if the whole is destroyed there will be no foot or hand, unless homonymously, as if someone were to speak of a stone hand.'[111] But Aristotle never refers to the state as a body.

The phrase 'the body of the *polis*' appears first in the work of Deinarchos and Hypereides in the second half of the fourth century. The former urges Athenians to think of the body of the *polis* so as to see that it is more worthy of pity than is Demosthenes. The latter claims that Demosthenes and Demades, having made money from decrees of the city and royal gifts, now take money 'against the body of the city'.[112] In neither of these two usages is the image being used to highlight the close organic relationship between citizens, such that they form a single body. Rather the body is here an image standing for something that is living and with which others can empathise.[113] By contrast, when the phrase 'body of the state' becomes a familiar one in Latin (*corpus rei publicae*),[114] it is as an image of the organic union of different parts, and it is in the Roman world that the fable of the parts of the body warring against each other, and so destroying the whole, was transferred from the context of warring brothers and of the army, to which it is applied in Greek texts, to the state.[115] In this strict sense, there is no body politic in the classical Greek world.

[109] On which see the classic analysis by Williams (1973), and G. R. F. Ferrari (2003). See more generally Brock (2006), esp. 352–3.
[110] Lucian, *Anacharsis* 20 (words ascribed to Solon).   [111] Aristotle, *Politics* 1253a18ff.
[112] Deinarchos I.110, Hypereides V col. 25.
[113] Compare Brock (2000) 25–6 on the absence of anatomical detail in political use of body imagery in Greek texts.
[114] Cicero, *On Duties* I.85, *Against Piso* 25, *Pro Murena* 51; Seneca, *Moral Letters* 102.6; *Digest* 41.3.30, 6.1.23.5.
[115] Xenophon, *Memoirs of Socrates* 2.3.18–19 (brothers), Aesop 132 and Polyainos 3.9.22 (army); applied to state in Livy 2.32.8–12 (cf. Cicero, *On Duties* 3.22 and Dyck (1996) ad loc.).

What of the larger question, of the extent to which the *politai* were classed together and separated from others? We have seen that *politēs* is indeed contrasted with *xenos*, but the contexts in which that occurs are almost always concerned not with the *politai* as a group but with the position of the individual *politēs*. When we have discussion of *politai* it is notable that they are rarely if ever contrasted with any other group. This is in one sense both unsurprising and trivial: any context in which an Athenian wants to contrast the citizen group with a body of non-citizens is likely to be a context in which it is better to talk of 'the Athenians' and a body of identified *xenoi* (e.g. Spartans). But the absence of circumstances in which reference to a citizen body was appropriate is itself a significant historical fact.

It is worth comparing the Roman situation. As early as the late third century BC Greeks themselves observed that Romans used citizenship differently. Philip V of Macedon in a letter to Larissa written in 215 argues that it is the best state of affairs for as many as possible to enjoy citizenship, and he adduces as proof that 'the Romans, when they manumit their slaves, admit them to the citizen body and grant them a share in magistracies, and in this way have not only enlarged their country but have sent out colonies to nearly seventy places'.[116] Modern scholars have proceeded to contrast Roman generosity of citizenship with Greek miserliness. But Roman generosity was combined with a strong differentiation between the political and legal rights of Roman citizens and of others, and with a Roman division of the world according to statuses ascribed by the Romans themselves. It was the Romans who had a census and listed citizens; the Athenians had no such list and only in exceptional circumstances attempted practically to differentiate the citizen body.[117] Greek miserliness was part of a world where possession of a particular citizenship remained primarily a local matter.[118]

The invisible citizen body

So far my discussion of the citizen body has revealed that the modern ambiguity over whether citizenship is simply a matter of having formal links to a community or is about how one behaves in that community can be traced back to ancient Greece. The same ambiguity is present in the most

---

[116] *SIG* 543.31–3, Austin (2006) no. 75.

[117] Notably in the *diapsephismos* of 346/5: Aischines 1.77, 86; Demosthenes 57; Isaios 12; cf. Plutarch, *Pericles* 37.4.

[118] It is indicative of the different nature of citizenship in the Greek and Roman world that various books explore Roman citizenship and the world of the Roman citizen (Sherwin-White (1973), Nicolet (1980)); no comparable work exists on citizenship at Athens or in any other Greek city.

insightful and extended ancient discussion of what it is to be a citizen, in Aristotle's *Politics*. And that ambiguity can be seen being formed as Greek authors take up two terms that mean belonging to the community of the town (*astu*) or city (*polis*) and develop diverging but overlapping uses of these terms to cover both qualitative and formal aspects of belonging. If a classical Athenian referred to someone as an *astos*, one could be pretty certain that he meant that that person formally qualified as a member of the Athenian political community, in the terms described by the Aristotelian *Constitution of the Athenians*, chapter 41. If a classical Athenian referred to someone as a *politēs*, it might well be true that that person formally qualified as a member of the Athenian community in those terms, but it would not be such qualifications to which the term *politēs* would be drawing attention. Rather to call someone a *politēs* was to suggest that they were part of the community and could be expected to act to other members of the community in particular ways.

One feature of the preceding discussion deserves to be stressed. This is that the term *astos* is a rare term in most classical authors. We have already seen that it is a term used just once by Lysias and just once by Isokrates. The more frequent use of the term by Plato is a direct consequence of his need to employ the term to define legal status precisely in *Laws*. For most Athenians most of the time, even when speaking in the lawcourt, drawing attention to someone's formal membership of the Athenian community was simply unnecessary. Much more to the point was the question of how others were behaving, whether they were behaving in the ways that one would want a resident of Athens to behave. But for all that Aristotle figured that the virtues of a good man were different from the virtues of a good citizen (*politēs*), one suspects that the distinction would be lost on most Athenians. Could one ever see a good, or bad, citizen (as opposed to a good, or bad, man)?[119]

Some art historians have indeed believed that they can detect a citizen body, or at least signs that a body is that of a citizen. German scholarship in particular identifies the knobbly stick carried by some bearded figures on Athenian fifth-century pottery (cf. 3.5, on p. 62) as a 'Bürgerstock', and the cloak which such figures wear as the 'Himation des athenischen Bürgers'.[120] Others see these same signs as being not of citizenship but of

---

[119] The bad citizen has recently been explored by Christ (2006). His bad citizen is self-interested and manifests himself by being a reluctant conscript (ch. 2), cowardly hoplite (ch. 3), or artful tax dodger (ch. 4).

[120] For the stick, Heinemann (2000) 332; for the cloak, Krummeich (1999) 67, n. 122; compare Lissarrague (1993) 210, writing of a satyr that 'his clothing, chiton and himation, gives him the dignity of a citizen'. See more generally Hollein (1988).

4.1 Two men with pigs, one bare-headed with a cloak (chlamys), one wearing his himation loincloth style and with a countryman's hat, on a Athenian red-figure pelike, *c.* 460 BC.

class, talking of the himation's turning satyrs into 'middle-class folk'.[121] Whether youths wear himatia or not is indeed an issue of contention in Aristophanes' *Clouds*, but the contention between 'Better Argument' and 'Worse Argument' is between different generations of citizens, not about displaying citizenship or class.[122]

There is no doubt that clothing can indeed 'make people' on Athenian pottery, but there is no reason to take the signals sent to be signals of citizenship.[123] Hats indicate roles – the *petasos* of the traveller (6.1, see p. 159), the *pilos* of the countryman at work (4.1); so too does the main garment worn – the *exōmis* is working-man's clothing, as is the garment tied round the waist.[124] But Athenian painters are remarkably inconsistent in marking out legal or political status with clothing. Although slaves can

---

[121] Lissarrague (1993) 210.   [122] Aristophanes, *Clouds* 987, cf. 964–5.
[123] For the phrase cf. Heinemann (2000) 332 'Kleider machen Leute'.
[124] Pipili (2000). For the development of distinctions between rustic and urbane clothing in the archaic period see van Wees (2005) 49.

be marked out by stature, physiognomy, marks on the body, or clothing, there are other cases where, although slave status seems probable from the context, neither physical size nor appearance (whether of body or of clothing) signals that status.[125] As Sian Lewis has noted, 'In most working scenes there is no clear indicator of status at all, from clothes, length of hair or facial appearance.'[126]

What is true of painted pottery is true also of sculpture. Again, art historians find themselves talking about, for example, 'the "mature citizen" type' constituted by the bearded man in himation, but this is careless talk. Momentary acquaintance with Athenian grave stelai reveals men identified as non-Athenian, and hence *xenoi* or *metoikoi* at Athens, sporting both beard and himation.[127] Clairmont claims that 'A hint at citizen status can be found in that a chlamys is draped over the shoulder of the deceased.'[128] But not only are there many citizens who are not so shown, but the chlamys picks out a particular form of activity (hunting) which, although particularly associated with young men of high social status, who will also normally have been citizens, cannot be held itself to be exclusive to or a mark of the citizen. Clairmont in fact lists only three occurrences of the chlamys in his whole corpus.[129]

Can we tell, then, when we look at a sculpted figure or a figure painted on a pot, whether we are looking at a citizen body? What happens if we hold an identity parade of statues of men from the late archaic and classical periods?

I begin with the kouros from Anavyssos (4.2), long associated with an inscription which provides both his name, Kroisos, and the circumstances of his death: he died fighting in the front ranks in war.[130] Is he a citizen? What should we take this sculpted body to signify?

---

[125] Oakley (2000). See further below, pp. 130–6.

[126] S. Lewis (2002) 79; cf. 138–41. See further Himmelmann (1971), (1994), and compare Clairmont *CAT* Introductory volume, pp. 35–7.

[127] For the phrase, see Stewart and Gray (2000) 273. For an Erythraian of that type cf. e.g. *CAT* 2.206 (*IG* ii² 8501a). Clairmont circumspectly notes that 'The long himation (mantle) is standard for men in their prime and the following two age groups' (*CAT* Introductory volume, p. 30). For further discussion of the mantle and the stick on grave stelai see Bergemann (1997) 76–8, who notes further of grave stelai of metics (p. 146) 'Doch gibt es dort gleichwohl alle von den Bürgern bevorzugten Bildthemen.' But when Bergemann talks of 'Die Assimilationsbereitschaft der Metöken' (p. 147) his assumption of citizen priority mistakes a quantitative for a qualitative phenomenon.

[128] *CAT* Introductory volume p. 31.

[129] *CAT* 1.364, 1.866, 2.268, listed at *CAT* 6 p. 93. Neither of the first two is inscribed and neither has a precise provenance.

[130] Athens NM 3851, Richter (1970) no. 136.

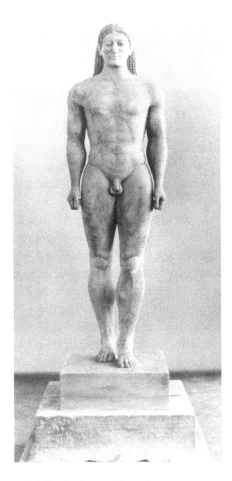

4.2 Athenian kouros from Anavyssos.

The question of whether this kouros displays a citizen body might be taken to be rather artificial. This was a statue that stood by a major road outside what was only a modest village in southern Attica. No one who lived in the village can have been ignorant of the man whose death was commemorated here. They will have known a great deal about him and his family. They will hardly have needed the statue to tell them that this was a citizen. Context, we might think, is everything here.

But we should pause before dismissing the question of identification. The whole point of placing graves beside major roads must have been to show off the glories of the community that they were approaching not to the villagers themselves but to a wider group of travellers, who at Anavyssos increasingly included the full range of those interested in the Athenian silver mines. This was not a monument purely productive of pangs of poignancy for relatives, it was a monument productive of community pride in the face of passers-by. And for anyone who did not know the village families, the inscription will have incited no small curiosity, for it gives the figure a name that is neither Greek in origin nor popular in Athens. This name, surely derived from the sixth-century Lydian king, is otherwise known from one fifth-century Athenian citizen, one fifth-century Athenian metic, working on the Erechtheion, and one or two certainly or possibly fourth-century men, known at Athens but of uncertain legal status.[131] If displaying citizenship was a concern one might expect the bearer of such a name to be particularly anxious to indicate that he belonged to the Athenian community.

Neither the body nor the inscription offers any indication of civic status. The inscription does not say where he fell in war or for whom he was fighting. The body of the kouros offers itself as a member of an international set, found all across the Aegean, in central and southern mainland Greece, and occasionally beyond. For all that the number of kouros monuments must not be underestimated, the very expense of a monumental sculpture like this will indicate the family's wealth.[132] But is this a distinctively Athenian body that we see? It is one of the features of sixth-century free-standing sculpture that the choices of male body-types, like the choices of how to represent clothed women, are highly regionalised. As Stewart notes: 'Though the *kouros* type does display a certain constancy in its portrayal of a uniformly athletic, beautiful, youthful, and happy clientele, archaic regional preferences as to physique were extremely diverse', and he offers a comparison of the slim, curvaceous and sparely modelled Naxian kouroi and the muscular, broad-shouldered and barrel-chested Parian.[133] But when Stewart goes on to relate the diversity of kouros body forms to 'the jealously guarded independence of the poleis themselves' he goes one crucial step too far. The classic analysis of the kouros by Richter does indeed divide kouroi into groups to which it gives geographical names, but those groups neither comprise material from a single *polis* nor subdivide neatly by *poleis*. 'Kroisos' belongs to a group dubbed by Richter 'The Anavyssos-Ptoon 12 Group', named for this statue and a statue at the sanctuary of Apollo Ptoios at Akraiphia in Boiotia. And while Richter does point out that Ptoon 12 is 'softer, less sturdy' than the Anavyssos and other Attic kouroi, this group includes a statue from Keos

---

[131] I follow the categorisation of *LGPN* II. Fifth-century citizen *IG* i³ 1183.17, metic, 476.12, 22f.; fourth-century figures *IG* ii² 11917, 11916.

[132] Snodgrass (1983) offers speculative calculations of the total number of kouroi produced that are likely to be of the right magnitude.

[133] A. Stewart (1990) 75.

which, while clearly distinguishable, is as close or closer to the Anavyssos kouros as are other Attic kouroi of the same period.[134] For all the distinct regional groupings, it is not *polis* particularism and political boundaries that we are seeing here.

But if Kroisos is not distinctly *Athenian*, is he distinctly a *citizen*? A more or less contemporary funerary relief also from the Attic countryside shows the profile figure of a hoplite, named Aristion. Of this figure we know nothing of the circumstances of his death, but in his beard we are given a clear indication of his maturity. At least this man was *old* enough to be a citizen. But kouroi have earned their name from the apparent youth conveyed by their beardlessness. How old is Kroisos? Presumably he should not be fighting unless reasonably mature, but can we know whether he joined up aged seventeen or nineteen?[135] Davidson has recently insisted that puberty came four years later in antiquity than now but, even if we allow for this, real men can rarely have remained quite without facial hair much beyond eighteen.[136] For all the enthusiasm of scholars for a Gombrichian model of 'schema and correction', kouroi are surely the products of projection rather than observation, but what they show is that projecting precise age and political status was not the sculptor's concern.[137] The lack of concern of sixth-century Athenian sculpture for distinguishing those too young for political involvement from those who have a claim to involvement might seem hardly surprising. Athens' government was in the hands of Peisistratos and his sons from shortly after the middle of the sixth century until 510 BC. Tradition held that the Peisistratids even preferred to use mercenary troops in this period. We might then expect that when we turn to the fifth century and the world of Athenian democracy we shall find that distinguishing the citizen from the non-citizen becomes more pressing.

Fifth-century sculpture does indeed quickly come to show great interest in showing age. The most famous of all early fifth-century Athenian free-standing statues, the Kritian boy from the Athenian Acropolis and dating to more or less precisely 480, is known as the Kritian *boy* precisely because

---

[134] Richter (1970) 113; the Keos kouros (Athens NM 3686) is no. 144.

[135] For A. Stewart (1996) 67: 'Well-fleshed, well-muscled, and the right age to be an *erōmenos* or "beloved", [the Anavyssos kouros] appeals to what has been called the glance's fetishistic, even narcissistic component which, so far from keeping aloof from what it sees, is captivated by it, desires to identify with it, wants to be at one with it and to emulate it.' I see in this kouros none of the distinguishing marks of the *erōmenos*, particularly in terms of facial hair.

[136] Davidson (2006), (2007).

[137] Gombrich (1960), which has been variously critiqued (Beard (1985), Elsner (2006), R. Osborne (2008d)) but remains explicitly the model behind A. Stewart (1990) 75. As to what exactly the sculptors' concern was, see further Chapter 7.

4.3 Roman copy of statues of the Athenian 'tyrannicides', Harmodios and Aristogeiton, by Kritios (cf. Fig. 2.1) and Nesiotes.

his youth is not in question. Although the physical signals given are not entirely consistent, most people think they can age this boy on sight. And it was Kritios and Nesiotes who were responsible for the group of the 'Tyrannicides', Harmodios and Aristogeiton, set up in the Athenian Agora to replace the monument taken away by the Persians in 480 (4.3). The age of the figures here is guaranteed by historical tradition: it was because Harmodios was a desirable youth that Hipparchos made the advances whose rebuff was the cause of the insult that Harmodios and his lover Aristogeiton avenged.[138] We can certainly see the age difference between Harmodios and Aristogeiton represented, though in the Roman copies of the statues, which is all that survives, this comes across primarily in the modelling of the face, the depiction of the hair and Harmodios' absence of facial hair.

One might expect the statues of the tyrannicides to be particularly interested in the political status of the two men. Herodotos' brief account of

[138] Thucydides 6.53–9 for the story told in this form.

the assassination is followed by an extensive discussion of the family background of the assassins. They were, he says, of the family of the Gephyraioi, and on their own account had come in the beginning from Eretria but, according to his enquiries, were in origin Phoenicians who had first settled at Tanagra in Boiotia and subsequently been made *politai* by the Athenians on stated conditions that excluded them 'from many privileges not worth mentioning'.[139] And if both men were on the edge of the citizen body because of their origin, Harmodios must have been on the edge of the citizen body in terms of age. Was he seventeen or was he eighteen? Was Athens rid of its tyranny through the actions of a man who would not have any political role in democratic Athens, or by a newly minted citizen? Can we read any of this off the statues? Harmodios and Aristogeiton are equal in height, and Harmodios must be taken to be fully grown, but that will not decide the question of age. For although Harmodios' body is markedly more mature than that of the Kritian boy, the total absence of facial hair links him to the Kritian boy rather than to any figure of greater maturity. Aristogeiton and Harmodios have hairstyles distinct from one another, but in both cases styles that can be paralleled in contemporary sculptures more or less certainly representing Athenians. In short, nothing about the copies suggests that the sculptors had any interest in the question of the non-Athenian origin of the pair or the precise age of Harmodios.

How surprised should we be that when sculptors become interested in age they appear to show no interest in the age distinctions that were politically significant – not just the age of eighteen but the age of thirty, at which Athenians could for the first time serve on the Council of Five Hundred and as generals?[140] There are two reasons for thinking that we should take this absence of these age indications seriously. The first is that, at least from time to time, painters of pottery choose to portray ages with very considerable precision. This is true of the indication of the onset of male maturity, where some pots show the various whiskery signs of maturity in great detail, and of the onset of maturity in girls, where Christiane Sourvinou-Inwood argued at length for the significance of the 'budding breast'

---

[139] Herodotos 5.55–7.

[140] Bernard Ashmole, in a classic discussion, has analysed the east pediment at Olympia, sculpted *c.* 460, in terms of its display of the 'seven ages of man'; in his view the sculptors 'have deliberately contrasted extreme youth with youth, with maturity, with old age', Ashmole (1972) 30. Yet it is notable that a set of figures concerned with the very young and the distinctly aged fails clearly to indicate the passage from youth to maturity: while the representation of the river Kladeos is as a youth, and the river Alpheios as a more mature figure, both rivers are shown beardless. But if maturity is not here, as in life, revealed in facial hair, absence of facial hair ceases to be an indicator of immaturity. Is the Kladeos eighteen or not?

4.4 'Warrior A' recovered from the sea off Riace Marina, Calabria, *c.* 460 BC. Reggio Museum.

phenomenon.[141] The second reason is the extraordinarily sensitive portayal of different bodily types of which sculptors of this period prove themselves capable.

The finest example of such sensitive portrayal of body types surviving comes in the Riace warriors (4.4, 4.5). These bodies are certainly over the age of eighteen, and most viewers would think they could place them quite precisely in middle age, but what of their political status? The close similarity of the pose of these figures only draws attention to their extraordinary difference from one another. Warrior A is firm fleshed, fighting fit without

---

[141] On pots and boys see Davidson (2007); for girls see Sourvinou-Inwood (1988).

4.5 'Warrior B' recovered from the sea off Riace Marina, Calabria, *c.* 460 BC. Reggio Museum.

giving any sense of artificial bodily development. Warrior B has flesh that is thinner and slacker, muscles that lack the tone. These two warriors live in the world differently. Bruno Latour has called for the introduction of the term 'multinaturalism', drawing attention to how productive 'the abandonment of the world into incommensurable and irreconcilable multiplicities' would be.[142] Precisely because Warriors A and B are in many ways so alike, the differences between them seem the more incommensurable and irreconcilable. Since the body is 'that through which we learn to be affected',[143] these two different bodies can only be taken to stand for different ways of being

---

[142] Latour (2002) 140.   [143] Despret (1999) quoted at Latour (2002) 140.

affected. Those differences are, for some modern Italian observers at least, different sexual orientations.[144] What they are unlikely to have been for any observer, I suggest, is different positions within the political status groups in the *polis*.

Kouroi, in their variety of body types, had put on display a range of ways of living in the world. But the uniform pose had combined with the body to suggest a certain irrelevance to the body form. Mature young men of all types, the kouros suggested, were readily facing up to the world, whatever the circumstances. Different natures, the message seems to be, are commensurable, for they are all ready to measure up to the same tasks. But the distinct body types of the Riace warriors point in a very different direction: here are two men whom we could expect neither to react nor to react in similar fashion. We cannot see in these bodies political status, but we might see the makings of a good or a not-so-good citizen.

No subsequent sculptures look like the Riace warriors. It is true that classical bronzes have survived only in exceptional circumstances and that the most famous of free-standing sculptures have survived only as copies. But those copies are not to be despised. Let us return to the *Doryphoros* ('Spear carrier') (2.2, see p. 42) of Polykleitos of Argos. When Pliny describes the *Doryphoros* he uses the words 'viriliter puerum' ('a boy but manly'), contrasting it with another of Polykleitos' statues, the *Diadoumenos* (2.3, see p. 43), which he describes as 'molliter iuvenem' ('a young man, but softly').[145] The copies support this contrast between the 'hard' *Doryphoros* and the 'soft' *Diadoumenos*, but if Pliny's terms 'youth' and 'boy' lead one to expect something particularly childish about the *Doryphoros* the copies disappoint. By contrast to the youthful – but how youthful? – *Diadoumenos*, the *Doryphoros*' virility denies the very youth that, amongst Greeks who did not shave, the absence of facial hair asserts. Rather than offering a body type resonant of a particular way of being in the world, the *Doryphoros* offers a body type whose reference to the world is confused and unreadable. Yet it is this statue that became already in antiquity the very embodiment of classical male beauty. Quintilian writes that 'the outstanding sculptors and painters, when they wish to represent the most beautiful bodies .... use the *Doryphoros*, a work suitable for both the military and the palaestra'.[146]

Polykleitos' *Doryphoros* is best seen rather as a symptom than as either cause or occasion for changing representations of manhood. For the same

[144] Taplin (1989) 88–9.   [145] Pliny, *Natural History* 34.55.
[146] Quintilian, *Institutes of Oratory* 5.12.21.

refusal of the challenge posed by the Riace warriors can be seen in the Parthenon frieze. Here the sculptors notoriously devote enormous attention to details of the appearance of horses and drapery, bringing out the throbbing veins and flaring nostrils of the former and both textural and technological detail in the latter (e.g. the distinctive appearance of the selvedge).[147] But when it comes to the representation of men, the cavalrymen who wrestled to control their lively mounts are given remarkably uniform bodies and facial appearance and are all rendered not simply as beardless young men but as youths – few observers could have any confidence that they have passed their eighteenth birthday.[148] There is no temptation here to talk of 'multinaturalism'.

Nor indeed is there much more temptation to talk of multiculturalism. Ancient lexicographers repeatedly identify those who carried trays in the Panathenaia as metics, citing Theophrastos, Menander and other fourth-century authors.[149] Tray-carrying in festivals does, indeed, seem to have been a trait that marked a man out as a metic, and the carrying of a hydria or parasol perhaps to have marked a woman out as a metic (just as carrying a wineskin on one's shoulders marked one out as a citizen).[150] In Dionysiac processions, and perhaps also in the Panathenaia the metic tray-carrier was further distinguished by a crimson cloak.[151] The cloaks of the tray-carriers on the Parthenon frieze, who are not well preserved (we rely largely on Carrey's seventeenth-century drawings), may have been coloured red, but enough survives for us to be confident that there was no indication that they were distinguished by facial or bodily features from the other participants, most of whom must represent citizens. In ritual contexts, it seems, it was important to make distinctions – just as distinctions were made within the citizen body so that how much sacrificial meat one received depended upon one's role in the city – but these distinctions were not considered to reflect any distinctions embodied in the individual so marked out.

Fourth-century sculpture becomes interested in pushing further the exploration of different male bodies.[152] They variously charted the softly sensuous (compare 7.10 on p. 212) and the slim and hard. And they became

---

[147] Outstanding among the horses is the rearing animal, West VIII.15; for detailed drapery see East VIII.59–61.

[148] On the politics of this see R. Osborne (1987). For observations on the limits of Parthenonian uniformity see Daehner (2005).

[149] Hesychios and Harpokration s.v. σκαφηφόροι, Photios s.v. σκάφας and συστομώτερον σκάφης, and other texts collected by Michaelis (1871) 330.

[150] Harpokration s.v. σκαφηφόροι, Photios s.v. συστομώτερον σκάφης, Bekker, *Anecdota Graeca* 214.3.

[151] Bekker, *Anecdota Graeca* 214.3.   [152] See above p. 43 on Lysippos, and Edwards (1999).

interested in presenting the appearance of specific historic individuals, in particular in the context of awarding them public honours for their services. After 394 the Tyrannicides were not alone among public benefactors in being represented in the Agora: they were joined by the Athenian general Konon and the Cypriot ruler Evagoras.[153]

Although the bases of a number of portrait statues survive, there are rather few cases when even a copy of a portrait statue of a known individual is preserved. Nevertheless scholars have considered that sufficient is known from copies to which names can be more or less plausibly supplied to suggest that what was at issue was 'role portraits'. That is, emphasis was not on the inner thoughts of the individual, but on presenting them playing their particular role in life – as general, political leader, poet, or philosopher.[154] The most recent study has emphasised that the variety of head types surviving among portraits to which no name can be supplied means that distinction in the heads was used to differentiate men shown in the same role, but this does not change the fact of presentation by role.[155]

What we can gather about portrait statues reveals two facts of importance. The first is that the roles that are differentiated divide up the citizen body, rather than divide it off from the body of non-citizens. Just as texts concern themselves with whether politicians present themselves appropriately to the public, so the statues of politicians can be read to display qualities such as moderation.[156] In as far as citizenship is at issue here it is the sort of citizen that one is, not whether or not one is a citizen. But in terms of Aristotle's distinction, portrait statues interest themselves in the qualities that make someone a good man, not those that make him distinctly a citizen. Although we have little evidence for how non-Athenians honoured with statues in the fourth century looked (no evidence for the appearance of Evagoras' statue survives), third-century and second-century evidence shows that citizens and non-citizens could not be distinguished. So the comic poet Poseidippos (from Kassandreia) (4.6) is not marked out by dress, treatment of the head or seated posture from his Athenian predecessor Menander (4.7), and the philosopher Karneades from Cyrene, the base of whose honorific statue has been found in the Athenian Agora, is not distinct in type from the Athenian philosopher Epicurus – except in as far as it is Karneades who wears chiton

---

[153] RO 11 for the decree ordering this monument; Shear (2007) 107–13 for the phenomenon. See also more generally Gauthier (1985) for honours and Dillon (2006) ch. 5 for the statues.

[154] For role-portraits see Pollitt (1986) 59–62.   [155] Dillon (2006) 76–98.

[156] So the exchange between Aischines (1.25) and Demosthenes (19.251; cf. Dem. 18.29). For advice on public presentation more generally see Giuliani (1986) 129–40. See also Zanker (1995) ch. 2.

4.6 Roman copy of a portrait of the comic poet Poseidippos of Kassandreia, after an original of the mid third century BC.

as well as himation, something that aligns him with portraits of Athenian politicians.[157]

The direction of my argument will have become clear. Not only do classical authors employ the term *politēs* loosely, feeling free to include within it all the residents of the *polis*, but when men are represented on pots or in sculpture no attempt is made to mark off either the actual from the potential citizen by age, or the citizen from the metic or foreigner by appearance. Political status is never visually flagged, even on monuments which represented Athens to itself, as the Parthenon frieze does. This absence of either verbal or visual marking out of members of the citizen body goes with an absence of concern to pick out and set apart the citizen body as a whole. Whatever modern scholars have heard behind *politai*, no reference

---

[157] It is interesting to note in this context that in claiming (against Zanker (1995) 83–9) that the statue of Demosthenes shows him as a model democratic citizen Klaus Fittschen argues for this not on the basis of any aspect of Demosthenes' appearance but on the content of the decree preserved in Plutarch, *Moral Essays* 850–1. See Fittschen (2001) 330–2 and Dillon (2006) 75–6.

4.7 Plaster reconstruction of the portrait statue of the Athenian comic poet Menander, of the early third century BC.

to either group could, without context, be assumed to pick out only either those who 'ruled and were ruled in turn' or those who had two parents who were both Athenian.

This is not merely a negative matter, some extraordinary negligence, but a positive matter. Athenians found themselves needing, in a range of different contexts, to talk about those who belonged in the Athenian community. Exactly what that community comprised, and with whom a contrast was being made by referring to the community, varied from occasion to occasion. The Athenians had a term for a person who belonged to the community, *politēs*, but used that term flexibly, defining the community by context, not by the term itself. If it was necessary to refer to the particular rules which determined who had political capacities in the community, they had an alternative term they could use, *astos*. But the default term was *politēs*, and the default emphasis was on playing a part in the city community, not on having or not having a set of political rights. So too classical sculptors, although demonstrating in works from shortly after the

4.8　Grave stele of Hegeso from Kerameikos Cemetery, Athens.

Persian Wars that they could distinguish individuals in extremely subtle ways and draw attention to the multinaturalism of the human world, chose rather to continue to stress, as their archaic forebears had done when they sculpted kouroi, what human figures have in common, and to do so by developing a convention for representation which stood free not just of petty jostlings for status in a particular culture, but of the particular combinations of features offered by nature itself.

Does this have a wider significance? I suggest that it does, and in two respects: for what we think about citizenship and for what we think about the body. Consider this most elaborately dressed woman seated demurely looking into a box brought by a female assistant in simpler attire (4.8).[158] This domestic scene is transformed by its public display on a gravestone placed on a conspicuous grave enclosure in Athens' main Kerameikos cemetery. Whatever private motives a woman may have for elaborating her appearance, the presentation of the contemplation of adornment to the public gaze

---

[158]　Athens NM 3624.

turns the gesture into one of display. However demure her pose, Hegeso is made here ostentatiously to declare her wealth and her difference. However accurate a representation of a wealthy Athenian woman at home this may be, the public display of the scene renders it remote from real Athenian life. Just as archaic korai with their elaborate garments represented women by representing a particular type of woman, so Hegeso and the other women on grave stelai represent a type of woman.[159] And both korai and Hegeso represent women in community – korai do so by the offering that they almost invariably hold out and by their, occasionally professed, nobility; Hegeso and the women of classical grave stelai do so by engagement with a serving girl or with a husband or wider familial group. Whether or not we take the reappearance of grave stelai and the dominance of women in their iconography to be itself a product of the insistence of the Periklean Citizenship Law upon having an *astē* as a mother as well as an *astos* as a father, this situation of woman in community should be seen as a depiction of woman as *politis*.[160]

Aristotle, we have seen, finds himself in *Politics* juggling narrow definitions of who is afforded political capacities in the *polis* against broader conceptions of what it is to be a citizen, conceptions which involve the quality of participation within the community. He does so, I suggest, because the *polis* in which he spent much time, Athens, had found it necessary to define who could take part in politics but continued to think in much broader terms of participation in the community and showed no interest in developing ways of formally marking on the citizen body in life or art any of the distinctions, of age or birth, which officially defined who was politically capacitated.[161] As soon as we lift our eyes from the Assembly, and think of classical Athens not merely as a matter of a gathering of men making political decisions democratically but as a community that constantly asserted and defended itself against other communities, Greek and non-Greek, it becomes clear that this was a community which could not afford to be exclusionary: *astoi* alone could never provide the men required for the navy or even for the infantry army, let alone for Athens' commercial involvement with the wider Mediterranean world.

Aristotle's legacy has been a dichotomous model which remains dominant and unresolved in contemporary talk of citizenship. Faced with a political move to restrict political capacities, the Athenians responded by developing a terminology to refer to those possessing the political capacities

[159] R. Osborne (1994) on korai.   [160] R. Osborne (1996/7), Stears (1995).
[161] Cf. Vlassopoulos (2007).

distinct from their regular way of referring to the community. The British Citizenship Act of 1981 hijacked the term 'citizen' for a restricted use when it wanted to distinguish between British subjects who had and those who did not have the right of residence in the United Kingdom. That it is now felt necessary to teach 'citizenship', that is teach what it is to be a good member of the community, suggests that modern Britain has been less successful than classical Athens in preventing the exclusionary use of the term from impacting upon community.

It is in this context that the classical citizen body has its importance. For if my argument is correct, part of Athenian resistance to dividing society between those who had and those who did not have political capacities was constituted by the creation of a classical body which resisted the claims of particularism and the possibilities for distinguishing bodies, whether as to their nature or as to their culture. There was neither a distinct body type for the Athenian male over the age of eighteen nor a distinct clothing for mature children of Athenian parents. What we have come to call classical idealism, and treat as a feature of art history, constituted an act of resistance to multinaturalism, as a male body combining features which nature kept separate was charged with positive force in representations of service to the community. At the same time it also constituted an act of resistance to multiculturalism as a fantasy of womanly domesticity was turned into a public display. The more closely the real citizen body was scrutinised for its age and its parentage, the more distanced the body of art became, and the more impossible it was to pin the distinctions of civic status made by language onto real bodies. What drove that resistance is a topic to which I shall return in Chapter 7.

5 | Foreign bodies

Is this a foreign body (5.1)? A man lies on a sturdy bed or couch, with a thick draped mattress. A lion standing on its hind legs, forepaws either side of the man's head, leans forward over him, head turned towards the viewer. At the foot of the bed stands another figure leaning forward over the corpse, this time a naked male figure of sorts, arms apparently stretched forward to push against the lion. Whether or not there is a head behind these outstretched arms has been much disputed; certainly where we would expect to find his head we find instead the prow of a ship.[1] This scene is the relief on a gravestone found in the Dipylon cemetery at Athens, and probably to be dated to the third century. A unique gravestone like no other. What is going on here?

The stone is headed by a Greek inscription which records the name 'Antipatros son of Aphrodisias of Askalon' and goes on, 'Domsalōs son of Domano of Sidon dedicated this.' This same information is then repeated in Phoenician. Bilingual inscriptions are not common at Athens, either among gravestones or more generally, but such bilingual inscriptions as we have are dominated by bilingual Greek and Phoenician inscriptions. There are in total nine bilingual Greek–Phoenician gravestones.[2] They variously translate or transliterate the names: here Aphrodisias is a Greek equivalent of Abdastart, but Antipatros is simply a Greek name substituted for Sem, while Domsalōs' names are essentially transliterated.[3]

But if we can identify the deceased as a hellenising Phoenician, that hardly offers an immediate explanation for the imagery of the relief. Some sort of explanation, however, is afforded by a further inscription below the scene. Here we find an epigram in Greek verse, of which the first two lines and

---

[1] *CAT* 3.410; Stager (2005) is the fullest description; compare Bäbler (1998) 136–7 (not known to Stager) on exactly what we should reckon to be visible here. I repeat some of my discussion here, but in a different framework, in R. Osborne (forthcoming).

[2] Bäbler (1998) 131. There is also one, third-century, decree with the main text in Phoenician and a concluding line in Greek which identifies the resolution as being by the 'community of the Sidonians' (probably a cult association worshipping Baal); *IG* ii² 2946; Bäbler (1998) 125–7, Amelung (1990).

[3] Bäbler (1998) 123, Herzog (1897).

5.1 Grave stele of Antipatros of Sidon, from Athens.

last two lines are hexameters, the third is a pentameter and the fourth two half lines which do not metrically fit together. Metrical irregularity is not unparalleled on gravestones,[4] but here the Greek too is full of oddities of spelling and usage, although the sense is more or less clear.[5] It says:

[4] Tsagalis (2008) 297–99.
[5] Hansen's notes in *Carmina Epigraphica Graeca* 596 tell the story: 'est error . . . vox hic tantum reperitur . . . Vox alioquin ignota . . . per soloecismum dictum . . . vox alioquin ignota est.'

Let no one of men wonder at this image, that a lion and a prow stretch against me. For a hostile lion came wanting to tear me apart, but my friends defended me and provided me with a tomb here, friends whom in my love (?) I wanted, coming from a sacred ship. I left Phoenicia; I have concealed my body in this land.[6]

The link between text and image is direct, with the text explicitly offering an explanation of the image. But what are we to make of this story of a man attacked by a lion, whose body is saved for burial by friends on a sacred ship? Most commentators have taken the story literally, looking for the place closest to Attica where a lion, or at least a large feline, is plausible (North Africa? Asia Minor?). They have supposed that Antipatros was attacked, mauled, rescued, taken away by his friends (either dead or dying) and given burial in Athens on arrival there. Since lions are hard to come by around the Mediterranean at this time, some have supposed, disregarding the picture as well as the text, that the beast must really have been a panther.

Recent interpreters have preferred a symbolic reading. Bäbler has insisted, following a suggestion a century ago, that the image can only be understood 'in the light of Semitic pictorial symbols', and in particular the oriental portrayal of underworld demons as lions. Stager thinks both prow and lion figure Astarte.[7] On these interpretations Antipatros was 'saved from the lion's mouth' of death demons or the goddess Astarte by being buried by his friends, and the prow-headed man may refer to Phoenician ships carrying protecting statues.[8]

Neither the purely literal nor the wholly symbolic interpretation is attractive. The replacement of the head by a prow of a ship offers a powerful visual symbol that we are not dealing with literal depiction. But, as the epigram claims, this is a tomb, and the other inscription confirms that friends did play a peculiar part in creating the monument. The image and the epigram need a place between the literal and the symbolic, and we might see them as alluding to the risk faced by a dead foreigner of not being given an adequate burial, a fate from which Antipatros on his decease has been saved because he has friends who have buried him.

What would an Athenian viewer have made of this stele? In formal terms the stele as a whole conforms closely to Athenian practice. The shape of the stele with its pediment is a standard one. The combination of recessed image and inscription above and/or below is regular. Epigrams are not found on most Athenian gravestones, but they are not rare, and some are found

---

[6] *Carmina Epigraphica Graeca* 596; cf. Tsagalis (2008).
[7] Bäbler (1998) 138–42 following Usener (1914) 449; Stager (2005) 439–43.   [8] Herodotos 3.37.2.

arranged very much as is this one.[9] However, an Athenian who looked at all closely at this image and read its epigram would find it strange in all its details. The use of 'dedicated' of the putting up of a gravestone for someone else is unattested on other stelai. All other stelai for Phoenicians, whether offering a bilingual text or not, limit their identification of the deceased to patronymic and city ethnic, not otherwise playing with Phoenicians' being quintessential sailors from lands of exotic animals. What looks like a standard stele proves on examination to be odd both in image and text.

The easiest element in the image to parallel is the ship's prow, featured prominently on the famous stele of Demokleides, where a young warrior, his helmet and shield behind him, sits on the deck of a ship behind the prow.[10] Lions can also be paralleled in an Athenian funerary context.[11] The element that is most strange is the naked body lying on the couch. There is nothing foreign about the body as such, but the presence of a dead body is itself foreign. For although from the earliest figure scenes on Athenian pottery, and the great Geometric funerary markers put up in this very Dipylon cemetery, onwards scenes of mourners gathered around the body of the deceased at the laying out of the corpse have been regularly shown on painted pottery, and they continued to be shown in the classical period on certain shapes of pot associated with funerary ceremonies, such scenes have never been shown on grave reliefs: the moment grave reliefs mark is a different one.[12]

The decision to show the corpse goes together with the decision to show and tell, in however allegorical a form, the fate of the dead person. Grave epigrams regularly refer to the way in which death has snatched the deceased from life and from family, often referring to fate, Hades, Hermes and other metaphysical paraphernalia, but, unlike some archaic personal epigrams and classical epigrams for the war dead as a whole, classical personal epigrams do not tell the events leading up to the burial. The closest we come to that is epigrams which indicate age at death (ages of 100, 24, 90, 70 and 21 are claimed).[13] Notwithstanding the opening injunction of the epigram, and indeed encouraged by it, Athenians would surely have wondered at this scene, even after they had read the verses.

---

[9] Sculpted stelai with epigrams are conveniently collected in Clairmont (1970).   [10] *CAT* 1.330.

[11] They are prominent in archaic Attic funerary iconography but can also be found in some classical monuments, see *CAT* 1 (stele for Leon of Sinope, first half of fourth century), 3 (from Dipylon cemetery; mid fourth century).

[12] Kurtz (1984), Oakley (2004) 76–87. While no clothing is shown on male corpses in Geometric images, later archaic and classical paintings show the dead clothed or covered with a sheet.

[13] Clairmont (1970) 55bis, 56, 58, 72, 73 (= *Carmina Epigraphica Graeca* –, 590, 531, 554, 580). Cf. Tsagalis (2008) 198–208.

Domsalōs, in setting up this memorial to Antipatros, chose to use an Athenian form of monument – and presumably an Athenian sculptor – but to inscribe upon it both in his own language and in what we can only assume to be his own idiosyncratic Greek. He chose to present in his verse and in the sculpted panel an image which tied in to a way of thinking about the world which was not Athenian, but the treatment of the figures in the sculpted image is not oriental but Greek. He chose to place this monument in what was probably Athens' most historic and conspicuous cemetery. And if the expert in the field is right about the date of the letter forms, Domsalōs chose to take advantage of his foreign status to put up a sculpted funerary stele during a period when, after the legislation of Demetrios of Phaleron in 317, Athenians were banned from putting up such monuments.[14] This is neither a case of a foreigner bringing his own practices to a city in which he is temporarily resident, nor a case of a foreigner choosing to adopt the practices of his city of temporary residence. This is a foreigner who chooses to display his identity by introducing into a monument, whose form and whose forms conform to local practice, conceptions and manners of expression which are quite alien. Image and words alike play out not simply to Athenians but also to Phoenicians – and insist that one can be both. In the language which post-colonial studies have made fashionable, this monument is marked by hybridisation.[15] In the terms of one of my colleagues, we see here, in both text and image, 'the stickiness of synthesis': as different cultural practices rub up against each other, every form of expression comes to bear the traces of the cultural encounter.[16]

But what made this synthesis so very sticky? Phoenicians were well integrated into Athenian society. The Phoenician merchants of Cypriot Kition were granted, albeit after some hesitation as the Council decided to forward the matter to the Assembly without giving it its formal blessing, permission to acquire land and build a temple of Aphrodite.[17] Athenian banking seems to have been strongly Phoenician. We know that a Phoenician Pythodoros effected introductions to the banker Pasion, and that other Phoenicians, Theodoros and an Antipater of Kition, were creditors of the bank.[18] We are

---

[14] Stephen Tracy's dating is quoted at Stager (2005) 427. For Demetrios of Phaleron's ban on elaborate grave monuments and for the continued presence of some elaborate monuments to non-Athenians see Bäbler (1998) 205f.

[15] For a fine recent discussion of hybridisation, in the context of the Roman Empire, see Jiménez (2011).

[16] I owe this phrase to Caroline Vout.   [17] RO 91.

[18] Pythodoros, Isokrates 17.4; Theodoros, Demosthenes 34.6; Antipater of Kition, Demosthenes 35.32–3.

almost certain that the banker Pasion himself and his slave protégé Phormio were Phoenicians too.[19] And Pasion and Phormio have the distinction of being the only certain examples we have of men who began life at Athens as slaves and ended as citizens.[20] If other non-Greeks became close to Athenian citizens, these non-Greeks actually became Athenian citizens.

Plausibly one thing that made it more possible for Pasion to be accepted as an Athenian citizen – and one reason why Domsalōs created so singular an image for Antipatros – was that Phoenicians had bodies effectively indistinguishable in physical features, if not in circumstances, from the bodies of citizens.[21] For many Greeks, to judge by explicitly theoretical writings, maintained that the world was mapped onto the bodies of its human residents. By placing in the very last chapter of his history the observation by Kyros the Great, founder of the Persian Empire, that 'soft lands breed soft men', Herodotos lends to that claim a potential explanatory power for the whole of his *Histories*: the course of history is determined by who lives where and what the natural environment has differentially done to human physical and mental constitutions.

The classic exposition of the importance of the environment for the human constitution comes in the fifth-century Hippocratic treatise *Airs, Waters, Places*. After an opening theoretical discussion of how climate affects the human body, the author turns to the distinction between Asia and Europe, aiming to show why the form of the peoples is so different. The equable blending of the climate of Asia, he maintains, makes everything grow finer and larger (ch. 12), but the absence of variation in the climate also means that they are lacking in courage and lacking in spirit (ch. 16). Variations within Asia are admitted, but they too are attributed to climate (ch. 16).[22]

Even in *Airs, Waters, Places*, however, the physical environment is not the only factor influencing human appearance and health. Men are able to mould their appearance, literally, by their customs. The Makrokephali

---

[19] Trevett (1992) 1; the evidence for the Phoenician origin is circumstantial: Phormio was non-Greek (Demosthenes 45.73, 81), which makes it highly likely that Pasion was, and since Phoenicians are the non-Greeks most closely associated with the bank, Phoenician is the most likely non-Greek origin. Apollodoros, son of Pasion, like Pythodoros, bears a name typical in form of Greek versions of Phoenician names (and cf. Antipater); cf. Diller (1937) 197–8; Bäbler (1998) 120–1.

[20] On the origins of slaves indicated in Athenian sources see Miller (1997) 82–3.

[21] So too it is noteworthy that there are no naked Persians on Athenian painted pottery: only clothing distinguishes the Persian from the Greek; cf. Raeck (1981) 215.

[22] Thomas (2000) 90ff.; note the parallel passage in Aristotle, *History of Animals* 606b17–20 cited by Thomas (2000) 96.

('Long-heads'), we are told, 'used to mould the head of the newly born children with their hands and to force it to increase in length by the application of bandages', though now children inherit this appearance from their parents (ch. 14). The Skythians 'grow up flabby and stout for two reasons. First, because they are not wrapped in swaddling clothes, as in Egypt, nor are they accustomed to horse-riding as children, which makes for a good figure. Second, they sit about too much . . . The girls get amazingly flabby and podgy' (ch. 20 trans. Chadwick and Mann).

The point of *Airs, Waters, Places* is to convince 'whoever would study medicine aright' of the need to consider the effect of seasons, winds and water, and so the major role played by custom is surprising. And we clearly cannot take Herodotos' concluding chapter to indicate environmental determinism on his part: for the whole rationale of his history is that one can understand present and past events only if one understands the customs of those involved. So when Xerxes and Demaratos discuss what makes the Greeks, and in particular the Spartans, what they are, both men acknowledge the force of qualities consciously cultivated as well as the force of natural circumstances.[23] The roles of *phusis* and *nomos*, nature and culture, were a topic of debate among late fifth-century intellectuals, but it is hard to find anyone who maintained that nature alone was wholly determinative.

Something of the same discourse on the role of original habitat and custom in distinguishing human bodies is to be seen in the way non-Greeks are shown in Athenian painted pottery.[24] Painters distinguish various non-Greek groups by their bodily features. In particular they may distinguish slaves by their miniature bodies, or by showing them with the colour or facial or other features distinctive to black Africans (5.2). They may distinguish Thracians by tattoos and Egyptians by circumcision (5.3). But what is striking is that whether or not any of these distinctions is made depends upon the context in which the foreign figure is represented. Foreign bodies are good to think with and worth thinking about, but not worth thinking about absolutely. They are worth thinking about only when the foreignness of the other offers insights into what it is for the self to be Greek.

Most frequently the context in which it is thought appropriate to indicate ethnic origin by showing particular bodily forms is mythological, and, as with Antipatros' stele, it is the frame, not the central characters, who carry the ethnic information. It is in the context of the myths of Bousiris and of Andromeda (5.4) and of Memnon, that the ruler's servants may be shown,

---

[23] Herodotos 7.101–4; see Thomas (2000) 109–11.
[24] For a survey of non-Greeks on Athenian pottery see Raeck (1981).

5.2 Athenian red-figure amphora from Vulci showing an older man followed by a small slave with black African facial profile, *c.* 470 BC. Name-vase of the Copenhagen Painter.

5.3 Athenian red-figure column krater from Sicily attributed to the Pan Painter, *c.* 470 BC. Thracian women attacking Orpheus.

5.4 Athenian red-figure pelike related to the workshop of the Niobid Painter,
c. 460 BC. Andromeda between two black Africans. Photograph © 2011. Museum of
Fine Arts, Boston.

in the sixth century and first third or so of the fifth century, as African.
Memnon himself, although literary sources make him of African origin, and
in the *Aeneid* he will be explicitly a black African, is never so portrayed in
vase painting. Similarly, although Andromeda is the daughter of Kepheus,
ruler of Ethiopia, neither daughter nor father is shown as black African,
though those who bind Andromeda may be so shown.[25] Both in the sixth
and the fifth centuries the Egyptians who, on the orders of Bousiris, attempt
to sacrifice Herakles, may be shown as black Africans, and on a pelike by the
Pan Painter, of *c.* 460, the short garments that the Egyptians wear are parted
to reveal circumcised genitals (5.5).[26] In all these cases the status of being
a protagonist with a name evidently precludes being given a foreign body.
The hero or heroine of the story must always, it seems, be a figure for whom
the viewer could substitute himself or his Greek friends. The division of

[25] Bérard (2000).   [26] Miller (2000).

5.5 Athenian red-figure pelike from Boiotia, ascribed to the Pan Painter, *c.* 470 BC.

the world into foreign and not-foreign is here a division on narratological lines, between those at the centre of the narrative and those who provide the necessary context for that narrative to make sense without individually having a particular role.

While these myths seem to have been thought systematically to demand setting in a world of foreign bodies, scenes relating to daily life are only occasionally so set. Some figures are marked as slaves by unrealistically diminutive bodies (5.2), recalling the habit of referring to any slave as 'child'; other figures are marked as slaves by black African features as well as by role or size.[27] They appear as servants at the symposium, carrying wine or accompanying women in graveside rituals.[28] Among figures not marked by colour, hair or facial features as black Africans, scholars have sometimes interpreted a short haircut for women, along with minor differences in

[27] On the representation of slaves see also above, Chapter 4, nn. 125, 126.
[28] Cf. Miller (1997) 212.

5.6 One side of an Athenian red-figure pelike attributed to the manner of the Altamura Painter, *c.* 460 BC.

stature, as indicative of servile status, but such distinctions are in practice extremely difficult to make.[29]

The problems of identifying slave women are nicely illustrated by a pot painted in the second quarter of the fifth century showing a transaction involving oil. On one side (5.6) we see a female standing figure, dressed in chiton and himation and with earrings and long hair (a braid hangs down her back to below the level of the shoulder blades), handing over an alabastron to a female seated on a chair with short hair and no earrings but of larger stature, also dressed in chiton and himation. A jar of the same shape as the pot that bears this image sits by the feet of the seated figure – presumably it is to be thought of as the source of the perfumed oil with which the alabastron will be filled. On the other side of the pot (5.7) there

[29] Oakley (2000) on maids. For problems of the identification of slaves more generally see Himmelmann (1971), (1994), S. Lewis (2002) 28–35, 79–81, 104–6, 138–41.

5.7 The other side of the Athenian red-figure pelike shown in Fig. 5.6.

is a slightly larger standing figure, well wrapped in himation over a chiton, with earrings and short hair. She dangles an alabastron that she seems to be about to give to a figure of very similar stature, seated on a stool, who is again well mantled in a himation, and has short hair but no earrings. Above the seated figure is a mirror, and behind the standing figure is a wool basket. The standard interpretation of this scene is that one side shows 'a maid buying oil from a female oil-seller' and the other shows 'a maid bringing oil home'.[30] But how can we tell the status of any of these figures? The figure supposedly buying oil is smaller in stature than the seller, but her hair is long and she has jewellery. So too the figure 'bringing oil home' seems more elaborately dressed than the figure to whom the oil is brought. Do we have a young woman small in stature because of age buying from a slave vendor? But if so, what are we to make of the status of the seated figure on the other side? The close mantling of the figures on this side might suggest

---

[30] So Bloesch (1943) caption to plates 36–7, and pp. 67–9, 172–3, followed by Beazley, *ARV* 596.1.

5.8 Athenian red-figure cup from Chiusi attributed to Douris, *c.* 480 BC.

modesty, and so free status, but nothing about their hairstyles sets them apart – indeed the young standing woman here has lost her long plait.[31]

Identification of male figures as slaves in pot painting, and indeed on grave stelai, on the basis of physical features is also very often highly problematic.[32] A look at two pots will show the difficulties. A red-figure cup attributed to Douris, and painted in the first quarter of the fifth century, shows, inside and out, images of a drinking party (symposium) (5.8).[33] The scenes on each side are very similar, with each showing three bearded reclining men, two seen from the side and one from the back, each wearing himatia in such a way as to leave most of their upper body bare, and being served by two smaller, beardless, naked youths. On one side the youth at the centre is playing the double pipes, on the other he stands empty handed. On both sides a still smaller youth stands at the far left of the scene holding out a wine strainer and a small pot to one of the symposiasts. Stature and action

---

[31] On which figures have long plaits see S. Lewis (2002) 27–8.

[32] Note that when we have grave monuments for slaves the representation of the slaves broadly follows the conventions for representing citizens. See Bergemann (1997) 149: 'Ihrer Bilder zeigen ähnlich denen der Metöken zum großen Teil ganze konventionelle Bildthemen, wie sie auch auf den Stelen attischer Bürger üblich waren.'

[33] For a full discussion of these scenes see Lissarrague (1999).

5.9 Athenian red-figure krater attributed to the Pan Painter, *c.* 460 BC.

point to the servile status of this figure, although nothing about his body reveals it as non-Greek or slavish. But what about the youth in the middle? Is he too to be seen as a slave? Or is he a young symposiast who has got up to parade his skills, and his bodily attractions, before the older partygoers? There are plenty of young men like him in scenes of revelling that no one has ever suspected of being servile. Here he is at the centre of the scene, the focus of our attention but also of the gazes of all the reclining drinkers, the object, it seems, of their game of kottabos and of their desire.

A wine-mixing bowl attributed to the Pan Painter shows a scene of grilling the entrails of a sacrificial animal over an altar in front of a herm (representation of the god Hermes) (5.9). On the left is a bearded man with a knobbly stick wearing his himation in classic fashion to leave free the right arm with which he holds out a cup over the altar. Next to him stands a beardless youth with his himation tied round his waist in the fashion of a workman, and holding the ritual basket. On the right, holding the spit on which the entrails are roasted, is another beardless young man, this time wearing a knee-length himation, draped in more or less the classic manner.

Both of the youths are the same height as the bearded man and the herm. Slaves certainly helped with sacrifices (as we see from the sacrifice scene in Aristophanes' *Peace*), and his dress identifies at least one of the youths here as at work, but that is not the same as identifying him as a slave. Nothing at all about these bodies – including their stature – suggests that they are slaves. It is less that these are definitely freeborn Greeks than that the question of status is not one that the painter is interested in. The truth is that there is no systematic attempt to suggest that slaves are physically different sorts of people. Whatever Aristotle would maintain in *Politics* 1, pot painters did not show slaves different by nature.[34]

Black Africans appear also in two particular classes of pot, the so-called 'Negro alabastra' and the 'head vases'. The former are a group of small pots intended as containers of perfumed oil. Alabastra are made and decorated in a number of different techniques and styles, but a group of alabastra in the white-ground technique mark their exotic content, and the way in which perfume enables its wearer to take on a different role, with scenes involving those who are 'other'. These alabastra show black Africans wearing trousers, along with Amazons and, in one case, a Skythian (5.10). All these are figures anomalous in terms of Athenian tradition. In two cases Greek youths in elaborate himatia are combined with Amazons.[35] Head vases are pots whose bodies are shaped in the form of human heads. Various heads are used, including heads of black Africans, white women (who may or may not be thought of as Amazons), Herakles, the god Dionysos and satyrs (5.11). Strikingly absent from head vases are white men.[36]

The 'Negro alabastra' and the head vases show how imagery *can* create the sorts of polarised oppositions which texts inevitably generate. The alabastra set up oppositions, showing a series of contrasting individuals and including as one pole of opposition the Athenian youth. The head vases, drinking vessels for use at symposia, show a range of heads – human, hero, god or satyr – all of which share the quality of not being heads of Athenian men. The practice on both classes of pot is undoubtedly discriminatory – classification and discrimination are what they are about – but although physical characteristics are the key discriminator in the head vases, physical characteristics are just one of the ways in which discrimination is made on

---

[34] Recent scholarship has argued that 'natural slavery' was a theory developed by Aristotle specifically in the context of his overall argument in *Politics* book 1. See Schofield (1990), Garnsey (1996) and, contra, Millett (2007b).

[35] Neils (1980).

[36] Standard red-figure imagery is to be found in decorated portions of some of these pots, near the rim. On head vases see briefly R. Osborne (2008a) 359.

5.10 Athenian white-ground alabastron showing a black African (on this example juxtaposed to a Skythian), *c.* 480 BC.

the 'Negro alabastra', and in neither case are the discriminations ones of social status.[37] But whereas texts inscribe discrimination upon a world that is separate from the reader, and experienced from afar, these pots effect an

---

[37] To such an extent is this the case that Bérard (2000) 409–11 claims that these vessels are 'beyond ideology' and that 'neither the perfumes of Aphrodite nor the wines of Dionysos put up with racism'.

5.11 Athenian black-figure 'head vase' *c.* 500 BC. Photograph © 2011. Museum of Fine Arts, Boston.

invitation to their users and viewers to assimilate to that different world: alabastra entice their users to think that by putting on perfume they make themselves other; the head vases encourage the thought that consuming the alcohol they contain opens up another world. The pots frame their own users' actions as attractively exotic, and in doing so parade the foreign world as a world of enticement.

Like natural differences, acquired physical attributes are also depicted to frame actions. Just as it is in a mythological context that Egyptians are once marked out by circumcision (5.5), so in mythological contexts, when they attack Orpheus or act as servant to Herakles, Thracian women appear with tattoos (5.3).[38] The tattoos serve both to indicate the geographical context, and to put a distance between the women who perform these extreme and cruel acts and other women. But in the case of acquired attributes history as well as myth can determine their presence. So when, more rarely, these

---

[38] The attack on Orpheus is supposed to have been the origin of the tattoos.

5.12 Athenian red-figure hydria attributed to the Aigisthos Painter, *c.* 470 BC.
Thracian women slaves at a fountain.

tattoos appear on women in contexts of Athenian life, as in the appearance
of women at a fountain or a funeral (5.12), they mark the women who have
a personal history as slaves, and offer a social context.[39]

Thracian men were picked out in vase painting not by tattoos but by their
clothing.[40] They are one among several groups of foreigners distinguished
not by their bodies but by what they cover their bodies with. Thracians wear
a distinctively patterned cloak (*zeira*), animal-skin cap (*alōpekis*), and boots
with turned-down tops.[41] Pot-painters employ these items individually or
together to mark out Thracians in myths, whether as framing figures, lis-
tening to Orpheus or the Thracian Thamyras performing, or protagonists
(the Thracian king Lykourgos, the personified North Wind, the Thracian
Boreas, the Thracian goddess Bendis).[42]

[39] Tsiafakis (2000) 372–6; Bérard (2000) 391; Oakley (2000) 241–3.
[40] And perhaps occasionally by their hair colour: see Tsiafakis (2000) 371–2.
[41] The costume is described by Herodotos at 7.75.   [42] Tsiafakis (2000) 376–88.

5.13 Satyr dressed up in Thracian cloak and boots as the god Hermes on a psykter (wine-cooler) signed by the painter Douris, *c.* 470 BC.

These figures from mythology are by no means the only figures on pots who wear items of Thracian dress. There are a large number of non-mythological figures on Athenian pots, too, who wear one or more items of Thracian costume, in particular the cloak and the boots. Some of these dress items may mark out their wearers as themselves Thracian. Thracians became extremely famous as light-armed 'peltast' troops, and when an Athenian painter shows in the tondo of a cup a light-armed soldier complete with all the elements of Thracian costume there seems no reason to deny that the figure would be seen as itself Thracian.[43] But in many other cases the context makes it certain, or all but certain, that the costume element carries no implication of Thracian origin or ethnicity. So Douris shows a satyr wearing the cloak and boots but also carrying the caduceus, to indicate that he has assumed the role of the god Hermes (5.13).[44] Thracian cloaks, boots and headgear appear in a wide range of other scenes, involving drinking and horsemanship. Most notably of all, some riders on the Parthenon frieze,

---

[43] Best (1969); Tsiafakis (2000) 267–72.   [44] *ARV* 446.262.

5.14 Cavalry in Thracian caps from the frieze of the Parthenon, North XLIV.

who are divided into tribal ranks and must stand for Athenian cavalry, wear elements of Thracian dress (5.14).[45]

Clothing likewise distinguishes Skythians. Skythians had no certain place in Greek mythology, unlike the Thracians, although some artists included them in scenes of the Kalydonian boar hunt when Atalanta was present.[46] But Skythians became associated with horsemanship and fighting as archers. Athenian vases painted between the middle and end of the sixth century show a very large number of figures equipped with one or all of the soft Skythian cap, the tight-fitting all-over garment and the bow and quiver of the archer (cf. 3.3, on p. 60).[47] Such a figure becomes almost indispensable during this period in scenes involving hoplites, a constant spectator, at least,

---

[45] E.g. the *alōpekis* in N. XLIV, and the whole of the first rank of six riders on the South frieze (S I–II), on which see Harrison (1984) 231. On the ranks of cavalry see Jenkins (2007) 41–3, 89, 132.

[46] Barringer (2004).   [47] Vos (1963), Lissarrague (1990).

in the arming, inspection of the liver of the sacrificial victim, departure, and combat of the heavily armed hoplite soldier.

But were these figures thought of as representing men hailing from Skythia? Texts attest to the presence of Skythian archers as a police force maintaining law and order at Athens from perhaps the second quarter of the fifth century.[48] But by that time painters of pottery had largely ceased to portray Skythians.[49] There is, indeed, an inverse relationship between the representation of Skythians on Athenian painted pottery and the presence of Skythians in Athens. For although there may have been Skythians employed as specialist troops in the sixth century, it was only in the fifth and fourth centuries that Skythians were regularly present in Athens. Yet the Skythian who appears all over late sixth-century black-figure pottery is conspicuously absent from fifth-century red-figure imagery, particularly after the first two decades of the century.[50] One scholar who has recently re-examined the data has concluded that it is an error to think that Skythian costume elements have anything at all to do with identifying actual Skythians or anything to do with ethnicity.[51]

Much of the explanation for the disappearance of the Skythian lies in the changing relationship of the Athenians to their own army. The extent to which Athenians had themselves been militarily engaged during the tyranny of Peisistratos and his sons is uncertain, but there is no doubt that the creation of the 'people's army', together with its startling successes first against the Boiotians and Chalkidians and then, at Marathon, against the Persians, came to be one of the features of the Kleisthenic revolution of which Athenians were most proud.[52] Whereas black-figure imagery of warfare had been heavily symbolic and laden with epic overtones, red-figure imagery rapidly comes to make explicit reference to contemporary warfare, not least in choosing to depict combat between Greek and Persian. As long as representations remained heavily symbolic, the Skythian served to point up the contrast between hoplite and light-armed troops, just as the Thracian helped to point up contrasts between hoplite and cavalry. But once going out to fight became part of what it was to be Athenian, the focus ceased to be on ideal warfare and the particular status of the heavily armed infantryman. Indeed all representation of light-armed troops and of cavalry fades, as the hoplite figure is made on pots to stand for all military enterprise.[53]

---

[48] Bäbler (2005).   [49] Vos (1963) 81.   [50] R. Osborne (2004b); cf. Lissarrague (1990) 132–6.
[51] Ivanchik (2005).   [52] Cf. Herodotos 5.78.
[53] R. Osborne (2000a) 34–40, (2004b). I discuss changes in the way soldiers are represented on Athenian red-figure pottery more fully in R. Osborne (2010b).

The essential independence of representation of Skythians on Athenian pottery from the presence of Skythians in Athenian experience, is further revealed by the other major context in which Skythian elements appear in the imagery of vase painting: the symposium. Skythians had a particular, if paradoxical, reputation for drinking. Herodotos records that the Skythians were milk-drinkers, drinkers of blood and drinkers of neat wine.[54] Some, he says, ascribed the madness of King Kleomenes of Sparta to the fact that he had acquired from some Skythian ambassadors the habit of drinking his wine unmixed.[55] Athenaios, who himself refers to Herodotos' testimony, notes that 'Skythian-style' was used to refer to a strong mix of wine, and quotes from the late-archaic poet Anakreon, who contrasts 'Skythian drinking' to 'gentle drinking with noble hymns'.[56]

Some painters at the beginning of the fifth century include a man or youth wearing the Skythian bonnet in an otherwise ordinary sympotic scene (5.8).[57] One Athenian painter, active at the same period and notable for his execrable style and for finding his market to a much larger extent than is common in parts East, rather than in Etruscan Italy, had a particular line in showing in the tondo of cups a solo symposiast, seen in back view with Skythian bonnet and drinking horn.[58]

The Skythian bonnet is not the only element of foreign costume to be sported at the symposium or in connection with drinking. The 'turban' or 'headscarf', 'mitra' or 'sakkos' which is worn by women in various scenes on pots is worn by men only in the context of drinking, either in the symposium or in the revelling of the *kōmos*.[59] In some scenes we find the headscarf worn by otherwise naked drinkers; in others it is combined with wearing not just a himation, but a himation with a chiton under it (5.15).[60] There is evidence from archaic poetry of something of a craze in Greece for the Lydian mitra, and Herodotos tells how the Lydians were encouraged by Kroisos to wear chitones under their clothes, and soft boots (*kothornoi*), and to play the

---

[54] Herodotos 4.2 (milk), 4.64 (blood). Hartog (1980) 176–85.   [55] Herodotos 6.84.

[56] Athenaios 427a–c; elsewhere he notes that one Hieronymos of Rhodes, who wrote a work *On Drunkenness*, claimed that the reason why Skythians are associated with heavy drinking is that their name is close to the name of a large drinking vessel, the skyphos: 499e–f. See further Miller (1991) 67–8.

[57] Lissarrague has suggested that this marks the figure out as a 'peerless drinker' or as the symposiarch (1987) 16, (1999) 30. On Skythian costume at the Athenian symposium see further Miller (1991).

[58] Works of the Pithos Painter, *ARV* 139.23–141.63; Lissarrague (1987) 86.

[59] Kurtz and Boardman (1986) 50–6; Frontisi-Ducrous and Lissarrague (1983).

[60] For the former see the Kleisophos painter's oinochoe, Athens NM 1045, *ABV* 186, with de Vries (2000) 360, who also draws attention to the boots worn by one drinker; for the latter, the Nikoxenos Painter's *kalpis*, Kassel A Lg 57.

5.15 Reveller with headscarf (mitra) and with a chiton under his himation juxtaposed to a reveller wearing a himation only, and in such a way as to conceal little, on the interior of an Athenian red-figure cup from Vulci attributed to Douris, *c.* 470 BC.

kithara so as to feminise them and dispel Persian fear that they might revolt.[61] We should surely see both effeminate and Lydian connotations to the dress choice of these drinkers.

Unlike Skythians, Lydians were associated not with a particular style of drinking but with a particular, soft and luxurious, style of life. A series of pots showing men in headscarves, wearing chitones under their himatia, and often sporting parasols or the form of lyre known as a barbitos, have become known as 'Anakreontics' because Beazley identified such figures with the barbitos as the lyric poet Anakreon.[62] Before coming to Athens Anakreon had spent time at the court of the Samian tyrant Polykrates,

---

[61] Herodotos 1.155–6. On the Lydian mitra see van Wees (2005) 49–50.
[62] Caskey and Beazley (1954) 55–61. On the parasol see Miller (1992).

which became renowned for its emulation of 'soft Lydian ways'.[63] It is not clear from the three images that explicitly make reference to him that the Athenians thought of Anakreon in these specifically Lydian terms, but there is little doubt that his popularity and the popularity of the Lydianising trend to some extent went together. The characteristics which mark out these 'booners' are the combination of marks of delicacy (the parasol, the chiton, the soft boots) with marks of ecstasy – the thrown-back head, the frontal face – induced by music, dancing and drink. The exotic dress serves to mark a lifestyle choice, and painters use figures so dressed to explore particular aspects of the social life of the symposium and the revel.

The Lydian style first appears on Athenian pots in the 520s and in black-figure technique; it attracts two of the finest artists of early fifth-century red-figure, Douris and the Brygos Painter, and continues to be represented in the 'mannerists' of the decades immediately after the Persian War. But by 450 painters have lost interest in these figures, who disappear from the iconography. Although the pictorial life of the Lydian was not as intense as the pictorial life of the Skythian, nor did the Lydian disappear from view quite so precipitately, nevertheless the history of the image cannot correspond with the history of Lydian presence in Athens or Athenian knowledge of the Lydians. The Kroisos whose kouros featured in the last chapter must have been given his name shortly after the middle of the sixth century, and by that time one fine Athenian black-figure pot painter was already signing himself 'Lydos'. So too Lydians continued to be familiar in Athens after 450. 'Lydos' became thought of as a stock slave name. A Lydos is found among those sold off in the Attic Stelai, and Euripides has Pheres in the *Alcestis* treat 'Lydian' as the equivalent of 'bought' and 'worthless'.[64] Six fourth-century gravestones of Lydians are known, all of them plausibly monuments to slaves or freedmen, and all but one to women.[65] The one monument with a relief is of low quality and marked as foreign not simply by the parental name given but by the fact that that name is a mother's name, but there is nothing foreign about its imagery of a woman on a couch approached by another woman.[66] A Lyde is among those listed in the manumissions marked by dedications of *phialai* in the third quarter of the

[63] Kurtz and Boardman (1986) 67–9. Athenaios 515d–516c, 540f for Lydian ways and the court of Polykrates.
[64] *ABV* 107–20; Cicero, *For Flaccus* 65; ML 79, p. 247; Euripides, *Alcestis* 675.
[65] Bäbler (1998) cat. nos. 24–8.
[66] The stele of Malthake daughter of Magadis: *CAT* 2.457; Bäbler (1998) 90–2.

5.16 A pipe-player wearing an *ependutēs* over a sleeveless chiton, Athenian red-figure amphora attributed to the Kleophrades Painter, *c.* 480 BC.

fourth century at Athens.[67] As with Skythians, what it is to look Lydian on Athenian pots is quite a different matter from being Lydian.[68]

More remarkably, what it is to look Persian on a pot turns out to be quite different from being Persian. Athenian artists show various items of Persian origin, particularly the sleeved chiton, the sleeved jacket known as the *kandus*, and the tunic known as the *ependutēs* (5.16).[69] The *ependutēs* seems

[67] D. M. Lewis (1959) Face A line 328.
[68] There is an abundant modern literature on the colonialist gaze and the gaze of the tourist which is relevant to these issues. See, for example, T. Mitchell (1988) ch. 1, Mackie (2000), Hight and Sampson (2002), especially Hayes (2002) 178.
[69] For what follows see Miller (1997) 153–87.

to have been taken up in Ionia when Persians conquered the area in the sixth century, and it is unclear to what extent it was thought of as Persian when initially shown as clothing of goddesses on sixth-century and early fifth-century Athenian pottery.[70] But fifth-century Athenian painters certainly considered the *ependutēs* to be an oriental garment, given the frequency of its appearance after the period of the Persian Wars on Amazons, Persians and generic Easterners.[71] The garment is then found in a wide range of contexts, worn by men and women in funerary scenes, by soldiers in departure scenes, by dancers, by women in ritual scenes and by a variety of figures in mythological scenes. Sleeved chitones appear in classical red-figure vases in a similar range of scenes, and from the last quarter of the fifth century there is an outbreak of *kandus* wearing by small children and women in scenes with ritual overtones (particularly scenes on the small jugs (choes) associated with the Anthesteria (5.17)), as well as in identifiably Persian scenes.[72]

The Persians were not a remote enemy as far as classical Athenians were concerned. There were Persians living in Athens. Along with nine other grave stelai of Persians, several bearing reliefs indistinguishable from reliefs commemorating Athenians, there is one stele with entirely Achaimenid iconography (5.18).[73] We do not know whether this hybrid stele, with its Attic workmanship as well as findspot, in fact commemorated a Persian, since the stele bears no name. The lower scene on the stele is paralleled by the reverse of an Athenian red-figure pot painting of late fifth-century date, which shows a fleeing man in Persian dress, and Athenian artists played with Persian imagery in a variety of circumstances. Similarly there is no reason to think that the fragment of a torso wearing items of Persian dress, which comes from a grave terrace in the Kerameikos, in fact commemorated a Persian. A stele showing a figure in a *kandus* who bears the name 'Myttion' appears to commemorate a slave, but not one for whom there is reason to postulate a specifically Persian origin.[74]

---

[70] E.g. Andokides Painter, *ARV* 4.10; early fifth-century Panathenaics nos. 24, 38–9, 45 in Neils (1992).

[71] Miller (1997) 171. This is almost certainly true of the wearing of the *ependutēs* by aulos players in festival or sympotic contexts from 490–480 onwards: Miller (1997) 175, n. 157 lists the images. There had been a forty-year gap since the earliest *ependutēs*-wearing auletai, whose connotations may have been merely Ionian.

[72] Miller (1997) 165–8.

[73] Bäbler (1998) cat. nos. 41–50; for standard Attic iconography see nos. 44, 45, 47, 48. The Achaimenid iconography appears on the 'Kamini' stele, Bäbler (1998) no. 41 and pp. 109–11, on which see also Miller (1997) 56.

[74] Bäbler (1998) 26–32; *CAT* 1.224. There were, of course, plenty of slaves in Athens who did come from lands within the Persian Empire, but specifically Persian slaves are another matter.

5.17 Small child wearing a *kandus* on an Athenian red-figure chous, *c.* 400 BC.

5.18 Athenian grave stele (the 'Kamini' stele) with Persian iconography, *c.* 350 BC.

All these elements of non-Greek attire are employed much as items of attire associated with particular parts of Greece itself were employed. Although they are harder to spot on pots, the Athenians knew a particular style of men's footwear as 'Lakonian slippers' and perhaps a style of walking stick as Lakonian.[75] Aristophanes has Philokleon in *Wasps* put on Lakonian slippers (along with Persian *kaunakēs*) when he becomes a well-dressed man.[76] There are indeed 'Spartan' overtones here: as we discover when Agathon is found to have no Lakonian slippers, these are serious manly wear.[77]

The burden of my argument will have become clear. Athenian artists, whether sculptors or pot painters, had a large number of resources at their disposal to differentiate role, social status and ethnicity. We have seen already in Chapter 3 that pot painters had a great deal of interest in the nuances of social positioning, often offering combinations of figures with differently elaborated dress. However, only rarely did painters choose to deploy clothing or other features to indicate formal status divisions. Thus only occasionally are figures picked out as specifically rustic country workers by their wearing of the fur hat, and only occasionally are female figures on funerary lekythoi marked by features, clothing or size as maids.[78] Indicators of ethnicity were employed readily enough to identify mythological scenes, but rarely does it seem to have been thought relevant to set scenes relating to daily life in a specific ethnic context. Only in the case of slaves are ethnic indicators employed in scenes that relate to life, and there the desire seems to be to indicate servile status rather than to determine a particular ethnic origin. It is as if in relations between free persons, features particular to the individual, not features shared by the individual and his whole native community, are what is at issue. Painters employ identifiably foreign clothes and accoutrements to mark styles adopted by individual Athenians themselves, rather than to identify foreigners. The Xenophontic *Constitution of the Athenians* notes that the Athenians were peculiar in deriving their dress from barbarian as well as Greek sources.[79] Whatever the relationship between life and art, this claim is very much of a piece with the sophisticated use of foreign items of clothing with which Athenian artists expected their viewers to be familiar.

---

[75] On the walking stick see Diggle (2004) 242–3; on the slippers Stone (1981) 225–7.

[76] Aristophanes, *Wasps* 1157–8. On the *kaunakēs* see Miller (1997) 154–5.

[77] Aristophanes, *Women at the Thesmophoria* 142; cf. *Assembly Women* 74, 269, 345, 508, 542. These men's shoes are opposed to the *persikai* worn by women – an element almost invisible in pot paintings but featuring repeatedly in Aristophanes; see *Assembly Women* 319 and Stone (1981) 227–9.

[78] See Pipili (2000) on hats.   [79] [Xenophon] *Constitution of the Athenians* 2.8.

The representations of Memnon and of Andromeda (5.4) are worth revisiting at this point, for they can now be seen to reflect artists' use of foreign clothing. Just as foreign clothing items are used to alert the viewer to the wearer's desire to operate on a more than local stage, so Memnon and Andromeda's foreign company situates them in a markedly foreign context. The decision to show the servants as black but to leave the protagonist as white simultaneously exploits the association of blackness with slavery and points out that the central character's story needs to be understood as happening in a world where such figures prevail. The Athenian viewer is able to put himself or herself into the position of Memnon or Andromeda because the heroes share the viewer's appearance, but at the same time the accompanying foreign figures warn that the nature of the experience the heroes are to be imagined to undergo is quite removed from the experience of living in the Greek city.[80]

There is some evidence for Athenians themselves showing some consciousness of the peculiarity of presenting foreign heroes such as Andromeda and Memnon in a way that effaced their personal foreignness. In a scene which has never been satisfactorily explained, the white-ground lekythos in Athens which Haspels made the 'name-vase' of the 'Beldam Painter' shows a woman with distinctively African features and pendulous breasts, tied to a tree and being beaten and variously tortured by satyrs (5.19).[81] What is happening here? The presence of satyrs requires the reference to be either to mythology or to cult activity, and the latter seems highly unlikely. The best candidate for a mythological woman tied up and maltreated is Andromeda. I suggest that, in the face of and with reference to the convention of representing Andromeda as if she were not foreign but Greek, this painter is here, in the spirit of satyr play, drawing attention to what happens if the heroine to be rescued is instead shown as foreign and black. Once Andromeda is black, and therefore slavish, and once her assailants are freed from any ethnic characterisation, the question of how the viewer reacts to her maltreatment comes to be seen in a rather different light.

In the last chapter I was concerned to argue that formal legal status was not something for which Athenian artists showed much concern: citizens cannot be visually distinguished from non-citizens, and among non-citizens metics cannot be visually distinguished from *xenoi*. The evidence now reviewed

---

[80] Bérard (2000) 395–406.

[81] Athens NM 1129, *ABL* 266.1, with discussion on p. 170. Haspels herself was uncertain that the woman was Negroid, but the combination of hair and pendulous breasts seems to me to put that beyond serious doubt.

5.19 Athenian white-ground lekythos, name-vase of the so-called Beldam Painter, *c.* 460 BC.

here shows that while painters are also very far from systematic in showing the distinction between free and slave, slave status is something which they can sometimes think it important to show.[82] Distinctions between slave and master or mistress are far from being always salient, but those distinctions can be crucial to understanding how figures relate. And the clearest means by which painters indicate slave status is by indicating that the figure in question is not by nature a Greek. Indicating ethnicity is here a means to an end. By contrast, those signs of ethnicity that consist in clothing are free-floating and may be worn reversibly by individuals identified by their context as barbarian or as Greek.

---

[82] There are a small number of grave reliefs for slaves and for metics which are iconographically distinct, showing the figure in a way that no citizen is shown. An example would be the stele for Sosinous of Gortyn the metalworker (a solo, seated male figure, see above, p. 70) or that for the slave Karion (shown carrying a bag): see Bergemann (1997) 147, 149. There are no grounds for thinking that the distinct iconography of some metic monuments marks these metics as ex-slaves (Sosinous of Gortyn was surely not), as Bergemann claims (1997: 149–50, 155).

The instrumental use of ethnic indications on painted pottery is in stark contrast to the expectations created by classical texts that ethnic differences are an ever-present and ineradicable feature of identity. Greek writers distinguished, and assumed that others also distinguished, both between those who belonged to a city community and those who did not, by dividing the world between *politai* and *xenoi*, and between those who spoke their own language and those who did not, classifying the latter as *barbaroi*. Herodotos provides us with explicit guidance on this, reporting that 'the Egyptians call men of other languages *barbaroi*' and drawing attention to the oddity that the Spartans call the Persians *xenoi* rather than *barbaroi*.[83]

The polarities of the world of texts are complex. Scholars who base themselves on textual sources find the Athenians distinguishing themselves from others not simply by the invention of the barbarian – where the absence of the concept of the barbarian from Homer coincides with the absence of the word itself – but by insisting on such marks of separation as their own autochthony.[84] If it took the pressure of the Persian invasions to compel a sense of Hellenicity, of there being a common quality of being Greek,[85] the defeat of the Persians offered the Athenians the opportunity to insist not simply that the world of the barbarians was quite other than the world of the Greeks but that they were Greeks like no others. According to Herodotos, the Athenians had insisted in 480 that they would never side with the Persians, citing as their reasons the common blood, manners, language and religion of all Greeks.[86] But that common blood was now distinguished into an unmixed Athenian stream and other mixed streams. The processes of division, upon which Plato will insist that knowledge depends, are employed to produce the knowledge that to be Athenian is not to be Spartan or Boiotian or Argive or Thessalian, or indeed a member of any of the cities allied to Athens in the Delian League.

Such division, and the very creation of categories by negation that the world of language encourages, can only with artifice be introduced into the world of images. Athenian black-figure artists applied white paint to women's flesh and left male flesh black, turning whiteness into a sign of

---

[83] Herodotos 2.158.5 for Egyptians; 9.11.2 for Spartans (but note that the Spartans are made to use *barbaroi* of the Persians at 8.142.2 and 5). Flower and Marincola (2002) ad loc. seem to get things precisely backwards in their note on 9.11.2 when they claim that failing to distinguish between non-Greeks and Greeks from other *poleis* is a mark of their xenophobia. On use of *xenos* in fifth-century texts see Gauthier (1971).

[84] 'Inventing the barbarian': E. M. Hall (1989); authochthony: Loraux (1981a), (1981b), Rosivach (1987).

[85] J. M. Hall (2002).   [86] Herodotos 8.144.

being 'not-male' sufficiently powerful that it could be used occasionally to effeminise a man.[87] But even such manipulations, like the manipulations involved in the various role-playing opportunities afforded by drama and the symposium, leave any but the simplest images questioning whether, rather than affirming that, the world divides between those who possess a certain quality and those who lack that quality.

The possibilities and limitations of producing binary classifications in visual images emerge nicely from a monument at Olympia described by Pausanias. The people of Apollonia, he tells us, set up a semi-circular pedestal, at the middle of which were Zeus, Thetis and Day. Spreading out from them, and paired off, were Greek and Trojan adversaries, ending with Memnon at one end and Achilles at the other. Other pairs were Menelaus and Paris, Odysseus and Helenus, Diomedes and Aineias, Aias and Deiphobos.[88] Pausanias tells us that Odysseus and Helenus were those who had the highest reputation for wisdom on each side, and we can work out why Achilles faces Memnon (because when the two come into battle Zeus has to decide which of their lives should end) and why Paris should oppose Menelaus (they are rivals for Helen). One way of conceiving of what the artist has done is that he has contrasted the Greek and the non-Greek. But is Greekness actually an issue here? The monument was set up by the people of Apollonia in Epirus in north-west Greece, a city founded from Kerkyra, to commemorate their victory over the neighbouring Abantes, and Pausanias explains that the Abantes had settled there after having been blown ashore at that point on their return from fighting at Troy. The war commemorated was not between Greek and non-Greek, and the qualities pitched here against each other (wisdom; the favour of Zeus) do not turn upon ethnicity. It is hard to think that anyone who gazed at this monument for long enough to gather who was represented could come away thinking that they were being shown how Greekness was different to non-Greekness. Rather they were being shown the range of different qualities and behaviours that find themselves pitted against each other in war. Where language so often promotes thinking in binaries, images resolutely promote the plural.

This is not simply true of the images created by artists; it is even more true of the world around us seen by the eyes. Everything seen by the eye is particular, potentially ascribable to any number of classes. But such ascription

---

[87] As famously with the representation on a Corinthian amphora of Periklymenos running off, having been caught in adultery (Paris, Louvre E 460). Carpenter (1991) caption to fig. 269 denies the significance.

[88] Pausanias 5.22.2–3. The remains of the base survive.

of an object seen to a class can only be on the basis of observable features – and these might be features of nature or of culture, features displayed on the body or features displayed by what the body wears or carries. The status of not being a citizen can hardly have been manifested by the physical body, but the Athenians might have chosen to flag it by what must or could not be worn. Certain non-Greek non-Athenians, at least, had little choice but to display on their bodies their genetic origin. Such features of the body might be salient to the observer, sometimes noticed, or entirely pass the observer by. Painted pottery helps us to see what among the many visible features of those among whom they lived Athenians had come to notice.

If texts tell the historian how the world was divided up for the purpose of ruling it and understanding it, pictures tell the historian the sorts of ways in which the world that was experienced was actually ascribed into classes; they tell us something of the contexts in which conceptual division became relevant real life distinctions. And when we look for pictures of foreign bodies and find instead the language of clothes being used independently of any distinctive bodily features, we have good evidence that Athenian priorities did not in fact lie with separating the world into either Athenians and *xenoi* or Athenians and *barbaroi*. Athenian priorities lay much more with discriminating roles within their own community or even roles in a particular situation. Not for the last time in history, the language and priorities of the political assembly did not translate into the language of the street. For the historian, taking the language of law and of the political assembly to be the only language in which communications are made can seriously damage your world-view.

If Antipatros knew the sorts of things that were said in the Athenian Assembly he may well have had reasons to fear that on his death the lions would have him. However, Domsalōs was able to prove that there were not at Athens simply Athenians and foreigners but many different ways of being in the community. The framework of civic life was like the framework of the stele with small recessed relief panel (*Bildfeldstele*): there were broad conventions which had to be accepted to count as a member of the community at all, but once those conventions were accepted, it was possible to combine elements in ways that were quite new, to create a life which was unique and even make others realise aspects of life which they had systematically repressed. Within the conventions of the symposium, with its careful regulation of the consumption of wine mixed in due proportion with water, the Skythian (5.7) raised the question of whether one should not be drinking wine unmixed (or drinking milk!). Within the conventions of a festival, the Anthesteria, at which infants were recognised as persons in their own right, the Persian *kandus* asked what guarantees there were that this infant would observe local conventions. Within the conventions of the standard Athenian gravestone, which might show a couch, naked young men, an animal or a ship's prow but would never put on display the circumstances of death or the way a man met his fate, Domsalōs created an image which forced the Athenians to confront just that. Against a verbal politics which imaged an Athens in which the foreign was the negation of the Athenian, the visual politics of life and art conspired to insist that the place to look for the foreign body was always within the body of the citizens. If writers see the foreign by holding up a mirror to the familiar, artists suggest that anyone who looks closely into a mirror will always find there his own body foreign.

6 | Dirty bodies

We might expect dirt to be something visible, but is it any more visible than citizenship? When a mother says to a child, 'You have got a dirty face, go and wash it', it is not dirt that she is seeing. What she sees is usually chocolate. Were she to see blood, she would be very unlikely to react in that way. Blood around the mouth is too significant to be merely dirt. Lord Chesterfield's much quoted and approved definition of dirt as 'matter out of place' is certainly no sufficient condition: much matter may be displaced without becoming dirty; only some matter in some displacements counts as dirt. But is it a necessary condition? Is it merely conventional that certain substances – say excrement – are reckoned dirty in all or almost all circumstances, whereas others, like chocolate, are only dirty in some circumstances?

If this is a puzzle over identifying what we can see as dirty, there is even more of a puzzle over metaphysical dirt. The injunction to 'Wash your mouth out with soap!' is occasioned not by the sight of chocolate but by 'foul' language. We regularly use this language of dirt of actions which produce no physical mark. Sometimes that language is more or less directly related to morality, as in links between promiscuity and dirty behaviour, or talk of stains on people's consciences. Quite often it is related to bodily substances. Blood is often reckoned to make someone dirty, whether it is menstrual blood or blood shed in death – 'he has got blood on his hands'. Physical and metaphysical dirt are not separate but intertwined, and in both cases the classification as dirt is not straightforward. How do we tell that this body is dirty (6.1)?[1]

Finding dirty bodies on Athenian pots and in Athenian sculpture is virtually impossible. Consider the pots and memorials that were part of funerary ritual. Almost any death was thought to render those who were closely associated with the corpse polluted. This is nicely shown

---

[1] In common with many writers in the field, I have chosen to use terms with a very broad and vague purchase, and terms that overlap. I do so because my interest is in verbal and visual classification of the unacceptable, not in uncovering or analysing views about how things come to be unacceptable. For a discussion of the language of taboo, pollution and contagion, and an insistence that things avoided as disgusting must be seen differently from things avoided because prohibited, see Valeri (2000) 44–5, 61–2.

6.1 On this Athenian red-figure column krater from Bologna, attributed to the Painter of Brussels R330, *c.* 440 BC., Orestes, in travelling hat and cloak and carrying sword and spear, approaches a seated Apollo, with laurel and lyre; Artemis and Pylades stand to the right.

in the section of a long law on purification from Cyrene in Libya from the last third of the fourth century BC. Concerning miscarriage the law stipulates:

If a woman miscarries, if it is distinguishable (*diadēlon*), they are polluted just as from someone having died; but if it is not distinguishable, the house itself is polluted as from childbirth.[2]

A small series of Athenian grave reliefs shows women who have died in childbirth. The vast majority of classical Athenian grave stelai show the deceased as they were in life (3.6–3.11 on pp. 64–72; 4.8 on p. 121), but these stelai show the occasion of death – the act of giving birth (6.2).[3] The

---

[2] RO 97.106–10.
[3] The stelai are conveniently collected and discussed in Demand (1994) 122–6.

6.2 Grave stele from Oropos, of Plangon who died in childbirth, *c.* 320 BC. Her husband Tolmides is also named and both are identified as Plataians.

woman giving birth in this representation is certainly polluted by the fact of the birth itself; those with her polluted either by the birth or by the death of the woman. But nothing about these figures marks them out as in any way unusual or different from the figures who appear on other stelai showing scenes from life.

So too with the figures shown on pots mourning a dead person laid out on the bier prior to the funeral procession. These so-called *prothesis* scenes occur on Athenian pottery from the eighth century onwards. A white-ground lekythos dating to the middle of the fifth century (6.3) shows a young man wrapped in a deep red winding sheet lying on a couch.[4] By his head stands a man, leaning on a stick, his similarly coloured himation pulled up round his head; at his feet a young woman with hair cut short and wearing a chiton of the same red hue places one hand on head, the other on the bier. In between, another woman, in a chiton of lighter hue, tears her

---

[4] On these lekythoi and the way in which they picture death see Oakley (2004).

6.3 White-ground lekythos attributed to the Sabouroff Painter, *c.* 450 BC.

hair with both hands; her very similar facial appearance has the effect of making these two women stand in for a whole family throng of mourners. Can we see that these figures are polluted? Two clues are possible. One is the short and unkempt hair of the female mourners. Women on Athenian pottery do not normally look like this. The second clue is the colour of the garments worn. Some cities seem to have obliged mourners to wear garments of a particular colour. So the city of Gambreion passed a law in the third century BC that women in mourning should wear grey clothes, and men white or grey clothes.[5] But neither colour of garment nor cropping of hair are at all stable indicators on Athenian pottery: many women in mourning scenes have uncropped hair, some women not at all associated with mourning have hair very like that shown here, and even on this lekythos

---

[5] Sokolowski (1955) no. 16: 'There shall be a law among the citizens of Gambreion that women in mourning shall wear clean grey clothes; and the men and the children in mourning shall wear grey clothing unless they prefer white' (tr. Arnaoutoglou (1998) no. 110).

the colour of the garments worn by the mourners is not uniform.[6] We must conclude that even in circumstances which we know to be polluting, no attempt is made by artists representing the scene to show that the figures are 'dirty'.

For the last forty years discussions of dirt have been dominated by a single work of anthropology, the late Mary Douglas' book *Purity and Danger: an Analysis of Concepts of Pollution and Taboo*, published in 1966. It is Douglas who gave Lord Chesterfield's definition of dirt new life. In a classic piece of structuralist analysis she insisted that:

Dirt then, is never a unique, isolated event. Where there is dirt there is system. Dirt is the by-product of a systematic ordering and classification of matter, in so far as ordering involves rejecting inappropriate elements.[7]

For Douglas in *Purity and Danger* 'people really do think of their own social environment as consisting of other people joined or separated by lines which must be respected', and a person is polluted who 'has developed some wrong condition or simply crossed some line which should not have been crossed and this displacement unleashes danger for someone'.[8] If some sorts of crossing generate pollution beliefs more regularly than others, the explanation is that social pressures are potentially more explosive in those areas.[9] Douglas developed and modified her ideas in a number of subsequent publications, but it was the model offered in *Purity and Danger* that caught the academic, and indeed popular, imagination.[10]

For the last twenty-five years discussions of dirt in classical Greece have been dominated by a single work of ancient history, Robert Parker's *Miasma: Pollution and Purification in Early Greek Religion*.[11] Parker notes, against Douglas, that 'not all pollutions can be seen as products of category violations', and that in reckoning the newly born and the newly dead to be problematic 'a disconcerting being has been declared a misfit by special

---

[6] For a *prothesis* scene without cropped hair see, for example, Lyon E 288.3, *ARV* 1385.5 (Oakley (2004) fig. 52), where one of the women has her hair clearly tied back, and cf. Oakley (2004) 152: 'artistic convention did not demand that the hair be shown as short, even at the *prothesis*'. On the relationship of the colours of garments on lekythoi to those in life see Oakley (2004) 77–80.

[7] Douglas (1966) 35.   [8] Douglas (1966) 138, 112.

[9] Douglas (1966) 157: 'Is there any reason why all these examples of the social system at war with itself are drawn from sexual relations? There are many other contexts in which we are led into contradictory behaviour by the normal canons of our culture. National income policy is one modern field in which this sort of analysis could easily be applied. Yet pollution fears do not seem to cluster round contradictions which do not involve sex. The answer may be that no other social pressures are potentially so explosive as those which constrain sexual relations.'

[10] For later developments see Douglas (1975), (1993).   [11] Parker (1983).

manipulation of the classificatory process'. But when Parker goes on 'The being is disconcerting not on logical, cognitive, or classificatory but on simple emotional grounds that it is hard to adjust to decisive change', he fails to create significant clear water between himself and Douglas, who admits that areas subject to greater social pressure engender greater pollution concerns.[12] Parker himself explicitly accepts Douglas' association of fear of pollution with the urge for order and control.[13] The degree to which Parker works within the framework established by Douglas is clearly revealed in the title of his first chapter: 'Purification: a Science of Division'.[14]

Under the influence of both Douglas and Parker, Jan Bremmer, when he came to write his *Greece and Rome* New Survey of work on Greek religion, introduced the issue of purity and pollution in the following words:

An important consequence of overstepping or breaking existing cosmological, social, and political boundaries was the incurring of pollution. The vocabulary of pollution and purity together with its concomitant practices was most frequently used in Greek religion to indicate proper boundaries or categories not to be mixed . . . The employment of this particular vocabulary with the corresponding rites of purification can, in one way, be seen as an important Greek way of dealing with maintaining religious and social norms and values in times when the legal process was still underdeveloped.[15]

Just as Parker questions Douglas' approach only to employ it, so also, in the most recent treatment of pollution in the Greek world, does Andreas Bendlin. Bendlin raises the objection that if social control is maintained through purity regulations, and purity regulations are a natural extension of social control, 'one would need to assume that the purity regulations are regarded as natural categorizations by most and under all circumstances'; 'is that really the case?', he asks.[16] But, leaving this as a rhetorical question, he immediately goes on to say that Douglas' approach undoubtedly has heuristic value, and he suggests that it helps us understand childbirth and death and the relationship of women to purity regulations. It is time to think more radically about dirty bodies.

It is essential to Douglas' construction in *Purity and Danger* of what it is that makes a thing polluted that pollution beliefs are consistent. If something

---

[12] Parker (1983) 62.   [13] Parker (1983) 64.
[14] Cf. the last paragraph of that chapter: 'It seemed useful . . . to begin with a way of looking that relates purification to the desire for order, and that treats it as a form of behaviour rather than as a product of an explicitly formulated set of ideas', Parker (1983) 31.
[15] Bremmer (1994) 5–6.   [16] Bendlin (2007) 182.

falls between categories then it will be polluted.[17] It is no accident that the examples which Douglas places in pole position, and which readers of Douglas remember most clearly, are the dietary rules of the Old Testament, discussed in her chapter 3, 'The Abominations of Leviticus'. Here the story is simple and appealing: some animals are anomalous between categories, their anomalous position leads to them being regarded as unholy or polluted, and since polluted they may not be eaten. End of story. As Valerio Valeri, in the most powerful critique of Douglas to date, notes, on her account 'Holiness is taxonomy. The cult of God is a taxonomic cult . . . he certainly is a God of taxonomists, maybe even of a follower of Aristotle.'[18]

I want to draw attention to two sorts of problems with a purely taxonomic approach to pollution and purification. First, pollution is rarely so simple a matter as in the flagging up of foods for avoidance. To incur pollution is in most cases not the end of the story, for purification is possible. Purification implies that pollution can be removed, but if pollution is a consequence of an action done, how can that action be undone? How can a categorical anomaly be rectified? Would purification not have somehow to move the category boundaries? The second problem is that the taxonomic approach implies that the circumstances in which pollution occurs will be consistent across all who share the same categorical division – and so presumably normally all who share the same language. But what pollutes is defined by societies in ways that defy categorical consistency. In real life pollution is restricted other than at category boundaries.

A law on funerals from the island of Keos, dated to the end of the fifth century BC, illustrates both of these points. This law lays down how funerals and subsequent rituals for the dead are to be conducted, and it deals with purification and pollution. It lays down that, on the day after the burial:

a free person must sprinkle the house with sea water first and then wash it with water, having sprinkled it on the earth. When it has been sprinkled, the house is pure and one can make the sacrifices at the hearth.[19]

How can sprinkling with water undo the pollution of the house? On a Douglasian view, a corpse in a house is 'matter out of place'. Houses are places for the living. But on this view the house should cease to be anomalous when the corpse has been taken away. Sprinkling with water will be neither necessary nor sufficient. Sprinkling treats metaphysical dirt as if it is real dirt. Whatever the original link between matter out of place and pollution,

---

[17] Something similar I take to be implied by Parker's decision to talk of a *science* of division.
[18] Valeri (2000) 75.   [19] Sokolowski (1969) 97, translated in Arnaoutoglou (1998) no. 109.

the way pollution is dealt with makes clear that what has been declared dirty becomes not an intellectual or cognitive problem but a social problem, in the sense that outward and visible signs are required that the problem has been dealt with.

Later in the same law we find regulation of who exactly is polluted by the death:

Where someone dies, when the person has been carried out, women are not to go to the house other than those who are polluted. The mother, the wife, the sisters and the daughters are polluted, but in addition to these not more than five women, the children of daughters and cousins, but no one else.

It is not hard to see why pollution might be identified as limited to the immediate kin of the dead man, in whose world things have particularly been put out of place. But that there should be a numerical limit on the more distant kin polluted, regardless of their relationship either to the dead man or to his house, is hard to square with pollution's being a matter of category. Once more, if there is a cognitive and intellectual problem, its solution is tempered by social concerns.

It is not that categories have nothing to do with pollution, but that categories offer a way, but not the only way, of defining what has already been identified as problematic. Valeri reads the Jewish dietary restrictions in just this way:

The classification of animals that is found in Leviticus and Deuteronomy is . . . a classification for the purposes of eating and touching. The rules for eating and touching animals are not a side effect, a mere application, of a taxonomic enterprise; they orient that enterprise because they are its end. The issue is not 'given this classification, what should we not eat?' but 'if we are to eat so as to reproduce our identity, what classification?'[20]

So too, I suggest, with the Kean law, the question is not, 'Given the purpose of houses what can we do about death?' Nor is it, 'Given the closeness of kinship, what can we do about these female relatives?' It is rather, 'Given that death upsets arrangements in regard to things and people who are closest to the dead person, whether physically or by kinship ties, and given that deaths happen, how are we to classify in order to minimise the turmoil death causes?' To that question there is no need for a simple answer based on a single principle: pollution can be limited by kinship relation *and* by

---

[20] Valeri (2000) 80.

number. Categorical boundaries are associated with pollution because they are potentially part of the solution, not because they are the problem.[21]

Let me return to my opening question: how do we identify a dirty body? What made bodies dirty in ancient Greece? The fullest guide offered in classical literature comes from one of Theophrastos' *Characters*, the 'Superstitious Man'. To this man it appears that all sorts of things are polluting:

> The Superstitious man is the kind who washes his hands in three springs, sprinkles himself with water from a temple font, puts a laurel leaf in his mouth, and then is ready for the day's perambulations. If a weasel runs across his path he will not proceed on his journey until someone else has covered the ground or he has thrown three stones over the road. When he sees a snake in his home he invokes Sabazios if it is the red-brown one, and if it is the holy one he sets up a hero-shrine there and then ... If a mouse nibbles through a bag of barley he goes to the expounder of sacred law and asks what he should do; and if the answer is that he should give it to the tanner to sew up he disregards the advice and performs an apotropaic sacrifice. He is apt to purify his house frequently, claiming that he is haunted by Hekate. If owls <*lacuna*> while he is walking he becomes agitated and says 'Athena is quite a power' before going on. He refuses to step on a tombstone or go near a dead body or a woman in childbirth, saying that he cannot afford to risk pollution. On the fourth and the seventh of the month he orders his household to boil down some wine, then goes out and buys myrtle-wreaths, frankincense and cakes, and on his return spends the whole day garlanding the Hermaphrodites. When he has a dream he visits not only dream-analysts but also seers and bird-watchers to ask which god or goddess he should pray to ... If ever he observes a man wreathed with garlic <*lacuna*> the offerings at the crossroads, he goes away and washes from head to toe, then calls for priestesses and tells them to purify him with a squill or a puppy. If he sees a madman or an epileptic he shudders and spits into his chest.[22]

Encounters with various animals in particular circumstances, with the dead, with birth, with dream visions, with men engaging in certain dubious practices or suffering madness, all of these are felt by this man to be polluting. What makes this man peculiar is not that he finds things polluting that no one else would regard as polluting, but that he reacts in ways in which not everyone would react. The Superstitious Man takes all potentially polluting actions to demand both pre-emptive and reactive measures. Other men, the implication is, would only concern themselves in more restricted circumstances (perhaps, for example, when physical proximity or kinship create a particular link with the dead or with those who have given birth).

---

[21] Cf. Parker (1983) 121: 'Pollution ... is not so much a rationalization as a vehicle through which social disruption is expressed.'

[22] Theophrastos, *Characters* 16, Diggle's translation, modified.

This peculiarity of the superstitious man makes him good evidence for the maximal range of sorts of things that might pollute. But he is by the same token also excellent evidence – otherwise the character sketch would not be amusing – for the expectation that these things should not *always* be thought of as polluting; that is, it is inconsistency that is expected. The Superstitious Man, like classification systems themselves, does not recognise fuzzy edges.

The wider evidence for pollution in ancient Greece reveals another sort of inconsistency: inconsistency across time. The ancient scholiast on *Iliad* 11.690 already observed that there was no Homeric instance of a murderer's being purified. The first mention that we know of purification for murder came in the seventh-century epic *Aithiopis*, in which Achilles was purified on Lesbos after he had been provoked into killing Thersites.[23] As George Grote put it:

> The idea of a special taint of crime, and of the necessity as well as the sufficiency of prescribed religious ceremonies as a means of removing it, appears thus to have got footing in Grecian practice subsequent to the time of Homer . . .[24]

This Homeric silence has been much discussed. Parker has emphasised that death in war, the most frequent death in the *Iliad*, was never regarded as polluting, so that the occasions on which pollution might be expected to be alluded to are few. At the same time he has drawn attention to the association between disaster and dirt that is displayed when Achilles pours grimy dust over his head after the death of Patroklos and refuses to wash until after his funeral. There is some tension between these two points, since the more the latter behaviour is assimilated to regarding Patroklos' corpse as polluting the more we would expect all deaths in war to be polluting. Parker admits that the 'metaphysical extension' of the physical symbolism of dirt employed in the case of Achilles and Patroklos is not to be found in Homer, but he nevertheless denies that that extension can be *proven* to be later. Similarly, Parker maintained that, with regard to purification, 'The celebrated silence . . . reduces itself almost entirely to the matter of the actual rite of purification . . . If the actual rites of purification were introduced in post-Homeric times – an importation from Lydia, perhaps – the importance of this innovation was slight . . .'[25] But what Parker belittles as of minor importance are the features which transform into a metaphysical matter the

---

[23] Proclus, *Chrestomathy* 2 (D. B. Monro and T. W. Allen, eds., *Homeri Opera*, vol. V, 105, lines 28ff. Oxford).

[24] Grote (1862) vol. I, 21.   [25] Parker (1983) 69, 134.

pollution and purification that in Homer 'is inspired solely by a proper and sanitary striving after cleanliness'.[26]

It is important to realise that there are a number of occasions in Homer where issues of purification for murder would be expected to arise. In *Iliad* book 2 Tlepolemos, having killed his father's uncle, flees and suffers many hardships before coming to Rhodes and settling there. He is explicitly said to enjoy Zeus's favour on Rhodes, but there is no mention of any purification.[27] Similar stories are told of Medon, Lykophron, Epeigeus and Patroklos.[28] In the *Odyssey* Odysseus invents a similar story and the pattern recurs in the stories of Theoklymenos and of an anonymous Aitolian.[29] The various stories, although structurally parallel, are told at very different lengths and with different degrees of elaboration, but not one version so much as hints at the need for those with another man's blood on their hands to be purified.[30] So too the famous trial scene on the shield of Achilles involves a case of manslaughter and how it is to be dealt with, but no suggestion ever arises that purification should be involved.[31]

The Homeric silence on pollution and purification is only the most striking of various historic changes to what was regarded as polluting and in need of purification. Two changes that have attracted particular attention relate to sexual intercourse and to menstruation. Concern that sanctuaries be kept pure from menstrual contamination occurs only in late texts for non-Greek cults.[32] The evidence for concern for purity from sexual intercourse is more complex. A sixth-century law from Olympia forbids sexual intercourse in the sanctuary and requires sacrifice of an ox and complete purification should it occur.[33] Herodotos observes in his account of Egypt that 'Apart from the Egyptians and Greeks, almost all humans have sexual intercourse in sanctuaries and go from women into a sanctuary without washing, considering humans to be just like other beasts.'[34] In the middle of the fourth century the Koans required the slaughterer of the ox to be 'pure

---

[26] Gillies (1925) 74.   [27] *Iliad* 2.661–70.

[28] *Iliad* 13.694–7 = 15.335–5; 15.430–2; 16.571–4; 23.85–90; cf. 24.480.

[29] *Odyssey* 13.258–75; 14.379–81; 15.272–8.

[30] The simile likening, with wondrous role-reversal, the astonishment of Achilles at Priam to the astonishment felt at the arrival in a strange community of someone who had killed a man is particularly striking in this connection (*Iliad* 24.480–3). Richardson (1993) 323 thinks that the surprise 'may not be so far from the later idea of pollution', but I incline rather to think that it is the wonder at a man who has done something terrible.

[31] *Iliad* 18.497–508; cf. 9.632–6.

[32] Parker (1983) 101–2, n. 112. On other societies where menstruation is not regarded as impure cf. Testart (1991) 254–5.

[33] *GDI* 1156; Buck (1955) no. 72.

[34] Herodotos 2.64.1; cf. Aristophanes, *Lysistrata* 912–13; Parker (1983) 74–5.

from woman and man during the night' prior to the sacrifice.[35] But it is first in the great late fourth-century purification law from Cyrene that those who have had sexual intercourse during the day are required to undergo purification before entering a sanctuary.[36] Then in the Hellenistic period such prohibitions become common.

Are these apparent changes to be explained in terms of accidental gaps in our evidence, or in terms of changes in practice or belief? Parker suggests that 'there was originally a connection between the three "polluted days" at the end of the month and menstruation', on the grounds that Aristotle claims that menstruation naturally fell at the month's end.[37] Such a connection seems implausible but, even if it is accepted, there is no doubt both that there is a change in the degree to which the need for purification is advertised, and that when the need for purification is advertised the practices enjoined in different places and at different times vary markedly. We find variation both in whether washing or lapse of time was required, and in whether the status of the sexual partner mattered (courtesans and adulterous liaisons prolong the time lapse required in some cases, virgins prolong it in two cases, and in one of those regulations it is stated that illegal liaisons permanently debar from entry to the sanctuary).[38] If the idea that sexual relations pollute was not itself new, these variations suggest that the question of what exactly was problematic about sexual relations was variously interpreted.

The significance of changes in beliefs about pollution over time depends upon what we take pollution to be. Douglas acknowledged at the beginning of *Purity and Danger* that 'danger-beliefs are as much threats which one man uses to coerce another as dangers which he himself fears to incur by his own lapses from righteousness', and that 'The whole universe is harnessed to men's attempts to force one another into good citizenship. Thus we find that certain moral values are upheld and certain social rules defined by beliefs in dangerous contagion.'[39] But the larger claim that Douglas wanted to make, that they 'have as their main function to impose system on an inherently untidy experience', required that pollution beliefs were not open to cynical manipulation, since the order of the world rested upon them.[40] While Douglas explicitly allows that ideas of impurity and purity were sensitive to change, and that the impulse to impose order continually modified and

---

[35] RO 62 A 40–2.   [36] Cyrene, RO 97.11f.; see Parker (1983) 74, n. 4.

[37] Parker (1983) 102, n. 113.

[38] Parker (1983) 74, n. 4 for summary. Sokolowski (1962) 91.12, 19, from third-century Lindos, for the banning of those involved in illicit relationships and the long period imposed in circumstances of *diakoreusis*.

[39] Douglas (1966) 3.   [40] Douglas (1966) 4.

enriched ideas of purity, the more she insists that 'primitive religions' have scope to meditate on 'the great mysteries of religion and philosophy', the more the investment involved in ideas of purity and pollution will prevent any significant change occurring.[41]

For Douglas, notions of impurity and danger belong to a primitive world-view which is personal, anthropocentric and undifferentiated.[42] In her treatment of pollution and morality Douglas suggests that taboo is reified and failed law, the failure being consequent upon 'the absence of sufficient power in society to sanction the law and to inflict punishment on its violators'.[43] With regard to the ancient Greek world, we have seen that Jan Bremmer expresses the view that pollution beliefs were a way of 'maintaining religious and social norms and values in times when the legal process was still underdeveloped'.[44] But once we accept that pollution beliefs are not a secondary product of a classificatory system, that they may well have entered the Greek world at a particular historic moment in the seventh century BC, that they differed from place to place in the Greek world and that certain sorts of pollution concerns developed or changed over time, then a rather different relationship to law suggests itself.

It is precisely from the seventh century, when purification is first attested, that we possess the first written laws from the Greek world. There is some dispute whether early Greek laws were isolated enactments or part of codes, but there is no doubt that over the period from the seventh to at least the fourth century law codes in Greek cities become increasingly elaborated.[45] Chronologically, at least, Greek pollution beliefs and purification practices develop in parallel with law.

Quite apart from the chronological parallels in their development, there are good empirical and good theoretical reasons for thinking seriously about the relationship between pollution beliefs and law. The empirical reason is that much of our evidence for pollution beliefs comes in the

---

[41] On the existence in Douglas of two conflicting views of taboo, a functionalist one and a cognitive one, which are never reconciled, see Valeri (2000) 406 and n. 103.

[42] Douglas (1966) 92, where she defends use of the term 'primitive'. This is at the end of the chapter 'Primitive worlds', which begins with the claim that 'it is impossible to make any headway with a study of ritual pollution if we cannot face the question of why primitive culture is pollution-prone and ours is not. With us pollution is a matter of aesthetics, hygiene or etiquette, which only becomes grave in so far as it may create social embarrassment' (p. 73). Both Douglas and those writing since have inclined to link pollution beliefs to individual psychology, while acknowledging that the link may not be a simple one (Douglas (1966) 127).

[43] Douglas (1966) ch. 8. I quote the summary of Douglas' view in Valeri (2000) 406. Valeri points out that it is not clear that this is consistent with Douglas' other claims.

[44] Bremmer (1994) 6.

[45] For early Greek laws as isolated enactments see Hölkeskamp (1990), (1999); for the case for early 'codes', R. Osborne (1997a).

form of explicit regulations, the regulations that have come to be termed 'sacred laws'. These are inscriptions prescribing practices and behaviour in relation to sanctuaries and the sacred.[46] Some offer both rules and sanctions, and they indicate where responsibility for the sanctions lies. Others simply indicate what is or is not to be done and leave it at that. Some identify themselves as having been agreed by a particular body, community or state, whereas others give no indication at all of the authority which issued them. Some of these laws are certainly or plausibly part of larger law codes; and the many that are plausibly or certainly isolated injunctions are exactly like laws about matters other than the sacred.

The theoretical reason for associating pollution beliefs and purification practices on the one hand, and 'laws', that is, formally articulated rules accepted by a community, on the other, is that both form part of a community's customs.[47] To belong to a community is to observe that community's pollution beliefs, just as it is to observe their laws and their less formal customs. Both the injunctions of law and the warnings of pollution beliefs are liable to be absorbed by individuals and form part of their experiences of honour and shame.[48] Any account of a group's behaviour needs to take into account pollution beliefs as well as formal laws and informal customs.

The way pollution beliefs and law work together is well revealed by Athenian homicide law. Athenian law notoriously made homicide an offence which only the injured party could pursue – in this case the injured party being the immediate family. And what is effectively the earliest Athenian law that we have, Drako's homicide law, stipulates the conditions in which a man guilty of involuntary homicide may be pardoned by the relatives, without any reference to pollution or purification.[49] The primary concern

---

[46] Lupu (2005) 3–112 for a summary; Parker (2004) for general discussion.

[47] Cf. Valeri (2000) 407: 'over time taboos become custom, so that one may also follow them to identify as a Huaulu or a member of a particular subgroup. The character of custom is thus one that the taboos share with many other habits and rules, but this by definition does not imply that they have the same cause.'

[48] Cf. Cairns (1993) 42: 'There is no justification for the unlikely claim that there are societies in which internalization of social and moral values does not take place, and none for the view that conscience is a phenomenon restricted to a very few cultural contexts.' Whether internalisation is a good thing can be doubted, cf. Nussbaum (2004) 334: 'Mill's argument in *On Liberty* has great value for the way in which it shows how social conformity, peer pressure, and the legal realization of conventional morality all damage the self-development of individuals.'

[49] ML 86, cf. Parker (1983) 116. Demosthenes 20.158 maintains that Drako insisted that the manslayer should be excluded from things sacred, libations, social gatherings ('mixing-bowls') and the Agora, but that if he did indeed keep clear of them he maintained that they were *katharos* ('pure'). For a scholarly desire to see Drako's law as a response to new fears about pollution, cf. Parker (1983) 115.

of law here is to regulate the relationship between the killer and those who have obligations to the person killed. Law steps in to prevent feud and to ensure that whatever settlement occurs between the parties is public and enforceable. Pollution, on the other hand, is not concerned with the relationship between killer and the kin of the killed, but between the killer and the rest of the world, human and divine, and does not distinguish between voluntary and involuntary killing.[50] The result might seem to be something of a tension: death in suspicious circumstances brought pollution on those responsible, but unless one was a kinsman of the deceased there was no provision for using the courts to pursue those responsible.[51] But this is only a tension for those who believe that the only proper way of dealing with killing is through the lawcourts; in a world where gods have power not only to act but to act over successive generations, to require purification is to require something still more vital than settlement in court. The most explicit of sacred laws on the subject, the law from Selinous, provides that any man who has killed and needs purification can ask for it wherever he wishes and whenever he wishes and can be purified by anyone – after which he will be free to eat with and board with anyone.[52] For all that in the context of homicide 'ritual and legal status are assimilated to the extent that . . . "pure" and "not subject to legal sanctions" are often synonymous', law and pollution beliefs turn out to be complementary, not identical.[53]

Both law and pollution beliefs are concerned, but differently concerned with homicide; many other actions and events which bring pollution are not the concern of law at all. Unusual or problematic animal movements, birth and death (as opposed to killing or burial), dreams, madness, none of these things that Theophrastos' 'Superstitious Man' worries about come into the domain of civic law, nor does sexual intercourse as such, or marriage, or miscarriage (unless artificially induced), which are other things regulated in other texts with reference to pollution.

One area where concern for pollution overlaps with an area that law did concern itself with comes as something of a surprise: the wearing of particular clothes or jewellery. A law from third-century Dyme in Achaia lays down:

---

[50] For the evidence see Parker (1983) ch. 4.

[51] This issue is raised in Plato's *Euthyphro* 3e–4c: note in particular the claim at 4c1–3, mixing court action and pollution, that whether or not the victim is related 'the *miasma* is equal if you knowingly consort with such a [killer] and do not render yourself and him *hosios* ('holy') by prosecuting that man in court'.

[52] Lupu (2005) no. 27.   [53] Parker (1983) 114 for the quotation.

At festivals of Demeter women are to have neither gold of more than an obol weight, nor decorated clothing, nor purple, nor to wear make-up, nor to play the aulos. If anyone transgresses the sanctuary she is to be purified on the grounds that she is impious.[54]

Although this is the only case where the language of purification is explicitly used, this regulation is one of a group, all from sanctuaries in the Peloponnese, dating between the late sixth century and the first century BC.[55] The earliest of the examples, from northern Arkadia reveals the seriousness with which the offence is regarded:

If a woman wears a garment made of animal skin, it is to be consecrated to Demeter Thesmophoros. If she does not consecrate it, may she die a bad death for her conduct unfavourable to the cult, and may the person who at that moment holds the office of demiourgos pay a fine of 30 drachmas. If he does not pay, he is to be convicted of impiety. This law is to be in force for ten years. This bronze plaque is to be sacred.[56]

But what precisely is the problem here?

One approach to these regulations takes the issue to be sex. Parker lists the laws in a footnote to his chapter 'The works of Aphrodite' and later, in his chapter on 'Sacrilege' remarks:

There is nothing intrinsically impure about a purple gown (indeed the offending object is sometimes required to be dedicated to the goddess); but it is polluting in this context because it offends against the ethos of a festival that requires women temporarily to renounce the paraphernalia of sexual attraction.[57]

There is no doubt that the items banned in the Dyme law were indeed items associated with women who sought to attract attention to their sexuality. Clement claims, for instance, that flowery clothes and gold jewellery were permitted at Sparta only to prostitutes.[58] But the Dyme restriction applies only to the festival of Demeter, an occasion which, particularly if it is the Thesmophoria that is in question, might be expected to be restricted to women only. Nor is it easy to see why sexually provocative dress (if that is what the *zteraion lōpos*, translated by me, following Dubois, as 'a

---

[54] Sokolowski (1962) 33.   [55] Sokolowski (1962) 32, (1969) 65.16–23, 68.
[56] Sokolowski (1962) 32, and see n. 59 below.
[57] Parker (1983) 83, n. 36 for footnote, 145 for quotation.
[58] Clement of Alexandria, *Instructor* (*Paidagogos*) 2.10 p. 220.6–9 St; Athenaios 521b ascribes similar regulations to Syracuse.

garment made of animal skin', should be reckoned to be), should be thought *dusmenēs* to the cult.[59]

An alternative approach is to see the regulations as essentially sumptuary: it is the elaborateness of the items of dress that is problematic because expensive outfits generate social competition, and, in a world where gods look like men, competition with the gods too. But a concern to restrict competitive expenditure sits uncomfortably with the concentration of the north Arkadian law on a single item – or should we think of the *zteraion lōpos* as the latest must-have fashion accessory? And it sits uncomfortably too with the prohibition on playing the aulos.

The latest of these Peloponnesian sanctuary restrictions on women's dress, the regulations for the conduct of the Mysteries at Andania, dating to 92 BC, gives the responsibility for policing to the magistrates known as 'woman-regulators', *gunaikonomoi*, and so aligns these regulations to other rules enforced by *gunaikonomoi*.[60] The explicit invocation of *gunaikonomoi* to enforce rules in relation to a sanctuary and to cult activity is unusual,[61] but the parallelism between what is regulated by pollution belief at Dyme and what is regulated elsewhere by the intervention of *gunaikonomoi* is important. Ogden concludes his recent study of *gunaikonomoi* with a list of the potential range of rationalisations lying behind dress restrictions and the observation that 'The Greeks understood fully the capacity of dress to be meaningful, and *gunaikonomoi* could no doubt be busy men.'[62] Dress, he implies, can be held to give so many messages that it provides all sorts of opportunities for intervening in women's lives.

I want to make two observations on the basis of these regulations of women's dress, jewellery and behaviour. The first is that it is *women's* behaviour that is regulated. Although some of the Hellenistic and later

---

[59] Both the *zteraion lōpos* and the phrase involving *dusmenēs* have caused problems to interpreters of this law. D. M. Robinson (1943) in his original publication took the first to be 'a hide-garment of Deraea' and the second 'if she is ill-disposed towards her religious rite and work'; Beattie (1947) objected and offered ' a brightly coloured robe' and 'being unfriendly as regards a sacrificial garment'. I have followed Dubois (1988), vol. II, 195–202 without expecting that the argument has now ceased.

[60] Sokolowski (1969) 65.25–8; on *gunaikonomoi* and their duties see Ogden (2002).

[61] Otherwise found in Sokolowski (1969) 127.5 (Methymna, fourth century BC, where the word is restored, in relation to a *pannuchis*), and Sokolowski (1955) 32.20 (arrangements for the cult of Zeus Sosipolis at Magnesia, 197–196 BC, where they are simply responsible for choosing nine maidens to take part). Ogden's claim that the core job of *gunaikonomoi* was 'selecting women for festivals and supervising their behaviour within them' (2002: 203) seems to me poorly supported by the evidence he himself gives, which shows a much more general and civic role, with responsibility in relation to cult activities at the margins of their responsibilities.

[62] Ogden (2002) 210.

gunaikonomoi seem to have been charged with regulating matters that involved men as well as women, the paradigm, as embedded in the magistrates' name, was clearly the regulation of women.[63] This despite the fact that, as we have seen in Chapter 5 in the discussion of wearing items of clothing of foreign origin or associated with foreign peoples, men were as liable as women to make claims to status and wealth by what they wore and how they wore it. The second observation is that our inability to find a convincing single explanation for the regulations applied to Peloponnesian sanctuaries or a single rationale, beyond imposition of 'good order', behind the regulations of *gunaikonomoi*, may be itself key to these rules: rather than a reflection of a single overriding concern, in both cases the regulations serve their purpose in important part by having *no* single overriding concern.

These two observations go together, I suggest, in the following way. Law requires that it can be more or less effectively policed. Advertising laws which cannot be put into operation, either because the offence cannot be detected or because even when it is detected no one is prepared to take action, undermines rather than reinforces the authority of the state. In the classical Greek world there were effectively no state prosecutors, and putting law into action depended upon the willingness of the injured parties to take their injuries to court or, where there was effectively no injured party, upon a third party's taking up the case. Injured parties could normally be expected to avail themselves of legal process, provided that the costs of that legal process to them were not greater than the injury sustained, and there are some reasons for thinking that states provided a variety of procedures at least in part to allow for injured parties of a wide range of resources.[64] Where there is no injured party the offence must seem serious enough to others to encourage them to take the case to law voluntarily. Offences against public order are problematic in this context, since the damage done to other individuals is slight. Where it can be thought that the offence will be so ill regarded by the gods that they will punish any community which does not itself 'take the law into its own hands', volunteer prosecutors may be forthcoming, but we might wonder whether anyone would believe that the gods, whose own behaviour is not rarely disorderly, have so keen an eye on individual human beings' disorderly behaviour as to strike a community which does not take the merely disorderly to court.

---

[63] For regulations that apply to men, compare the reports of a 'new law' limiting numbers of diners imposed by *gunaikonomoi* in Hellenistic Athens: Athenaios, *Teachers at Table* 245a–c.

[64] A claim I first made in R. Osborne (1985b). For a recent assessment of that claim see Carey (2004).

In the archaic and classical Greek city state, I suggest, law was able to deal with actions other than major offences only if the offence significantly damaged another citizen. Once there was a citizen who was willing to act, the city could provide a framework of law and courts which would ensure that that action was regulated, recognised and effective. But what of actions that needed to be discouraged but caused little direct injury to another citizen? There were, I suggest, two possibilities. One was to control such actions by the direct intervention of magistrates. This was a real possibility when the offenders were those who had no direct political voice and who could therefore be relatively easily coerced. The largest class of those over whom this sort of control could be exerted were women, although much the same was possible with regard to children. Hence the comparative prominence of *gunaikonomoi* (and to a less extent *paidonomoi* and other magistrates charged with looking after the behaviour of the under-aged).[65] But where the offender had a political voice magisterial control was more problematic: how could punitive action be taken without allowing the citizen to speak in his own defence? And how could magisterial authority ever be maintained if citizens could challenge and overturn it? The authority of powers not open to challenge was required. So the second way in which to discourage actions that were inappropriate in a community even though not directly damaging to other citizens was to enlist the agency of the gods. Declaring that a form of behaviour was impious, impure and demanded purification served to bring the offender into the public gaze and justify treating him or her as needing to be separated from and then reintegrated into society. To insist that anyone who did that was dirty and needed public purification was to issue an antisocial behaviour order.

The late sixth-century Arkadian law about the *zteraion lōpos* well illustrates the choice. The wearing of this garment is declared impious, but confidence that such a declaration itself will be sufficient to prevent the practice seems small. The Arkadian community spells out the threat of divine intervention by adding a curse, that she die a bad death. But those who proclaimed this regulation also thought it necessary to invoke magisterial aid, even though they were clearly uncertain whether they could persuade the *dāmiourgos*, the magistrate in question, to enforce the ban. Faced with a behaviour not obviously damaging but which they desired to discourage, those who moved this law try all the weapons in the arsenal at once. Later regulations of women's clothing in Peloponnesian sanctuaries have decided one way or another what should be done. The Demeter

---

[65] For the coercive powers of magistrates see Harris (2007).

sanctuary at Dyme seems to have been confident that the requirement of purification was enough to effect its regulation of women's jewellery, clothing, make-up, and music at its festivals, and no magisterial aid is invoked. The sacred authorities at Andania, however, go down the other route, and leave it to the *gunaikonomoi*.

If we turn from these regulations of women's appearance and behaviour to other areas of life in which pollution is invoked, we can see a similar pattern. I have already suggested that we should see a connection between the treatment of bloodshed as polluting with the problematic status of homicide at Athens as a charge that could be brought only by the injured party. Where a man had no kin or where the kin were not prepared to act, insistence on the purification of homicides was a way of forcing the offence into the public eye. But if there was a problem even with making murderers face the formal apparatus of law, there were many other areas of life where regulation might be desired but the formal apparatus of law was either not possible or not appropriate. Parker pointed out the role that ideas of pollution played in discouraging perjury – or even the contemplation of perjury.[66] He described this as an example of 'religious protection for the exposed', linking it with the special pollution which was held to obtain when suppliants or heralds were violated.

Pollution serves also in areas where society has an interest in actions which cannot be regarded in any way as antisocial or offensive. Modern states require registration of births, marriages and deaths and the certification of the mad, but the ancient city had no apparatus for such bureaucracy. The considerations which led to registration being a legal requirement, on the other hand, applied equally in antiquity. The classification of birth, marriage, death and delirium as polluting served a publicity function comparable in effect to official registration: all these are events of which a community needs to know, if it is to remain a community. And given that we used to insist on the licensing of dogs (and in some parts of the United Kingdom still do), we might reckon even the superstitious man's regarding of the presence of unexpected animals as polluting not totally beyond explanation in terms of this need for the community to know.

It turns out, then, to be fundamental that you cannot tell that this is a dirty body (6.1). You cannot tell by looking at a person whether he or she has committed homicide or has just married. Yet these are things that we feel we need to know. In the modern world we rely on the effectiveness of

---

[66] Parker (1983) 186–8. The most striking story of a 'pre-emptive strike' is that told by Herodotos about the Spartan Glaukos, Herodotos 6.86.

police and courts to guarantee that the person we meet in the streets is not a murderer. We still expect that generally a ring on a particular finger will indicate marriage. Where people might have conditions we feel we should know about but which will not show up, there are debates about the ethics of enforced registration, whether of those with infectious or contagious physical conditions or of those considered to have dangerous mental proclivities. The idea of pollution served in classical Greece to encourage individuals, if it could never compel them, to treat invisible conditions as if they were written on the body and needed to be washed off. If the gods can tell whether I am diseased, or have just had a dream by which I will become obsessed and a danger to others, then I must act to right myself in their sight.

Pollution and shame are surely closely related here. Bernard Williams has suggested that shame 'requires an internalised other, who is not designated merely as a representative of an independently identified social group, and whose reactions the agent can respect. At the same time, this figure . . . embodies intimations of a genuine social reality – in particular, of how it will be for one's life with others if one acts in one way rather than another.'[67] Pollution externalises that other, putting in their place the gods, whose very power compels respect and ensures that one is in no doubt how it will be for one's life if one does not take appropriate action. And by externalising that other, it becomes possible for fellow-men to take that other's part, to insist that they know what that other insists upon. If shame does not curb a man's behaving in a mad way or a woman's dressing or behaving inappropriately and in ways liable to cause a public incident, pollution can be invoked.

In a close-knit community one might reckon that shame alone adequately controls behaviour: it is obvious how it will be for one's life with others if one does or does not act in a particular way. It is when ordinary day-to-day interactions are taking place within a group broader than the household that it becomes less clear how interactions will be affected by one's particular actions. *Aidōs*, the Greek term which comes closest to our 'shame', is indeed prominent in Homer, where ideas of pollution are absent and where dispute settlement does not rely on comparing behaviour to formal rules but on personal arbitration.

Various classical authors explicitly explore the relationship between *aidōs* and pollution.[68] The most fully developed discussion comes in Euripides' *Heracles* after Herakles has murdered his family while out of his mind. Initially Herakles contemplates killing himself to avoid the *duskleia* that

---

[67] Williams (1993) 102.   [68] Cairns (1993) 291–5; Parker (1983) 316–17, cf. 189–90.

his actions will bring, but as his *philos* Theseus draws near he worries
that even the sight of himself may be polluting (*musos es ommath' hēxei*),
and he veils his head; but in doing so he explicitly refers to his shame
(here *aischunē*).[69] When Theseus discovers what has occurred he insists that
Herakles should look at him, that he is willing to face the consequences of
pollution (*musos*) being conveyed by Herakles' addressing him.[70] Herakles
expresses concern that Theseus is uncovering his head and insists that he
should keep away from unholy pollution (*anosion miasma*), but Theseus
denies that the gods can be polluted or that avenging spirits can pass from
one *philos* to another.[71] There follows a debate in which Theseus convinces
Herakles that his shame at his actions should not lead him to kill himself.
Theseus' arguments include that the gods themselves have done shameful
things (adultery, dishonouring their fathers) yet still live on Olympus, and
he summons Herakles to be purified in Athens.[72] Herakles, in famous and
problematic lines, rejects such stories of the gods, asserting that the god
who is rightly a god needs nothing; but he agrees to go to Athens since he
now considers killing himself to be cowardice.[73] Faced with the question of
whether he should abandon or take the weapons with which he murdered his
family, and which he imagines will constantly draw that act to his attention,
he nevertheless decides that he cannot be parted from them since they are
also the weapons by which he has managed his glorious deeds.[74] The shame
of his act goes with him; but the pollution of the act can be removed by
purification.[75]

Both the overlap and the distinction between pollution and shame are
well brought out in this passage. Herakles must learn to bear the shame,
which can be neither removed nor shared. Shame cannot be passed on to

---

[69] Euripides, *Heracles* 1146–60, cf. 1199–1201 and the case of Orestes, Euripides, *Orestes* 459–61;
cf. Cairns (1993) 292: 'Heracles' *aidōs* and his awareness of his pollution and its effects on
others are inextricably linked, as indeed such concerns will tend to be . . .'; Parker (1983) 316:
'as always, the line between internal guilt and shame before the world cannot be sharply drawn.
Inseparable from the hero's perception of his own pollution is his knowledge that he will be
henceforth a polluted being in the eyes of the world.'

[70] Euripides, *Heracles* 1214–20.

[71] Euripides, *Heracles* 1231–4. There is something of a tension between the view that homicides
should be secluded from the gods and the view that others should not have to be under the
same roof as they; all Athenian homicide courts were open-air, Antiphon 5.11; [Aristotle],
Constitution of the Athenians 57.4; Pollux 8.118.

[72] Euripides, *Heracles* 1314–25.   [73] Euripides, *Heracles* 1340–50.

[74] Euripides, *Heracles* 1376–85.

[75] Cf. Douglas (1966) 135: 'most pollutions have a very simple remedy for undoing their effects.
There are rites of reversing, untying, burying, washing, erasing, fumigating, and so on, which
at a small cost of time and effort can satisfactorily expunge them.'

others in the way that pollution can. To risk becoming polluted is not to do anything shameful but is an act of friendship, an affirmation that social relations can be restored. But the decision to share pollution cannot come from the polluted.[76] Purification offers a public and formal recognition of that. It also offers closure.[77] If the strength of shame is that it attaches to the mental disposition to act and serves as a restraint and a deterrent, the strength of pollution is that it attaches to the act itself and can be brought to an end. The relation of pollution to disease is revealing here. Not only were diseases held to pollute, but purification was a way of dealing with disease. As with disease, so with pollution, it is possible to be restored to a sound state.[78]

The argument which I am pursuing here is that notions of pollution in the classical Greek world serve to reach parts, types of behaviour, which formal law cannot reach, and where the society is not sufficiently small and close knit for shame, which is entirely without threat of sanction, to be relied on. Pollution invokes an outside agency, the gods, and offers a means of resolution, purification. Because pollution may be incurred either voluntarily or involuntarily it carries in itself no judgement. Whether or not some things are universally regarded as dirty, our propensity to think that there are circumstances in which reactions of disgust are natural serves further to distance the state of being polluted from the agency of the person involved.[79] But if pollution and disgust both start from the dirty, pollution and disgust differ in that pollution never arrogates to itself the moral high ground that is part and parcel of claims to be disgusted.[80]

To treat pollution as an idea through which a community regulates itself is to treat it in a way rather different from the way it has been treated by anthropologists. It is at odds with Douglas' view that notions of pollution

---

[76] Hence Oidipous draws back from embracing Theseus in Sophokles, *Oedipus at Colonus* 1132–4. For another friendly action in disregard of pollution see Helen in Euripides, *Orestes* 75–6, read too cynically by Parker (1983) 311.

[77] Someone else's taking on the pollution and its link to purification is literally embodied in the *katharma*, or *pharmakos*, the scapegoat who takes away pollution from the community, where the two terms offer the two parallel models (cleansing and healing) intimately associated with pollution. In Athens the dispatch of the scapegoat was part of the festival of the Thargelia. See Parker (1983) 24–6, 258–60.

[78] Parker (1983) chs. 7–8.

[79] See Nussbaum (2004) 91 for the claim that 'wastes, corpses, and most bodily fluids are ubiquitously objects of disgust. Societies have great latitude to determine how ideas of contamination extend to other objects, but they seem not to have latitude to make these primary objects nondisgusting.'

[80] As caricatured in the signature 'disgusted, Tonbridge Wells'. On the problems of disgust see Nussbaum (2004), esp. conclusion at 346–9.

are the result of cognitive discomfort experienced when confronted with ambivalence, ambiguity or anomaly.[81] It is also at odds with more recent suggestions that pollution ideas are centred on the body and that fear of pollution arises when 'decaying living matter or matter that is subject to decay as soon as it leaves the body – such as semen, blood, sweat – threatens to gain access to our body and thus to make it decay and die too' or that 'The embodied subject's fear of disintegration through the body and by the body is the ultimate basis for the notion of pollution.'[82] If Douglas' view ultimately situated pollution in language and made it a by-product of our attempt to establish a cognitive grip on the world, the view which puts the body at the centre of pollution, like the view which puts the body at the centre of shame, makes pollution a deep psychological reaction to fear of mortality and animality.[83]

Classical Greek ideas of pollution, like our own ideas of environmental pollution, build upon some fundamental and common experiences. Some form of aversion to at least some bodily waste-products is so close to universal among animals as well as humans that it is implausible to deny the natural origin of the reaction. But just as the inevitable existence of anomalies and ambiguities cannot of itself account for why anomalies and ambiguities become charged with significance, so the universal existence of reactions of disgust cannot explain why such reactions become charged with a significance that is then extended to other phenomena where no such universal aversion is experienced.[84] Pollution ideas exploit both cognitive and affective crises, they feed on what body and mind find hard to cope with, but they are not explained by those difficulties. To understand how notions of pollution develop, we need to see them not in relation to the individual mind or body but to society.

What do we have to be able to see in order to see whether a body is dirty? I suggest that we have to enter into shared values. Just as the child's washing chocolate from his face requires a recognition that chocolate round

---

[81] Cf. Douglas (1966) 4: 'I believe that ideas about separating, purifying, demarcating and punishing transgression have as their main function to impose system on an inherently untidy experience.' But Douglas did variously flirt with a rather different functionalist view which saw pollution as a replacement for human puhishment when that was impossible or as rendering offences inaccessible to police action (Douglas (1966) 14, 134, 142; (1975) 54).

[82] Valeri (2000) 102 (summarising the work of Anna Meigs), 111; cf. 356.

[83] For the view that 'Disgust concerns the borders of the body: it focuses on the prospect that a problematic substance may be incorporated into the self', see Nussbaum (2004) 88.

[84] Cf. already Douglas (1966) 121: 'Each culture has its own special risks and problems. To which particular bodily margins its beliefs attribute power depends on what situation the body is mirroring.'

the mouth is unacceptable, not just to his mother but to a wider group from whom approval is needed or desired, so for a murderer or a woman who has given birth or a madman to out themselves and seek purification depends on recognition that these states are not acceptable to a wider group from whom approval is needed: the gods. Pollution focuses on changes of state not because of some deep anxiety about things which are impossible to categorise, but because to suggest that something has moved from one condition to another constitutes a *prima facie* argument for the gods' interest and involvement. Pollution focuses on the body not, in my view, because of some deep psychological anxiety about our bodies, but because our bodies confirm the importance of unseen dangers, and because our bodies are that by which we are affected. It is because what happens inside our bodies has a profound effect upon us without being manifested on the body surface, and because the body produces from within substances over whose nature and production we have at best limited control, that we find it easy to believe that there are conditions invisible to the eye which fundamentally affect not just the individual but the relation of the individual to the community. And it is because we need our bodies and cannot relate to the world without them, because any restriction to our bodies has more or less immediate effect upon our lives, that we are necessarily highly sensitive to everything, seen or unseen, that might disturb our bodily condition.

In Chapter 4 I drew attention to the way in which citizenship status is invisible in figurative representations in classical Greek art and suggested that the failure to represent it corresponded with a low priority to making the distinction between citizen and non-citizen in life. In Chapter 5 I argued that the ways in which foreign appearance was advertised or ignored in classical figurative art required us to construct a more subtle view of relations between Athenians and non-Athenians, and particularly non-Greeks, than scholars have formed on the basis of the polarities that they have found in texts. In this chapter I am again drawing attention to the way in which the distinctions which texts urge upon us between the clean and the unclean, the polluted and the pure (or purificated) are neither represented in art nor could be seen in the flesh.

But what should we see as the consequence of the invisibility of the polluted? In the case of citizens, the failure to mark them out in art or life indicates, I suggest, a lack of concern for the citizen/non-citizen boundary. Citizens might have been made different from others, and the significant fact is that they were not. In the case of the foreigner, the application of distinguishing features in a sporadic fashion, and to indicate performance as often as to indicate nature, indicates, I suggest, that the foreign was seen as providing varied resources for thinking and acting, rather than as a block of unmitigable opposition. Foreigners, including some Greek foreigners as well as non-Greeks, almost certainly could be told apart with a fair degree of certainty – much as one can with a fair degree of certainty distinguish visitors from Europe or the United States or Australia from those brought up in the United Kingdom, despite a more or less common genetic heritage. The significant fact is that Athenian artists take little interest in exploring, or caricaturing, these distinctions.

In the case of the polluted, however, their invisibility was arguably an essential condition of their pollution. One might even think that had the murderer, or the woman who had recently given birth or recently married been visible, like the storybook gangster in his stripy tee shirt, there would have been no need for them to be polluted. To claim that a murderer, a newly wed, a woman who has given birth, a kinsman of the newly dead, or whoever, is polluted, is to claim that, although the present appearance of those in this condition does not mark them out to the human eye, there are eyes that can indeed see that what they have done or suffered has made them different. The invisibility of the pollution is itself testimony to the exceptional power, and so to the claim to authority, of the gods.

When Herakleitos complains that to purify someone from blood guilt by application of sacrificial blood makes as little sense as for a man who has stepped into mud washing with mud, he draws attention to what purification does: it makes the fact of pollution visible.[85] So too when the taking of a forbidden object into a sanctuary is to be purified by dedicating that object in the sanctuary, the polluting act is rendered visible as well as unrepeatable. The power of the notion of pollution is directly connected to its invisibility. It is because you cannot see pollution that you need to worry about it. Because if you do not worry about it, those who *can* see it and do worry about it may decide to make it visible, and to make you worry about it. As Oidipous discovered in the face of plague, ignorance is no defence and no excuse. Sight and knowledge are, as in Sophokles' play, closely entwined, and without knowledge there can be no certain control.

Pollution acknowledges the subordinate position of men to gods and puts the gods at the centre of the social order. Controlling other men demands seeing what the gods see. But whose eyes do the gods see with? The features of Greek pollution beliefs which have argued against seeing them as a straightforward and direct product of the cognitive system or of human psychology (the way in which beliefs change over time, express

---

[85] Herakleitos B5 Diels–Kranz.

themselves differently from place to place, and are neither systematic nor expected to be systematic) point to the ways in which the eyes of the gods are the eyes of men dwelling in very particular places and times. Acts polluted if, and only if, people could be persuaded that acts polluted. But because the formal arbiters of pollution were the gods, the initiative to regard an act as polluting, or to disregard the pollution alleged of an act, might come from anyone. Theophrastos' 'Superstitious Man' is an object of ridicule only because he has not persuaded others to regard as polluting what he regards as polluting. In principle anyone's initiative in practising purification might persuade others (though no doubt some, such as religious exegetes, other recognised 'religious experts', and those who could afford to put a leading question to a respected oracle, were in a better position to convince). The gods always needed human assistants and their reputation depended on those assistants' fallibility. Pollution beliefs have the great advantage over law that their constant renegotiation demands no formal procedure – simply new insights into the gods' vision.

But seeing what the gods see required seeing the gods. It is to the issue of how men see the gods that I turn in Chapter 7.

7 | Godsbodies

Describing godsbodies

Herodotos had no doubt that the Greek gods were textual constructs. In the course of his discussion of what the Greeks owed to the Egyptians, Herodotos says it was Homer and Hesiod four hundred years before his time who had given the Greeks an account of how the gods came to be and had defined what the gods were called, what their reputations and means were, and their forms.[1]

Greek intellectuals not infrequently adopted a viewpoint akin to that of Herodotos, giving priority to the textual description of gods. In a story told much later by Strabo, Panainos, the nephew of the sculptor Pheidias and his collaborator at Olympia, asked him 'after what model he intended to make the image of Zeus', and Pheidias 'said that he would make it to the image set out by Homer when he wrote: "Kronion spoke, and nodded assent with his dark brows, and then the ambrosial locks flowed from the immortal head of the lord and he made great Olympos quake."'[2]

Pheidias' Olympian Zeus has not survived, and although the excavation of Pheidias' workshop at Olympia has recovered moulds and templates which show something of the detailed appearance of some parts of the statue, our knowledge of its appearance is dependent upon ancient descriptions and the inadequate images struck on coins of Elis (7.1) or carved on gemstones. Nevertheless we can be confident that, for all that Pheidias may have succeeded in creating a god who looked as if he might nod assent with his dark brows and cause Olympos to quake, Homer's descriptions of Zeus, either in this or in other passages, provided no basis at all for most of the features displayed by the statue.

---

[1] Herodotos 2.53.2: Ἡσίοδον γὰρ καὶ Ὅμηρον ἡλικίην τετρακοσίοισι ἔτεσι δοκέω μευ πρεσβυτέρους γενέσθαι καὶ οὐ πλέοσι. οὗτοι δέ εἰσι οἱ ποιήσαντες θεογονίην Ἕλλησι καὶ τοῖσι θεοῖσι τὰς ἐπωνυμίας δόντες καὶ τιμάς τε καὶ τέχνας διελόντες καὶ εἴδεα αὐτῶν σημήναντες.

[2] Strabo 8.3.30, quoting *Iliad* 1.528–30. The idea that Pheidias' Zeus embodied Homer's description is already found in Polybius 30.10.6, where that view is put in the mouth of Lucius Aemilius Paulus. Dio Chrysostom has Pheidias elaborate on his conception of Zeus in *Oration* 12.55–83.

7.1 Roman Imperial bronze coin minted in Elis in the reign of Hadrian representing Pheidias' statue of Zeus.

As with the lines from *Iliad* 1 quoted by Strabo, and as Herodotos' own comment stresses, what Greek texts indicated about gods was their effects. From Homer and Hesiod we gain a very extensive idea of what the gods could do, what their interests and motivations were, and of how the gods interacted with one another and with mortals. But even, perhaps especially, when gods make an appearance to mortals, the question of what they looked like is always elusive. They are somehow not quite like men, carry a certain radiance and produce amazement, but none of those qualities indicate anything precise about their appearance.[3] Gods who appear to mortals regularly assume the appearance of some other creature, whether it be an animal, a person of a particular type or a particular human individual. So in *Odyssey* 1 Athena appears to Telemachus in the form of Mentes, leader of the Taphians, and disappears in the form of a bird.[4] In *Odyssey* 2 she appears again in the form of Mentor, an elderly Ithakan, and, having taken a lengthy part in proceedings, disappears in book 3 as a vulture.[5] Later, when Athena

---

[3] For reference to ancient texts on the supernatural stature and radiance of gods when they appear, and the amazement they create, see Richardson (1974) 208 (and cf. 252).

[4] *Odyssey* 1.105 (appearance), 320 (disappearance).

[5] *Odyssey* 2.268 (appearance), 3.371–2 (disappearance). Other appearances of Athena in human form occur in *Odyssey* 8.8 (as Alkinoos' herald), 22.206 and 24.503, 548 (as Mentor again), *Iliad* 2.280 (as herald), 4.86–7 as Laodokos. Other gods that appear in the form of men include Iris (*Iliad* 3.122), Ares (*Iliad* 5.462), Poseidon (*Iliad* 13.45) and Hermes (*Iliad* 24.347). Athena's descent to the Trojan plain at 4.75 is 'like a star'.

watches Odysseus fight it out with the suitors she does so as a swallow.[6] In all these cases part of what is at issue is not wanting to be recognised: it is important that human actors, or at least some human actors, remain ignorant of divine intervention. But that is not all that is at issue.

If writers describe what gods look like only when the gods take on a form other than their own, they nevertheless repeatedly hint that the gods do have a form of their own.[7] When Aphrodite intervenes in battle to save her son Aineias from Diomedes, we are given a glimpse of the white arms she flings around her son. It is ichor, not blood, that flows, causing the flesh to darken, as Diomedes with a spear pierces her in her hand upon the wrist above the palm. This unique event elicits 'a dramatic theological innovation' in the form of an explanation for why it is that gods have ichor and not blood, but no further hint is given of her bodily appearance.[8] More remarkably still, even at the point at which her seduction of Aineias' father, Anchises, is described in the *Homeric Hymn to Aphrodite*, Aphrodite appears in her own form, but the description works by simile and by concentration not on the body but on the clothing:

Aphrodite the daughter of Zeus stood before him, being like an unbroken maiden in height and form . . . When Anchises saw her, he marked her well and wondered at her form and stature and shining garments. For she was clad in a robe out-shining the brightness of fire, a splendid robe of gold, enriched with all manner of needlework, which shimmered like the moon over her tender breasts, a marvel to see. She wore twisted brooches and shining earrings in the form of flowers, and round her soft throat were lovely necklaces.[9]

And when Aphrodite has assured Anchises, falsely, of her status and he takes off her clothes before making love to her, it is the clothes that we are told about, not the body that is revealed:

And when they had climbed into the well-constructed bed, Anchises first took off the shining jewellery from her flesh, the pins and the twisted brooches, earrings and

---

[6] *Odyssey* 22.239–40 (compare both Athena and Apollo assuming bird forms to watch the fighting in *Iliad* 7.58–9).

[7] For Homer generally offering little in the way of descriptive features cf. Dio Chrysostom 21.17 on Homer's descriptions of Hektor and Achilles. One exception to this is when Aphrodite comes to Helen in the guise of an old woman, only for Helen, when her desire has been stirred by the old woman's speech, to perceive her real identity as she recognises her 'very beautiful neck, desirable breasts and flashing eyes' (*Iliad* 3.396–7). On the issues involved here see A. D. Stevens (2002) 112–15.

[8] *Iliad* 5.311–54. The quotation is from Kirk (1990) on lines 339–42.

[9] *Homeric Hymn to Aphrodite* 81–90.

necklaces, and he loosed her belt and stripped off her bright garments and placed them upon a silver-studded chair.[10]

Even when she wakes Anchises next morning, and reveals herself as a goddess, the poet makes reference only to the fact that 'immortal beauty shone from her cheeks' and that Anchises realises that she is a goddess on seeing her 'neck and lovely eyes'.[11]

The absence of description of the body of Aphrodite in these passages does not, of course, mean that as far as the reader is concerned she has no body. The whole thrust of the seduction of Anchises would be lost if the reader took the view that what is not described in the text does not exist. The comparison to the unbroken maiden has the reader conjure up a young girl's body: it is by imagining the body of the young girl that we see the body of the goddess.[12] Because Aphrodite's body is not described it is necessarily indistinguishable from a woman's body. Richard Gordon's insistence that 'the non-existent, the fantastical, can be thought only in relation to that which has already been granted a place in the network of significations' is vital here.[13] Anchises may have been willingly complicit in his failure to tell the goddess's body apart from a girl's body, but the indistinguishability of god's body from human body is of vital theological importance. For just as what goes undescribed is nevertheless relied upon to give the narrative sense, so more generally the guarantee that the chaos that we observe on the surface of the world actually corresponds to a deeper order is provided by the fact that, however fantastic the particular actions attributed to the gods, gods act in ways just like our own. To quote Gordon again, 'fantasy worlds are not the pointless products of "wild" imagination: they are necessarily better structured than the "real" human world. And if we cannot predict fantasy worlds, we can always in principle reconstruct their logic.'[14]

If that is all rather abstract, inscribed stories from the sanctuary of Asklepios at Epidauros provide a wonderful concrete example.[15] In those stories, inscribed in the late fourth century to advertise the power of the god to visitors to the healing sanctuary, the god does all sorts of fantastic things – causing the blind to see, the dumb to speak, the lame to walk, and those pregnant for several years to give birth. But the mechanisms by which the

---

[10] *Homeric Hymn to Aphrodite* 161–6.   [11] *Homeric Hymn to Aphrodite* 174–5, 181.

[12] We might compare the way in which Plato has the beauty of the boy offer to the mind a glimpse of the Form of Beauty in *Phaedrus* (in a passage strongly contrasting with passages in other dialogues which insist that the senses are useless guides); see Nightingale (2004) 162–6.

[13] Gordon (1980) 20.   [14] Gordon (1980) 19–20.

[15] *IG* iv² 1.121–4. See RO 102, offering commentary on the first stele in particular.

god does so are always mechanisms which can be understood in human terms – binding a bandage around some marks a man has on his forehead so that they come off on the bandage, pouring a drug into an empty eye-socket to make an eye, cutting a man open to remove leeches inside him and sewing him up again, putting a drug on a man's head to cure his baldness. More than that, the stories construct a god with a character, who makes jokes (causing a woman to be pregnant but not to give birth since she had only asked to be pregnant, not to be delivered of the child; causing one who tried spying on what went on to fall from a tree onto stakes which blinded him – only then to heal him). The structure of the fantasy here is precisely the structure of real life; the techniques of the healing god and the techniques of doctors are the same: gods, like doctors, need to be hands-on and interventionist – but the god's techniques always work.

Perhaps the nicest demonstration of just how strong the sense that the god must be physically present is comes in two stories on the second stele from Epidauros.[16] In the first, Aristagora of Troizen dreams that Asklepios was away from the sanctuary and his sons try to cure her by cutting off her head to remove a tapeworm but then cannot put it on again, and only when Asklepios returns is her head put back on, her belly cut open and the worm removed. In the second, Sostrata, from Pherai, fails to have a distinct dream and is uncured in the sanctuary. But on her way home she meets a man of fine appearance (*euprepēs*) who operates on her there and then, revealing himself at the end of the operation to be Asklepios. Evidently she had failed to be cured in the sanctuary because the god was not there.

The theology of godsbodies

As both Asklepios and Aphrodite illustrate, when gods appear in texts they inevitably do things. What they do is theologically crucial. Already in the early fifth century Xenophanes of Kolophon complained that 'Homer and Hesiod have attributed to the gods everything that leads to blame and abuse among men – stealing, committing adultery and deceiving each other.'[17] Such complaints are echoed by Plato, who proposes in the *Republic* to censor the stories that are told, eliminating those that make a bad representation of what gods and heroes are. He targets Hesiod's stories of Kronos' castration of his father Ouranos, and of Kronos' subsequent swallowing of his own

---

[16] *IG* iv².1 122.10–19, 26–35.
[17] Xenophanes B11, quoted by Sextus, *Against the Mathematicians* 9.193.

children, and then Homer's stories of arguments between the gods leading to Hera being bound, and Hephaistos being thrown out from heaven.[18] But although the problem of the gods' actions is most obvious when those are actions which men regard as immoral, the problem that the gods' actions may not provide an appropriate model arises almost as soon as they do anything. And Plato will indeed go on to suggest that episodes need to be rewritten in which Homer describes the children or close relatives of the gods, let alone the gods themselves, showing grief for men – reserving special criticism for Zeus's grief at the death of his son Sarpedon.[19]

Xenophanes seems to have seen what the consequences were if one rejected immoral tales about gods: one could tell no tales about the gods at all. He claimed, accordingly, that there was 'one god, greatest among gods and men, in no way like mortals either in body (*demas*) or thought'.[20] Xenophanes' god had senses and could perceive but he did not move: 'without toil he shakes all things by the thoughts of his mind'.[21] Subsequent philosophical theology will come to very similar views.

Just as no one could write about the gods without making them do something, no one could create a visual image of a god without giving the god a body. The body that texts only imply, visual artists had to supply. If Xenophanes was right about god's being not like mortals in body or thought, then god could not be represented in a form that was like the form of mortals and became incomprehensible.[22] Representing gods with bodies that were not human bodies was indeed an option occasionally taken in the Greek world, with so-called 'aniconic' images. Such images might indeed have effects (laughter, in one famous story), but they gave away no idea at all of how the god might be expected to work and to act on the world.[23]

Whenever any action is attributed to a god who is not like a mortal in any respect, it is inevitable that whoever read or hear about this action import assumptions about how and why humans act in order to make the action comprehensible to themselves, but in importing these assumptions readers

---

[18] Plato, *Republic* 2.377b–378e.

[19] Plato, *Republic* 3.388a–c. The other examples are Achilles' grief for Patroklos and Priam's for Hektor.

[20] Xenophanes B23, quoted by Clement, *Miscellanies* 5.109.1.

[21] Xenophanes B24–6, quoted by Sextus, *Against the Mathematicians* 9.144 and Simplicius, *On Physics* 23.11 and 20.

[22] So, for example, Antisthenes the Sokratic maintained that 'god is not like anyone, and that is why no one can recognise god from an image' (fr. 40 Caizzi, variously quoted by Clement, *Miscellanies* 5.108.4 and *Exhortation to the Greeks* 6.71.1, Eusebius, *Preparation for the Gospel* 13.13.35, and Theodoret, *Cure of the Greek Maladies* 1.75).

[23] On aniconic images see Doepner (2002), Gaifman (2005); cf. P. Stewart (2007). For laughter at such an image see Athenaios 14.614a–b.

or hearers turn the god into a human. Xenophanes, again, famously observed that if cattle or horses or lions could draw they would draw the forms of the gods like cattle, horses and lions: 'they would make their bodies such as they each had themselves'.[24] What was surreptitious in the case of texts was immediate in the case of visual images: if god was not like mortals in body or thought, then god could not be given a body that was like mortals, or indeed the body of any animal or object known to mortal thought. But if god was not like anything that men and women know, then how could men and women conceive of what it was to be god, and how could god relate to humans?[25]

Greek writers are aware that there were people who did not think of their gods as like men – and who did think of their gods as like animals. Herodotos explains the absence of images of the gods, temples and altars in Persia 'because they do not consider that the gods are human in form as the Greeks do'.[26] He finds ways of explaining why the Egyptians represent gods whom he identifies with Greek gods in animal form, or he simply passes over the form in which their gods are represented.[27] Much later Philostratos will have Apollonios of Tyana ridicule the Egyptians for their theriomorphic gods.[28] He claims that such representations cannot carry respect, and that the Egyptians would be better off if they had no images and left it to visitors to temples to imagine the form of the gods.

These discussions show how difficult Greeks found it to imagine a role for a god who did not relate to humankind by being in human form. For Herodotos the whole complex of Greek religion, temples, altars and cult statues, was bound up with the gods' being like humans. It is perhaps not surprising, therefore, that Xenophanes and subsequent philosophers for whom god properly was just thought, had little influence on classical religious practice. But this does not mean that Greeks outside the philosophical tradition did not also think that gods could be too like humans.

If Plato found much to censor in the Homeric and Hesiodic poems, there are some signs that that tradition was itself already censored. Gods may grieve in Homer and they may be wounded either by one another or,

---

[24] Xenophanes B15, quoted by Clement, *Miscellanies* 5.109.3.

[25] There were, of course, objects closely associated with gods that were 'aniconic', but the sense in which these are 'images' of the gods is very weak, and no god is ever exclusively associated with aniconic objects. See Faraone (1992) 5–7.

[26] Herodotos 1.131.1; cf. 4.59.2 on the absence of images, altars and temples among Skythians except to Ares.

[27] So Herodotos 2.41 on Isis having ox horns; 2.42.4 on Zeus with a ram's head; 2.46 on Mendes as goat and Pan; 2.38 for passing over the form of Epaphos/Apis, while observing that bulls are held to belong to him (but contrast 3.64.3).

[28] Philostratos, *Life of Apollonios* 19.3–4.

exceptionally, by mortals, but not only do they not die, they do not shed blood. As we have seen, it is ichor that flows in their veins, not blood.[29] Gods may have sex with each other and with mortals, but it turns out to be sex without any of the uncertainty that surrounds mortal sexual relations. When gods have sex with mortals, at least, there is invariably progeny, and divine pregnancies inevitably come to term, even if something drastic happens to the mother in the meanwhile – as we see in the case of Dionysos, and indeed of Athena, let alone the case of Erichthonios. Unlike mortal bodies, gods' bodies are never dirty bodies. The god's body enjoys what Vernant has called 'corporeal plenitude', and it is by comparison with that super body that the human body is marked with 'the seal of limitation, deficiency, incompleteness' that is pollution.[30]

The issue of what the gods are like is implicit in every actual representation of a god. As scholars have observed, although it is possible Greek usage to talk of the image of a god, it is regular to talk of images simply as the god.[31] A vivid example of this is provided by Pausanias at Olympia. When he describes the temple of Zeus he first of all describes how if you ascend into the galleries you can view the cult statue, but then when he turns to the statue itself he says, 'The god is sitting on a throne; he is made of gold and ivory', and he continues to describe 'the god' in similar terms.[32] When he describes the dedications in the sanctuary he first singles out the statues of Zeus, beginning with the 'Zanes', the images of Zeus erected as fines for bad behaviour in the Olympic games. He then goes on to other images of Zeus, and once more he moves between referring to them as *agalmata* (literally 'things of delight', but which came to mean statues, in particular statues of gods) and simply referring to them as 'Zeus',

As you go on Zeus is turned towards the rising sun . . . the Phliasians dedicated Zeus and the daughters of Asopos and Asopos himself; the images are arranged in this way . . . Individual men of Leontinoi erected Zeus not at state expense . . . As you pass by the entrance to the Bouleuterion Zeus stands without an inscription, and again as you turn north there is an *agalma* of Zeus . . . In front of this Zeus is a bronze tablet . . .

and so on.[33]

---

[29] Cf. Vernant (1989[1986]) 26.   [30] Vernant (1989[1986]) 23.

[31] The classic discussion of this is Gordon (1979), introducing the issue on p. 7. Compare also Schnapp (1988); Steiner (2001) 157–60, and Graf (2004) 125 who draws attention to Artemidoros, *The Interpretation of Dreams* 2.39, who says that to dream of the statue of a god is equivalent to dreaming of the god.

[32] Pausanias 5.10.10–11.1.   [33] Pausanias 5.22.5–23.4.

This usage, which is exactly paralleled for men, where the image is similarly treated as being in an important sense the person it represents, does no more than recognise the ineradicable power of the image: if the image represents a god, then in some sense it is that god; if god has the features of the image then in some sense god is the image. But in what sense? Does the image share every feature with the god, or only some features? If so, which features? And do all images of a god share the same features – are they all not just equally but similarly the god? When the young man in the story variously told by Pliny the Elder and by Lucian was so smitten with Praxiteles' naked Aphrodite of Knidos that he left his mark on the marble, we might be tempted to think that he is making a category mistake, acting towards a statue as if it is the sort of thing to which one can make love.[34] But the fact is that he *does* make love to it, the statue was what had inspired his passion. In a very real sense, and however hard a time he had, this statue *was* Aphrodite for him.[35] The gods themselves are made to recognise this in a similar, if less well-known, story told of a pilgrim who was smitten with one of two statues of boys in the Treasury of Spina at Delphi. The pilgrim gets himself locked into the treasury, and leaves a wreath on the statue as the price of his intercourse. The Delphians arrest the man but are told by the oracle to let him go since he had paid the price. This is not an image that is desecrated but a relationship properly celebrated.[36]

The story of Aphrodite of Knidos is paradigmatic of the way in which the appearance of the goddess, what the goddess looks like in her statues, is the appearing of the goddess, her presenting herself before men. This is not a matter of reducing the gods to elemental forces, where Aphrodite becomes the name for sexual desire. Rather it is a matter of taking seriously the way in which all representations, whether textual or visual, three-dimensional or two-dimensional, call forth reactions and establish relationships. The term *agalma*, which in the archaic period is used of statues of various sorts that bring pleasure, comes in the classical period to be restricted to statues of gods, that is, the pleasure that is marked by the word comes to be thought of as pleasure to the gods, and these statues are the means and record of that pleasing relationship.[37]

---

[34] Pliny, *Natural History* 36.20–21, Lucian, *Erotes* 15–16.

[35] And when the story in Lucian ends with his throwing himself off a cliff and down into the waves, it is tempting to see the detail that his body was never seen again as an acknowledgement that Aphrodite had indeed duly received him.

[36] Athenaios, *Teachers at Table* 606b, in a collection of similar stories.

[37] On the development of the usage of *agalma* see Stroud and Lewis (1979) 193.

The gods are, for any individual, the sum of what they have been represented to be, the accumulation and overlaying of one story upon another, of one statue upon another, of one picture upon another. It is on the basis of these accumulated representations that worshippers know the gods with whom they have ongoing relationships marked out in prayer and sacrifice – and occasionally in divine epiphany. Ancient writers persistently employ terms for statues that suggest precisely the qualities which statues lack, or deny those which they have, using *zōon* (living thing), *eikōn* (thing that (only) seems), or *andrias* (embodiment of the manly). This 'gamble with the impermissible' is an acknowledgement that, contrary to appearances, people can and do have living relationships with these images, can and do conjure with them in their imagination, can and do rely on their performance of gender.[38]

One conclusion that we might draw from all this is that it is no good denying that god has a body. Banning visual images of god is pointless, because visual images always lurk behind textual claims.[39] If god really has no body, then while we have our bodies, at least, we have no hope at all of entering into a relationship.[40] But that is a theological point. The conclusion, I want to emphasise in this context, is that if god has a body, then that body is not outside history. And the history of that body is important not simply for what humans think about god, but for what they think about themselves.

The history of godsbodies

The first god we can recognise in Greek vase painting is Athena (7.2), and we recognise her from her context. Faced with a decapitated Gorgon, two Gorgon sisters, and a male figure disappearing stage right, separated from the Gorgon sisters by a female figure, there is not much doubt that the story is the story of Perseus and the Gorgon, and the female figure is Perseus' protector, Athena.[41] But if we ask whether there is anything about the body

---

[38] For the vocabulary used of statues and the 'gamble with the impermissible' see Gordon (1979) 9–10.

[39] Compare C. Osborne (1987).

[40] For Plato 'godlikeness' comes to be dependent on escaping the body, and on the assumption that the soul has parts and one part of the soul is not essentially connected to the body and not affected by what affects the body. See *Timaeus* 90b–d and discussions by Annas (1999) ch. 3 and Sedley (1999). Plato never explains how or why his cosmic god involves himself with the changeable world; Aristotle, in adopting the view that we must leave our body to get close to god who has no body, makes god exclusively intellectual: *Nicomachean Ethics* 10.

[41] Protoattic amphora from burial Gamma 6 of the north-west cemetery at Eleusis, now in Eleusis Museum; Mylonas (1957).

7.2 Protoattic amphora from Eleusis attributed to the Polyphemos Painter.

of Athena that distinguishes this as a god's body, the answer is pretty clearly that nothing does. It is true that this is a woman of stature – as with the Gorgon sisters, her head presses against the top picture margin, and perhaps if Perseus himself survived better he would be smaller. It is true, too, that this figure wears an extremely elaborately decorated garment. But although these are signs that this is a woman of status, they do not definitively mark her out as divine. Nor will the staff that she holds in her hand do so.

There is a positive as well as a negative side to this manner of presenting Athena. Just as it has to be at least plausible that Aphrodite can deny her own divinity to Anchises, and that in the *Homeric Hymn to Demeter* the queen Metaneira can ask Demeter to serve as nursemaid for her, even though when Demeter enters the room 'her head reached the roof and she filled the doorway with heavenly radiance', so too visual representations of gods' bodies must come within the range of the humanly plausible and plausibly human if humans are to relate to them.[42] The dangers of a human encountering the god outside the range of human experience are nicely illustrated by the fate of Semele: according to Apollodoros, after Zeus and Semele had made love he offered to do for her whatever she asked, and she asked that he should come to her 'such as he came courting Hera'. Bound by his promise, Zeus came in a chariot with thunder and lightning and hurling a thunderbolt. Semele, who in other versions is destroyed by lightning or thunderbolt, in Apollodoros' version 'expired from fright'.[43] Gods act in ways no human can match, but while the particular equipment which a god carries, and which distinguishes him or her and makes identification easy, may be equipment men could never use (like Zeus's thunderbolt), gods' bodies remain bodies that might belong to mortal men and women.

On painted pottery the articles that figures carry and the context in which the figures are shown, quite apart from the explicit labels that are often given, mean that ambiguity over the divine or human status of a figure is ultimately rare. The same applies to architectural sculpture, where allusion to some story or other is common and where difficulty in identifying deities is unusual. But free-standing sculpture is a different matter. Statues, small, modest, large, and colossal, were to be found in every sanctuary, often in very large numbers. But in the case of many surviving archaic Greek sculptures we remain uncertain whether or not they represent gods. Even in the case of what are often taken to be the earliest surviving cult statues, the beaten bronze figures from the temple of Apollo at Dreros, it is context alone that suggests the identification, and we cannot absolutely exclude that these figures are votaries.[44] And when a figure of a heavily armed warrior, now without his shield (7.3), is dedicated to Apollo at Thebes at more or less the same time, engraved with the inscription 'Mantiklos offers me as a tithe to Apollo of the Silver Bow; do you Phoibos, give me a gracious favour in return', should we take the figure to represent Apollo, to represent Mantiklos, or to represent neither – or both?[45]

---

[42] *Homeric Hymn to Demeter* 188–90.

[43] Apollodoros, *Library* 3.4.3. Graf (2004) 125 takes this story to mean that the anthropomorphic form is not 'the real image' of the divinity, but it is not degrees of reality that are at issue here: Semele really is made pregnant by the anthropomorphic Zeus. Rather, what is at issue is how to conceive of the otherness of the gods without rendering them beyond communication. 'The unanswerable question Kierkegaard repeatedly asks is, How can the other speak and be heard without ceasing to be other?', Taylor (1990) 600.

[44] There was no ancient Greek term to distinguish a cult statue from other statues (Nick (2002) 9–28). I use the term 'cult statue' to refer to the statue singled out for pride of place inside a temple. The Dreros statues are Heraklion, Archaeological Museum 2445–7.

[45] Boston, Museum of Fine Arts 3.997.

7.3 Mantiklos' Apollo, Late Geometric or Early Orientalising Period, *c.* 700–675 BC, Thebes. Bronze figure, height 20.3 cm (8 in.). Photograph © 2011. Museum of Fine Arts, Boston.

The problem of whether a figure is mortal or divine is particularly acute for the two largest classes of archaic Greek free-standing statues, kouroi and korai. Neither kouroi – naked, beardless men, their arms by their side, one foot advanced and, until the end of the archaic period, their hair long – nor korai – young women, standing and with feet together, variously and more or less elaborately clothed, and holding some sort of offering in a hand outstretched or folded across the breast – are plausibly to be identified as always and everywhere representations of gods, though scholars in the past have sometimes made such claims. Both statue types are, for instance, as we have already seen, used as grave markers. Much more difficult is the issue of whether they are *ever* to be thought of as standing for a god or goddess. Certainly kouroi are turned into Apollo with the addition of the minimal attributes of bow and libation bowl, as with the bronze Apollo recovered from the Peiraieus harbour (7.4), probably with the colossal Naxian statue on Delos (which, however, describes itself in its inscription as an *andrias*, statue of an *anēr*), and with various images of such figures with bows in conjunction with temples on later vase paintings.[46] Whether korai are ever turned into goddesses is less clear. Keesling has recently argued that we should see the extended forearm gesture, which is a feature of all the korai from the Athenian Acropolis, except for six early ones, as the mark of a deity, on the grounds that cult statues are shown and known to have had extended forearms.[47] Keesling sees these korai as Athenas, except for the famous 'Peplos Kore' which she thinks may have held a bow and an arrow and thus been an Artemis.[48]

Giving a woman a bow clearly marks her out as different. In many contexts on painted pottery it would mark her out not as divine but as an Amazon, but in the context of a man being attacked by (his own) hunting hounds, or of the shooting of young men and women, a woman with a bow is readily identified as Artemis.[49] So too an isolated female figure with a bow in a sanctuary would also have to be Artemis. By contrast, the motif of the extended hand holding out a piece of fruit or a bird is not one that is strange to mortal women and demands no special context. Indeed that it can occur both in the context of dedication and in the context of the grave, where the figure represented is unlikely to be unequivocally identified as a goddess, emphasises the gesture as one at home among mortals. The extended hand signals not just giving but reciprocity, drawing attention variously to links with the gods and with the dead by calling upon our experience of relations with other humans.[50] That the gesture recurs on statues which from their context undoubtedly represent gods only serves further to emphasise how much gods and men share. There is arguably nothing that a god does that in

---

[46] Cf. A. Stewart (1986) 57.   [47] Keesling (2003) 124, 149–58.   [48] Keesling (2003) 135–9.

[49] As in the name vases of, respectively, the Pan Painter, where the reverse shows Artemis and Aktaion, and the Niobid Painter, with its shooting of the children of Niobe.

[50] On this view of the kore see R. Osborne (1994). On reciprocity generally see Gill, Postlethwaite and Seaford (1998) and Seaford (1994).

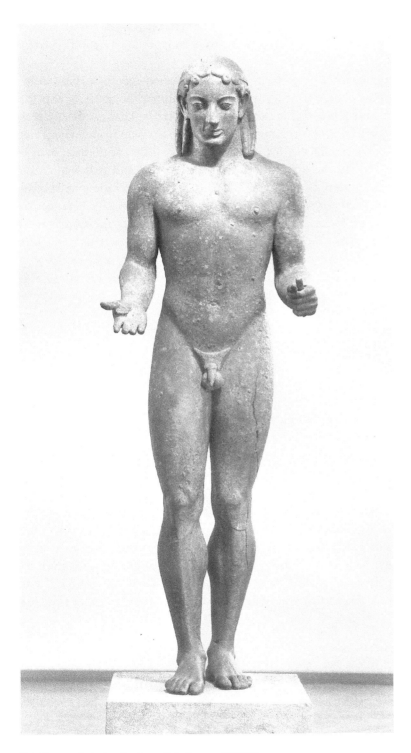

7.4 Late archaic Apollo from Peiraieus, *c.* 510 BC.

certain particular contexts a mortal might not be seen or fantasised doing.[51] Only in a particular context can a given body, even in action, become a god.

If it is impossible to tell from the body alone whether an archaic sculptural representation is of a divine or of a human being, it is also the case that rather little is here theologically at stake. That is, archaic statues offer strictly limited reference to the familiar visual world. They offer sufficiently rich reference for us to distinguish male and female, to register that this figure is richly dressed and adorned and that figure not, to note the absence of signs of old age, but they offer little purchase for our questions about what sort of a person we are observing. The regular 'archaic smile' does not distinguish mirth from sadness, the regular male nudity does not distinguish the athlete, the limited range of poses says nothing about how energetic is the engagement with a wider world. Neither abundance nor absence of power is on display. These are inscrutable figures. If these are gods they commit themselves to little more than formal anthropomorphism.

Almost no statue which was the main object of devotion within a temple has survived from archaic Greece, excepting the statues from Dreros, if they are such. Our knowledge of archaic cult statues relies on texts, and it is subject to the distortion of texts. Pausanias and other antiquarian authors such as Plutarch and, rather earlier, Kallimachos, tell of a time before the skill of carving had developed when planks or unworked stones represented the gods, but this was a story based on assumption not knowledge.[52] Nevertheless when relief sculptures and painted pottery in the classical period represent statues of gods they often represent them in archaic forms, and it is arguable that, at least in the case of the olivewood statue of Athena Polias on the Athenian Acropolis, there *was* something of a process of embellishment of a very simple form towards the end of the sixth century, with the addition of a gorgoneion, jewellery and a libation bowl.[53] If this is true, then Athena's body was made more distinctive, and the identity given by her context was reinforced by attributes which made of her both a goddess and Athena. From this same period come the lead griffin protomai from the

---

[51] Giving birth from the head, as Zeus does to Athena, might count as an exception to this claim.

[52] Donohue (1988) 195–7 quoting Pausanias 3.20.9, 7.22.4, 9.24.3; Kallimachos, *Causer* fr. 100 Pf; Plutarch, *Moral Essays* fr. 158 Sandbach; cf. also Donohue (1997), who points out that 'cult image' is also a modern construct, and that any image of a god was religiously powerful. This is clearly true, and the premise of what I have said above, but it remains the case that some images, because of their setting in temples, acquired particularly 'iconic' status. See also Scheer (2000).

[53] Keesling (2003) 156–7; Kroll (1982).

7.5 Chryselephantine head from the Halos Deposit (restored), late sixth century BC.
Delphi Museum.

temple of Athena at Emborio on Chios, which have been thought to have
adorned the helmet of the wooden cult statue of Athena there.[54]

The embellishment of these two Athena statues may be more or less
contemporary with the creation at Delphi of the most elaborate of all known
gold and ivory work from the archaic period, the three life-size figures from
the 'Halos Deposit' (7.5).[55] Various remains of ivory or gold-and-ivory
figures survive from the eighth century onwards, and it is clear that ivory
was a peculiarly precious substance regarded as particularly suitable for
dedication to the gods, but not restricted in its use to figures of gods.[56]
This is reinforced by the literary evidence, particularly that of Pausanias.
Pausanias pays special attention to cult statues, and most of the archaic
chryselephantine work that he mentions is in statues of gods, but on occasion

[54] Boardman (1967) 203–5.   [55] Lapatin (2001) 57–60.
[56] Lapatin (2001) 42–55. Ironically, Plato at *Laws* 956a objects to the dedication of ivory objects
on the grounds that ivory comes from a living animal.

he notes that associated non-divine figures may be of gold and ivory also.[57] This appears to have been the case with the figures in the Halos deposit, where the identity of the eight smaller figures, in particular, cannot be established but where the most plausible candidates include figures such as Horai, Graces or Muses. While there is good reason to think that gold and ivory was primarily associated with the gods, the association was not, and never became, exclusive.

In the fifth century gods were given a new body.[58] This new body was a direct product of fifth-century politics. When the Athenians decided, shortly after 450, to rebuild a temple to Athena on the Acropolis, following the destruction by the Persians in 480 of the old temple of Athena Polias and the part-built earlier Parthenon, they took the decision from the beginning to make room for a monumental cult statue, adopting an unusual, indeed architecturally revolutionary, eight-column rather than six-column façade, in order to achieve this.[59] The result was Pheidias' colossal twelve-metre-high gold and ivory statue of Athena that has become known as the Athena Parthenos.[60] In every way the impact of this statue was maximised. By using an amphiprostyle design for the cella (7.6) the architect achieved a much shallower porch than was customary with *in antis* arrangements. This brought the door of the cella closer to the exterior peristyle columns and so maximised the amount of light entering, but this light was further boosted by the addition of novel windows in the front wall of the cella. The division of the cella between an eastern and western chamber, and the provision of an interior colonnade carried round the west end of the eastern chamber, as well as along its north and south sides, meant that the statue itself, far from lurking in the gloom of the westernmost part of the interior, was actually in the centre of the temple, much closer than any visitor who had just come in from the Propylaia along the flank of the Parthenon would have anticipated. The massive base of the statue, 8.1 m wide by 4.1 m long, filled the lateral space between the interior colonnade, and in front of it was a shallow pool of water, approximately ten metres square. Pausanias identifies this as necessary to keep the humidity sufficient to conserve the ivory, but the reflection of the light in the pool can only have increased the dazzling effect of the statue.[61]

---

[57] E.g. Pausanias 2.1.7; in the classical period gold and ivory continued to be used for non-divine figures, e.g. that of Eurydike, mother of Philip II of Macedon, at the Philippeion at Olympia, Pausanias 5.17.4.

[58] Compare Weitman (2002).   [59] Coulton (1984) is fundamental.

[60] On the Athena Parthenos see Nick (2002), Leipen (1971).

[61] Pausanias 5.11.10 with Lapatin (2001) 85. See also G. P. Stevens (1955). The pool was created after the statue was installed, but we do not know how long after, probably very shortly.

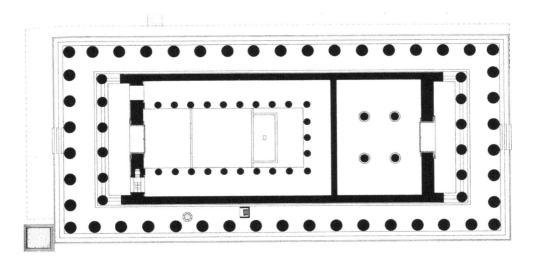

7.6 Plan of Parthenon.

The Pheidian revolution and the alternatives

Nothing like the Athena Parthenos had been known before, but it immediately set a standard. The authorities at Olympia decided that their new temple of Zeus needed such a statue too, called in Pheidias and acquired for themselves the monumental gold and ivory Zeus, described by Strabo in the passage quoted at the beginning of this chapter.[62] The best modern estimate is that this statue too was just over twelve metres tall, on a base a metre high, with a reflective pool, this time of olive oil and made of black limestone, in front of it (7.1). One massive gold and ivory statue might have been simply a curiosity; two set a pattern. To the question 'what does a god's body look like?', there was now a new answer: 'completely out of scale with the bodies of men'. The radiance and superior size of the gods that is a recurring feature of literary epiphany is here given a very material instantiation.[63] These statues fill the temple (7.7): from inside the temple no worshipper can take in the whole statue at once; only through the doorway do Zeus and Athena present themselves as a whole, so that to engage with these gods is to engage with them at a distance, framed within the temple façade and flattened into a picture.

Few sanctuaries were as well funded as Olympia and the Athenian Acropolis, but Pheidias' statues established a new fashion for what a cult statue

[62] Lapatin (2001) ch. 5 is the fullest description of 'The Pheidian Revolution'.
[63] Cf. Tanner (2006) 51–2.

ought to be like. Monumental chryselephantine cult statues are known from literary sources to have been produced for Pellene, Megara, Argos and Epidauros.[64] But such statues existed side by side, sometimes in the same temple, with other statues and statuettes of gods that were of wood, marble, bronze or terracotta; they might be on the scale of human bodies, or well under that scale, and might be highly naturalistic or not naturalistic at all. So how significant was the invention of the monumental gold and ivory statue for conceptions of gods' bodies?

Monumentality was no more a Pheidian invention than was the use of gold and ivory. In the early sixth century there was something of a competition in colossal kouros creation across the Aegean, with figures upwards of three metres high sculpted in Attica, Delos and Samos.[65] From the early fifth century we know of a three-metre cult statue of Artemis Delia on Paros. But although the stature of gods is often emphasised in descriptions of their epiphany, and large stature is one thing that persuades people that what they are seeing is a god, neither large stature within the bounds of the humanly possible nor monumentality beyond the human marked a sculpture as representing a god. What the Pheidian statues did was combine colossal size with both highly precious material and exploitation of the relationship between image and framing building: these were dazzling and amazing statues in every way. If every statue of a god made that god present in some way, these statues made the god present in a newly overpowering way. For the first time a Greek was faced with the visual equivalent of the shocking effect of divine epiphany that texts relate; now statues of the gods might come close to inspiring the fear which stories associate with those who see the gods themselves.[66]

One way of looking at the revolution effected by the Pheidian statues is to see it as a revolution in visuality. Jaś Elsner has argued that alongside the 'visuality of naturalism' in the ancient world there was a quite distinct ritual and religious visuality. He stresses that in the latter the vision of the god is 'the culmination of a ritual process' and that that process divests 'the spectator of all the social and discursive elements which distinguish his or her subjectivity from that of the god into whose space the viewer will come'.[67] Because the viewer is deliberately coming into the presence of the god, coming to gaze rather than happening to glance, the viewer enters the

[64] Lapatin (2001) 62–3, 96–111.   [65] Hermary (2006), cf. R. Osborne (2005).
[66] Cf. Dio Chrysostom, *Oration* 12.79–82.
[67] Elsner (2007) 23. For discussion of the religious implications of naturalism see also Tanner (2006) 72–89.

7.7 Reconstruction of the Athena Parthenos.

god's world and the god manifests him or herself in an epiphany, leading
the viewer to discover 'his or her deepest identity in the presence of the
god'.[68]

Elsner's description of religious visuality does indeed capture the experience which I have argued to be new to viewers of Pheidian cult statues. Any

---

[68] Elsner (2007) 24.

of the alternative ways Elsner offers of defining 'ritual-centred visuality' –
the acquisition of a cult-generated identity, the surrender of individuality
to collective sacred subjectivity, or the provision of a deity who is a vessel
into which pilgrims pour their devotions[69] – can be considered possible
responses to the Athena Parthenos or Zeus at Olympia. But for Elsner this
religious visuality applies not merely to the Pheidian cult image but to all
cult images; the revolution which I have argued to be brought about by size
and material, as well as setting, Elsner sees as a product of setting and of the
way in which the worshipper is brought face to face with the deity. For him
the relationship to the viewer is a matter of the correct ritual preparation and
attitudes, and only a matter of the god's appearance in as far as it is important that the worshipper see the god face on. However 'naturalistic' a cult
statue might be 'the correct ritual preparations and attitudes could prevent
the viewer from succumbing to the dangers of voyeuristic projection'.[70] For
Elsner it is the context that determines the nature of the visuality involved.

But can *how* one sees be uninfluenced by *what* one sees? Images evoke
memories of other images, both images of persons and things and images
of representations of persons and things. They may refer more richly to features associated with representations or more richly to features associated
with life. The context and setting of an image will certainly influence the
evocation, but so too will its form. Setting and form may conspire together
to persuade a viewer to react as he or she would to a religious icon or to a
photograph in a family album, or setting and form may send contradictory
signals, leaving the viewer poised between different kinds of viewing, different regimes of visuality.[71] In the context of sculpture, the mode of viewing,
the nature of the visuality, is always going to be affected by the body that is
displayed.

Size, material, setting, all made the colossal chryselephantine statues
suggest that gods' bodies really were different from men's bodies, that they
were both dazzling and distant, massively substantial yet also flattened
into a single frontal view. Important also was the removal of these gods
from narrative. The Athena Parthenos bore representations of battles with
Amazons on her shield and other narratives on her base, sandals, and so on,
but she herself simply stood, helmeted and with Victory on her outstretched
hand – a martial goddess for sure but not engaged in martial acts. So too
the Zeus at Olympia had all sorts of scenes on his throne and footstool,

[69] Elsner (2007) 25.   [70] Elsner (2007) 25.

[71] Elsner moves towards a recognition of this in the Epilogue to *Roman Eyes* (esp. (2007) 301–2),
but throughout he underplays the importance of the form of the image.

but Zeus himself sat with Victory on his right hand.[72] In neither case was it episodes in which the god or goddess in question played a sole or particular part that were displayed in conjunction with the images. Both were thus presented as presiding over the course of myth-history, but not as figures with particular involvement in it.[73]

This separation of Zeus and Athena from *histoire événementielle* is reinforced by the style. Although we know the Athena Parthenos only through copies, and the Zeus still less well, the evidence is sufficient to indicate that the statue was markedly old-fashioned.[74] This is seen in the long locks of hair falling over the chest, the way in which the fall of the drapery does little or nothing to betray any sense of bodily form beneath, and the repeated horizontal accents, which make the whole seem heavy.[75] Far from offering us the sort of ultra-specific body forms that contemporary sculptors, if not Pheidias himself, had explored in such works as the Riace bronzes (4.4, 4.5, see pp. 114, 115), the Parthenos brought back to the Athenian Acropolis the generalised female face that had been buried with the korai after the Persian destruction.

It is fundamental to the Homeric picture of the gods that gods and men cannot be securely told apart. The gods might be grand in stature, beautiful in form, radiant in complexion, fed by ambrosia and enlivened by ichor not blood, but, even when they do not choose to adopt the appearance of a mortal, their bodies are merely superior human bodies. Likewise, although gods have powers that enable them to do things that no human can do, their activities are fundamentally the activities of men – feasting, conversing and quarrelling, making love. Both archaic and classical pot painters showed the gods in action looking, apart from their distinctive accoutrements, just like humans. From what we can tell, archaic sculptors too presented gods in the same manner in which they presented men. But the Pheidian images were not at all like contemporary images of men. For all that he appeals to Homer as his inspiration, Pheidias presents gods who are distinctly different – different from earlier sculptural representations of gods, and different from humans. Pheidias' gold and ivory gods who could not be mistaken for humans are not beings who take part in the actions of this

---

[72] Pausanias 5.11.1–11 for our fullest ancient description.

[73] This was not in itself entirely novel: the figures of Zeus and Apollo on the east and west pediments at Olympia, respectively, provide a parallel, and this use of the centre of the pediment is to some extent anticipated at Aigina and on the old temple of Athena Polias at Athens (cf. R. Osborne 2000b).

[74] On the relationship of the copies to the Athena Parthenos see Gaifman (2006).

[75] Cf. Ridgway (1981) 167.

world: they are gods who preside at a distance over the affairs of the world. While Xenophanes would no doubt continue to object to the presentation of gods in human form at all, Pheidias offers images of the gods which go some way to answer the burgeoning philosophical criticism of the Homeric picture. He has instantiated a new theological paradigm.[76]

The Pheidian theological revolution was extremely important, but it was also partial. For every viewer transported by awe at the sight of Zeus, there was another who worried what would happen to the roof of the temple if Zeus stood up.[77] The attempt to keep anthropomorphism while changing the scale had its disadvantages as well as its advantages. So too did the chryselephantine technique: splendid the surface might be, but could one take seriously a hollow god?[78] What is more, only some gods could be presented in this form, which therefore emphasised power. It is not by chance that the other colossal gold and ivory statues were either also of Zeus (as at Megara) or Athena (as at Pellene), or of Hera (at the Argive Heraion) or the healing god who was in the classical period the epiphanic god *par excellence*, Asklepios (as at Elis). These were all gods who exercised their powers and made their presence felt by direct intervention in human lives. It is not by chance, either, that human rulers have wished to have themselves portrayed in the guise of Zeus, associating with themselves both his power and his distance.[79]

Other gods were represented, in the classical period as in the late archaic period, in gold and ivory, but, and this is theologically crucial, not on a monumental scale, and not in this style. Pheidias himself is said to have produced a statue of Aphrodite Ourania for the city of Elis. We owe our knowledge of this to Pausanias, who writes: 'They call the goddess in the temple Ourania. She is of gold and ivory, the work of Pheidias. She stands with one foot on a tortoise.'[80] Although we cannot be certain of the appearance of this statue (the ancient texts which mention it offer little description), there is some evidence that points to its presenting the godsbody in a very different manner.

Our best evidence for how Pheidias' Elis statue of Aphrodite looked is a sculpture probably related to, if not identical with, a second Aphrodite

---

[76] Dio Chrysostom in *Oration* 12 (*Olympian Oration*) uses Pheidias' Zeus statue as the occasion to explore the theology of statues of gods, so acknowledging Pheidias' central position in the theology of divine representation. For a summary and analysis of that speech see Betz (2004).

[77] So Strabo 8.3.30 (343C).

[78] So, repeatedly, Lucian, *Zeus Rants* 8, *Gallos* 24. Cf. also Arnobios, *Against the Heathen* 6.16.

[79] Cf. Suetonius, *Gaius* 22; Dio Cassius 59.28.3–4.

[80] Pausanias 6.25.1; Lapatin (2001) 90–4, *LIMC* s.v. Aphrodite 174.

Ourania by Pheidias mentioned by Pausanias, this one set up in her sanctuary in the Athenian Agora (7.8).[81] This very slightly over life-size statue also has its foot upon a tortoise, and the possibility that it relates in form to the Elis statue is strengthened by the fact that the flesh parts were added in a separate marble, perhaps Parian, giving a contrast in texture and surface which paralleled, if it could hardly reproduce, the contrast between gold and ivory. What is certain is that this statue is closely comparable in its style to the style in which the goddesses lounging on Olympus to observe the birth of Athena are presented on the east pediment of the Parthenon. The chiton is shown slipping from one shoulder and falls in abundant folds that create the impression of a bodily form beneath. Aphrodite's power was not expressed through commands but through seduction and the alluring promise that pleasures wait to be uncovered. An Aphrodite without a narrative, without a plot, would not be Aphrodite: this is not a goddess with whom one comes face to face but a goddess who diverts one from one's course.

Aphrodite was the limit case for any attempt to insist that the gods were other. She is similarly the limit case for any attempt to keep religious viewing separate from 'naturalistic' visuality.[82] The religious impact of Aphrodite is inseparable from her sexual attractiveness. How could one have a goddess of love who was not of the flesh? Incommensurable gods could do shock and awe, but desire? Desire demanded that the worshipper construe himself as invited into Aphrodite's world. If Pheidias' statues of Aphrodite Ourania showed his acknowledgement of this, it received its most emphatic emphasis in the fourth century with Praxiteles' Aphrodite of Knidos (7.9). Praxiteles did three revolutionary things. He stripped Aphrodite naked; he motivated that nakedness with allusion to bathing; and, as the tradition of display in a round temple affirms, he offered the worshipper a number of different angles of view which corresponded with potentially different narrative positions – as the invited lover, as the stranger blundering in to a private moment, as an unseen voyeur.[83] All of these together served to tease those who came to the temple with the possibility that Aphrodite was theirs, whether as a picture or as a body, while at the same time leaving it impossible either to confirm that chance or to rule it out.[84] Zeus and Athena watch what men do but

---

[81] Pausanias 1.14.7; *LIMC* s.v. Aphrodite 177; Lapatin (2001) 91–4. Ridgway (1981) 217 argues against its being a genuine fifth- or fourth-century piece.

[82] As even Elsner comes close to admitting: (2007) 25, 115–17, 301.

[83] On this statue see most recently Corso (2007) 9–186, who discusses the evidence for the round temple on pp. 32–7.

[84] R. Osborne (1994), (1998a).

7.8 Late fifth-century BC statue of Aphrodite from the Athenian Agora.

are not concerned with whether men watch them;[85] Aphrodite's power, on the other hand, depends on being able to attract, and distract, our gaze – it comes precisely in cultivating 'to-be-looked-at-ness'.[86] It is not by chance that the classic seduction scene which I analysed earlier when establishing the human nature of the gods was an epiphany of Aphrodite.

Praxiteles did not limit his forceful reassertion that gods share bodies with men and women to Aphrodite. His Apollo slaying a lizard (7.10) portrayed

[85] Though of course there was theological mileage to be had from thinking of circumstances in which Athena might not be so uninterested in being watched – but mileage achieved only by humanising the goddess. A literary example of this is Kallimachos in *Hymn Five, On the Bath of Pallas,* with the cautionary tale of Teiresias at 57–136. It is crucial that the consequence for Teiresias of seeing Athena bathing is acquisition of superhuman powers: he can no longer see the things of this world, but he can see into other worlds. For a sculptural example see the reliefs of the Athena Nike parapet on the Athenian Acropolis, where humanising Athena is essential to a particular construction of victory; see R. Osborne (1994).

[86] For the concept, see Berger (1972).

7.9 Roman copy of Praxiteles' Aphrodite of Knidos, *c.* 350 BC.

the god who in myth slew the great monster Pytho at Delphi as an immature young man, who, rather than doing battle with a fearful opponent was simply biding his time waiting for a moment at which crushing a harmless lizard would bring him greatest pleasure. Together the nature of the god's (in)action and the treatment of the young body and its smooth flesh raise the question of what sort of a body this god possesses: Apollo may be male, but is he manly?[87] It is not by chance that Apollo is a god strongly associated with the senses – not in this case with sexual desire but with music and the arts. Like Aphrodite, Apollo is a god who presides over the ways in which humans relate to each other, and those relations can only be conceived of in fully human form. Not for nothing is it Apollo who is in question when the painter of an Apulian pot in the fourth century (7.11) explores

---

[87] R. Osborne (1998c) 23–5 for Apollo.

7.10 Roman copy of Praxiteles' Apollo Sauroktonos, *c.* 350 BC.

the contrast between an archaic cult statue and 'the god himself'.[88] All the questions about what particular sort of anthropomorphic body the gods have, which are avoided by Pheidias when he reverts to late archaic styles of representation, are bodied forth in Praxiteles' very specific presentation of a languid youth. As with the Aphrodite of Knidos, so here, Praxiteles gives the gods bodies that are aggressively our bodies.

Nevertheless, for all the continuation of old traditions, and the devising of radical responses, once Pheidias had offered his vision that gods' bodies might be quite different, that possibility could not be dismissed. As it happens, one of the best extant tokens of its continuing power comes also from the island of Knidos. In 1812 the Society of Dilettanti excavated the marble body of a just over life-sized seated figure (7.12). Now in the British Museum, and reunited with its head, which was found later, this statue is universally acknowledged to represent the goddess Demeter and thought by

---

[88] Allard Pearson Museum, Amsterdam, inv. 2579. See Spivey (1995) 451–2, and more generally de Cesare (1997).

7.11 Fragment of an Apulian pot, fourth century BC.

some to be the work of the sculptor Leochares, perhaps dating to *c.* 330.[89]
As Ashmole has shown, this is a more complex figure than appears at first
sight, the superficially stately and static air proving on closer analysis to
be marked by restlessness not only in the drapery but also in the turn of
the head. Ashmole speculated that the statue belonged to a group, paired
with a now lost Kore. He also stressed, particularly with regard to the head,
that the sculptor must have been a 'man who has often walked on the
Acropolis... and has looked up at the Parthenos'.[90] Whoever the sculptor was, here he takes the formula Pheidias had pioneered in the Athena
Parthenos in order to dazzle with divine power, and he stages instead the
very different power of Demeter, a power manifest in maternal concern
and the ability to withhold from humankind their means of livelihood.
Demeter's calm and inscrutable gaze cannot, as Ashmole rightly observes,
be understood from the front. It is not a gaze with which the worshipper
can interact. Rather, what is played out in front of the viewer is the relationship between Demeter and Kore, and a reminder that human fate depends
upon relations between the gods over which humans have no control. This
is a godsbody which there is no need to measure on the human scale –
incomprehensibility is part of its message.

[89] For a classic description, and the case for Leochares, see Ashmole (1951).
[90] Ashmole (1951) 15.

7.12 Statue of Demeter from Knidos, second half of fourth century BC.

As far as Plato was concerned it was a problem both for theology and for human communities that gods might be presented as acting in ways that contravened the behavioural standards he regarded as necessary in a human community. The consequences for human communities of conceiving of gods as having bodies that are different in order from the bodies of humans were no less problematic. If godsbodies share only the *appearance* of human bodies – if, in Greek terminology, they are merely *eikones* – and are not otherwise commensurable, then, in as far as all experience is mediated through the body and the body is, in Latour's phrase, 'that through which we learn to be affected', the experience which humans have of the world and the experiences which gods have will be incommensurable. Humans will be reduced to looking on as divine power operates by its own unfathomable conventions. But how could men influence the gods or expect the gods to take any concern for the pleasures and pains of human life, if gods do not share the same experiences? In Greek terms, statues can be *agalmata*, things of delight, alike to men and to gods, only if gods and men are commensurable.

Incommensurability between gods and men means that there can be no sympathy between them. Gods of any shape may indeed have power over men, but once they no longer share bodies and bodily experiences with humankind the basis on which the gods have authority over men comes into question. If gods' bodies are fundamentally different, then man must look after himself and make up his own rules. The authority that gods who share a body with humankind possess by nature, gods who have a quite different body can have only by convention.

The theological problem that there can be human understanding of the gods only if the gods are in some important sense like men but that gods can have the sorts of powers that make them gods in human eyes only if they are in some important sense not like men is fundamental to all religions. In Christianity we see this in the long debates in the early church about the divine and human nature of Christ, a debate intimately bound up with the debate between iconoclasts and iconophiles over the use of images. In the Greek and Roman world the debate over the use of images never became as prominent or as violent, and images have largely been ignored in modern discussions of Greek theology. But the question of how the bodies of the gods were conceived of and how they were represented is crucial to our understanding of Greek religion. Upon the history of godsbodies we see writ large the history of Greek theology.

8 | Telling bodies

The previous chapters have emphasised the histories that are *not* written on the classical Greek body. Classical Greek texts take for granted status distinctions between citizens and non-citizens, Athenians and non-Athenians, Greeks and foreigners, the pure and the polluted, men and gods. None of these divisions manifest themselves in contemporary images of human bodies. Athenian artists, like other ancient Greek artists, produce images in dialogue with daily life in which status is simply not a concern – in which distinctions between belonging to one Greek state or another Greek state and between being a citizen and not being a citizen are invisible, and where even the distinction between being a slave and being a citizen or a potential citizen is often not marked.

Pictures and sculptures are certainly not unmediated visual equivalents to what they portray. Artists have always already chosen which features of the observed body they will reproduce when they make images of humans in sculpture, painting or drawing. Some features of the physical body they will ignore, other features, and above all movement, sound and smell, they have only very limited means of reproducing. But for my purposes the gap between the image and its referent is not a barrier to understanding; for the selectivity of the artist reveals what that artist considered to be important and gives a guide to what viewers thought they needed to know in assessing any image. For this reason sculptures and painted pots are good evidence for what was observed.

The gap between the visual discourse of pot-painting and sculpture and the verbal discourse of literary and epigraphic texts reproduces a gap in real life between the categories into which knowledge was sorted by education and by formal and informal conversation, and the categories into which people sorted the evidence of their senses about what they met on the street. But what does the existence and nature of this gap tell us? What does it mean for our understanding of Athenian society that divisions between citizens, metics and slaves, between Athenian and non-Athenian, between those who were and were not polluted, between beings with and beings without supernatural powers were not apparent to visual observation? In what way is our story of Athenian political, social and religious life going to be different if we work with the body of the visual arts, rather than with the body of texts? Our answer to this is going to depend upon what we think the Athenian community was like.

In some circumstances a gap of this sort would not matter. Suppose, for instance, that everyone knew about everyone else in a community on the basis of having been told each of their life histories. In those circumstances, whether a person's past history or current status was written on his or her body would not matter at all. Moses Finley, the last Wiles Lecturer to speak about Greek history, once suggested that classical Athens was indeed a 'face-to-face society'.[1] The notion of a 'face-to-face society' had been coined by Peter Laslett, for whom the prime example of such a society was the family. Laslett suggested that the mark of face-to-face societies was that responses were intuitive, and interpersonal communication not a matter of propositions but 'exclamations, apostrophes, laughter and silences'.[2] In such a society people will know without looking whether a man is a citizen, a metic, a Theban, a Thracian, and will know without looking that a woman has just given birth, that her husband or father has just died, even perhaps that she has had sexual relations with her husband (or with someone else) the previous night. It is somewhat unlikely even that other Greek communities, where citizen bodies might not reach a thousand in number, approached the condition of the face-to-face society. It is not simply that intuitive communication seems implausible even in a body of fifty, unless they permanently reside in close proximity, but that the very existence of formal decision-making institutions and communication by decrees advertising propositions demonstrates that laughter and silences, exclamations and apostrophes were not sufficient means of communication.[3] As for classical Athens, a community numbering in total perhaps 300,000 persons, with 30 to 60,000 adult male citizens spread over 120 and more communities scattered over an area the size of Derbyshire, it can never as a whole have remotely approached the condition of a 'face-to-face' society.[4] Even the various subdivisions of the Athenian *polis* can rarely have been face-to-face societies in the sense in which Laslett used the term.[5] Certainly one might

---

[1] Finley (1973) 17. [2] Laslett (1956), quoting from 158.

[3] For one small city where we have good demographic information see Reger (2006) 750–1 on Koresia.

[4] Cf. R. Osborne (1985a) 64–5, 89.

[5] There were 'at least about thirty' phratries, but even if there were twice that number we are still dealing with, on average, five hundred adult male members in each (Lambert (1993) 19). The 139 demes varied in size by a factor of forty-four, to judge by the numbers of representatives they had on the Council of Five Hundred, which varied from one every other year to twenty-two annually. A population of 30,000 implies an average of sixty adult male citizens per *bouleutēs*, so

reckon to know by sight two hundred people, and so be able to distinguish demesmen from non-demesmen, but knowing births, deaths and sexual relations within two hundred families is already potentially a different matter. It is not by chance that demes and other subdivisions of the Athenian *polis* adopt the same decision-making procedures as the city as a whole.[6]

Such *a priori* reasoning can be reinforced with reference to specific historical moments about which we are informed by ancient texts.[7] One of the most revealing is Thucydides' description of the events in Athens following the Athenian defeat in Sicily in 413. The Athenians are not certain what to do, become anxious that the mistaken decision to invade Sicily in the first place shows that the democracy is incapable of sensible decisions and start to wonder whether it is time for a new order. Suddenly a classification not previously important becomes vital: some people want to end democracy and replace it with oligarchy; some people continue to back democracy. It becomes vital to be able to tell who is who. Vital, but impossible. Thucydides remarks that the success of the oligarchic coup in 411 came about because

An exaggerated belief in the numbers of the conspirators also demoralized the People, rendered helpless by the magnitude of the city, and by their being uncertain about each other, and being without means of finding out what those numbers really were. For the same reason it was impossible for anyone to speak his mind to a neighbour and to concert measures to defend himself, as he would have had to speak either to one whom he did not know, or whom he knew but did not trust. Indeed all the popular party approached each other with suspicion, each thinking his neighbour involved in what was going on, the conspirators having in their ranks persons whom no one could ever have believed capable of joining an oligarchy; and these it was who made the many so suspicious, and so helped to procure impunity for the few, by confirming the commons in their mistrust of one another.[8]

Even more revealingly, Lysias' preserved speeches include one in which he seeks to demonstrate that one Pankleon is not an Athenian.[9] Pankleon claimed to be a Plataian, and the Plataians had, following their expulsion from their own city by the Spartans, been given Athenian citizenship. This

---

any deme with four or more representatives on the Council would have had upwards of two hundred adult male members, not all of whom, and in the case of some demes perhaps rather few of whom, would live in their ancestral village which bore the deme name (on mobility see R. Osborne 1991).

[6] Cf. R. Osborne (1990a).

[7] These and further incidents are discussed by Vlassopoulos (2007), who argues for a similar conclusion about the impossibility of maintaining clear categorical distinctions between legal status groups at Athens. He is more inclined than I to think this peculiar to Athens.

[8] Thucydides 8.66.3–5, trans. Crawley.   [9] See further on this case Todd (1993) 167–70.

involved registration in a tribe, phratry and deme. The prosecutor in this case seeks to demonstrate that Pankleon is not a citizen on the basis that his name is known neither in the deme of which Pankleon claims to be part, Dekeleia, nor among the other Plataians. David Whitehead observed that 'To discredit the claim of Pankleon to be a Dekeleian ... all that was necessary was to establish that the Dekeleians had never heard of him.'[10] But matters are not quite that simple. First, although Lysias can bring into the court 'those of the Dekeleians I have questioned', he cannot show that no Dekeleian knew Pankleon, nor can he prevent Pankleon from calling upon other Dekeleians who might claim to know him as a fellow-demesman. More significantly, Lysias does not rest his case on the ignorance of the Dekeleians, he also consults the Plataians. What follows is highly revealing:

I first asked Euthykritos, who I knew was the oldest of the Plataians and I thought would be most sure to know, whether he knew a Plataian called Pankleon, the son of Hipparmodoros. Then, when he replied that he knew Hipparmodoros but was not aware of any son, either Pankleon or anybody else, I asked also everyone else whom I knew to be Plataians. All denied knowledge of his name, but they said I would obtain the most accurate information by going to the fresh-cheese market on the first day of the month, because the Plataians assemble there every month.[11]

So here, although it is in the speaker's interests to present discovering whether or not someone belonged to a particular group as straightforward, he produces as a star witness someone whose testimony indicates that one might know a person but not know for sure whether or not he had any son. He follows this with several members of the group attesting that they considered it entirely plausible that there might be a member of the group whom they did not know. Admittedly we are dealing here with a group that is a whole city, and one in exile, but nevertheless the expectation of incomplete knowledge is clear.

The case of Pankleon is revealing at the institutional level. Whether or not demes kept a list of current members has been disputed, but, if they did, it is conspicuous here by its absence.[12] But it is even more revealing at the social level. There may have been all sorts of social reasons why other Plataians were wary of declaring either that they did or that they did not know Pankleon, but the claims not to know whether or not Pankleon was a member of the group must have been plausible. Athenians did not, it appears, expect that everyone knew all the other members of the various subgroups of the

[10] Whitehead (1986) 226. [11] Lysias 23.5–6.
[12] On the *lexiarchikon grammateion* see the rather differing views of R. Osborne (1985a) 72–3; and Whitehead (1986) 35, 98, 103–4.

city to which they belonged. But if even forensic investigation was often inconclusive, the importance of what could and could not be read off the body for day-to-day encounters is revealed as vital. Classical Athens is seen to be the sort of place in which intuitive knowledge did not spread very far, but where formal methods of establishing identity were still rudimentary. Athenians were unable to map onto the bodies they met the distinctions which their political discourse, and even the letter of their law, required them to make, and this had consequences for how Athenians behaved, and for their attitudes to each other and to rules, on a day-to-day basis.[13]

Further evidence that Athenians often could only access the information that they needed in order to carry through the requirements of the state by tapping into communities much more intimate than tribes, phratries and demes comes from Athenian law enforcement. The inadequacy of formal mechanisms of policing in Athens, and hence the importance of informal policing, has been stressed by Virginia Hunter.[14] The Athenian police force of Skythians, which we met in Chapter 5, had a rather limited remit, which did not include the investigation of crime or the monitoring of compliance with the law. Magistrates had some powers of law enforcement and some obligations to see that particular laws were enforced, but these were limited.[15] Although public prosecution of crimes was undertaken in some extreme circumstances, prosecutions that came to the courts were primarily brought by individuals who either claimed to be the injured party in an action or had voluntarily taken upon themselves the role of prosecuting an offence. Such volunteer prosecutions were possible only in a limited range of cases, and a powerful discourse developed, backed by legal sanctions, which discouraged such people and cast aspersions on their motivation.[16] Hunter emphasises the way in which informal policing methods made up for the absence of formal policing; in the contexts of the present discussion it is striking that kinsmen and slaves within the household are the chief alternative agents in enforcing acceptable behaviour. Hunter's work therefore reinforces the picture of Athens as a community whose institutional aspirations were not matched by the practical means by which they could be systematically and effectively operated day to day.

These observations further emphasise the historical importance of the gap between the discriminations encouraged by verbal discourse and the discriminations made by visual discourse. In each of the cases discussed

---

[13] Vlassopoulos (2007) similarly makes use of this case.
[14] Hunter (1994). I have discussed the role of pollution beliefs in informal policing in Chapter 6.
[15] Harris (2007).   [16] R. Osborne (1985b), (1990b), Harvey (1990).

above, the operation of Athenian politics and of the formal will of the state (as expressed in the law code) is impeded by the inability to know from people's appearance on which side of a political or legal category division they fall. The cases show both the self-serving nature of many of these categorical divisions and their fundamental importance to state organisation. Finding out about Pankleon's status matters only if one invests heavily in the importance of being or not being a citizen. But finding out whether a person is responsible for some antisocial act or has subversive political views can be vital to community relations.

It is in this connection that the interplay between visual and verbal data, and not just their difference, becomes important. I have described a world in which visual discourse (Chapter 3) marks gender and keenly observes the signals that individuals give out about how they want to relate to others, and how they want others to relate to them in return. Images on pots and classical funerary sculptures pick up what is performed, messages that are more or less consciously sent by choice of clothing or action. Those performances draw attention to age only occasionally, to signal position on one side or another of just a few divisions, between the elderly and the merely mature, between the child and the adolescent, between adolescent and adult, or, in the case of this last distinction, to negotiate a position precisely on the cusp. They draw attention to wealth or poverty irregularly. And they have almost no interest in distinctions of descent, whether of different families within a community or of members of one city or ethnic group or another, except where telling a (mythical) story requires such distinctions. If we think of the images as giving information on a 'need to know' basis, what Athenians expected to need to know was the sort of personal behaviour, of public or private performance, that would be manifested by those whom they met. In marked contrast to the modern, or even the Roman, world, visual images give no grounds for reconstructing separate class-based 'low' and 'high' cultures.[17]

Of the various discourses which texts emphasise, that which comes closest to mapping onto the visual discourse of pots and sculpted stelai is the discourse of shame. Certain motifs in painted pottery, and particularly the complete muffling of a figure in a cloak, have indeed been identified as signals of modesty and shame.[18] But shame has both a public and a private aspect. Shame depends on individuals being self-conscious, regardless of whether

[17] For the modern (French) world see Bourdieu (1984); for Rome see above Ch. 3, n. 49, and p. 105.
[18] G. P. Ferrari (2002) ch. 3.

or not others know. Individuals may wish to signal, more or less loudly, their modesty or that they are ashamed. But they may also wish to exhibit the shame that they feel either to no one else or only to selected people. The public discourse of pollution relates closely to expectations about shame, but it does not map exactly even onto the public aspect of shame, since pollution may arise from situations which are not at all shameful (being related to someone who has died, for example). The notion of the dirty body, at first sight so visual a notion, turns out to be one which stands in a highly oblique relationship to what Athenians expected to be able to see expressed on the bodies of those they met.

In my discussion of the dirty body in Chapter 6 I argued both that notions of pollution were increasingly, rather than diminishingly, prevalent over time, and that the behaviour regulated by notions of pollution complemented the behaviour regulated by law. If we take seriously the absence of ideas of purification and pollution in Homer, the parallelism between the development of ideas of metaphysical dirtiness and the development of codes of law becomes manifest and should be reckoned of fundamental significance. Metaphysical dirt comes to operate in places which law cannot reach and relies precisely on the fact that it is *not* written on the body. Given the way in which pollution relates to but does not map directly onto shame, this development suggests not that the institutional framework of the city came to map more and more closely onto those features of the world which were manifest to people's vision, but that it made use of more and more features that were invisible. The more the demands of the state were formalised, the more important the invisible came to be to proper civic life.

The relationship between the importance of the invisible and state power is not accidental. Had distinctions of status been visible, written on the body, there would have been no need to assert them. It is notable, for instance, that the visible distinctions of gender are taken for granted, not laid down in the laws of Greek cities. Asserting the importance of differences not visibly written on the body both requires that there is an authority powerful enough to make the assertion and reinforces the power of the asserting authority. Classification is essential to the claim of the institution to power and is supported by those whom the claims privilege. Division and classification are self-serving and aspirational, and states regularly seek to increase their power by complicating the classification and adding invisible classifications to those that are visible. Political history is marked by some animals always becoming more equal than others.

The increasing importance of the invisible to civic life emerges clearly in the arguments of Chapters 4 and 5 about citizenship and the identification of the foreign. In those chapters I argued for a developing gap between how the state legally defined the citizen and the way in which citizen terminology was used in everyday parlance. The definition of what it was to be a citizen changed both in detail and in nature over time, coming to be a strongly exclusionary concept backed up by increasingly severe sanctions against any attempt to breach the rules. But the quality of being a *politēs* remained, by contrast, more or less constant, with the focus upon participant membership of the community, not on either local or genetic origin. Participant membership of the community was something manifest, manifest in actions over time, but also visible to the eye at a glance in the way a person managed their relations to others. By contrast, there were no clear marks of local or genetic origin. The ever more closely defined rules for belonging to the community ensured that the gap grew wider and wider between what could be seen and what law required one to know.

One of the products of increasingly exclusive definitions of who could share the duties and privileges of legal and political citizenship was a corresponding increase in those reckoned to be foreign. Men who might have married Athenian wives and either become citizens themselves or had children who would be citizens were now kept apart in a world in which they could not intermarry with Athenian women. The more rigid policing of the category of the foreign, coupled with the economic attractiveness of Athens as a place in which to live and do business, meant that the Athenians increasingly enjoyed the presence among them of significant numbers of non-Athenians, both other Greeks and non-Greeks. That very presence is plausibly causally connected to the change in the way in which the visual language of the foreign – in particular foreign items of clothing – is used to imagine an other world. The repertoire of visual images indicates little interest in registering foreign bodies, as such, and limits its interest to using conventional signs of foreignness to draw attention, for approbation as much as for criticism, to unusual status or behaviour. The more the city became concerned to distinguish foreigners from citizens, the more citizens played the foreigner – not in contradistinction to playing the citizen, but as part of the very act of being a citizen, of performing the more high profile of their civic duties. Visual signs which might have been restricted so as to serve the interests of concepts to which the state was committed were instead deployed in ways that blurred and confused those concepts.

Classical Athens was notoriously restrictive in the rights it was willing to extend to any who were not part of the narrowly defined descent group of citizens. This manifested itself not only in the new rules for citizenship, the effective banning of marriage between Athenians and non-Athenians and the highly restricted circumstances in which those not born Athenian were given citizenship, but also in the taxation of resident non-Athenians, and the absurdly low limits on the property that could be held in her own right by any woman. It might seem, therefore, that the growing gap between the discriminations that law insisted on making and the discriminations that those in the Athenian streets were in a position to make was a peculiarly Athenian feature. However, not only are the developing notions of pollution even better attested outside than inside Athens, but, for all that Athens played a crucial part in at least some aspects of their development, the changing conceptions of the gods were exported well beyond Athens. Here at least are distinctive classical, not merely Athenian, or democratic, developments.

When it comes to the gods, we can trace a movement from there being no visible sign that distinguishes gods' bodies from human bodies to the creation of bodies for the gods to which humans may not aspire. This movement from invisibility to visibility matters, because the possibility and potential nature of communications between men and gods and gods and men depends upon the extent to which they share the same body. The powerful statement of abandonment of any commitment to a shared body that we see in the fifth century in two of the most prominent of all Greek sanctuaries, the Athenian Acropolis and the sanctuary of Zeus at Olympia, undermined the grounding of human morality in the world of the gods more fundamentally than any moral failings displayed on Olympus by all-too-human gods. But, more important than that, if gods might not share fully human bodies, the need for and relevance of bodily knowledge must be questioned. If the body by which we are affected is not the body by which the gods are affected, then our bodily senses cannot be reckoned to inhabit the same world that the gods inhabit. It is not for nothing that Plato's theory of knowledge would suggest that true knowledge is of objects which have only a distant and uncertain relationship to the objects experienced by our senses.[19]

Just as I suggested that the Pheidian conception of the gods as having superhuman bodies was challenged by the difficulties of coming to terms with gods such as Aphrodite, and by sculptors such as Praxiteles who put such deities at the centre of their presentation of the gods, so the Platonic theory of knowledge was challenged by others, most obviously by Aristotle. But such challenges do little to reduce the significance of Pheidian or Platonic

[19] This is closely linked to the appropriation of the idea of *theōria* to refer to the rational 'vision' of metaphysical truths: see Nightingale (2004).

conceptions. The very existence of those conceptions is indicative that there was no expectation that knowledge – of the gods or of anything else – depended upon what could be experienced.

The gap between what could be seen and what might be otherwise known was not new in the classical period. Those lying tales in the *Odyssey*, for instance, feature prominently false identifications, which rely on its not being obvious whether a man is a Taphian or a Cretan or whatever. But the more that official categorisation of individuals came to be important, the more that rules about participation in the community were constructed to rest upon identities which were not written on the body, the more human life came to involve two parallel worlds. On the one hand, there was the world in which official identities were all that mattered, where status as a citizen, metic or *xenos*, as a Greek or non-Greek, as possessed or deprived (*atimos*) of civic rights, as pure or polluted, as falling into one census class or tax-liability group or another, determined possible roles in the state. On the other hand, there was the world in which potential behaviour was what had to be assessed, where what mattered was how a person was likely to interact with others of their own age and gender or of other ages and genders, where one wanted to know whether they were nice to know, either absolutely or in relation to a particular circumstance or opportunity. Commercial advantage, intelligence, craft skills as artist or doctor, athletic prowess, capacity for friendship and love – none of these things had anything to do with the identities which the city regulated or was interested in, but all had a fundamental bearing on what happened from day to day in individual interactions.[20]

The increasing gap between the world that could be observed written on the body and the divisions which were important for political purposes had profound effects on history. Arguably, indeed, it invented History. Relations that are conducted on the basis of the history written on the body are conducted in the present and demand no history. They give little scope for insistence on distinctions between the peoples of one state and another. Homer's vaunted panhellenism – the fact that his epic is not made up of episodes attached to or giving preference to one Greek state rather than another – is just one reflection of a world in which people's interest was mostly in the identities written on the body. Being able to read the body is important, and much can be made of men's inability to read the stories

---

[20] Although the city did mark some, at least, of these qualities with civic honours. On the cardinal virtues celebrated by the city's honorific decrees see Whitehead (1993); and cf. above p. 84 (Ch. 3, n. 67).

written on others' bodies. Semonides' famous poem in which men's wives are compared to animals is a good example of capital being made out of the way that individuals fail to read the visible signs.[21] But relations between Greek states had always required some knowledge that was not written on the body, and as relations within states came similarly to demand such knowledge history became increasingly significant.

Understanding the significance of who had done what to whom depended crucially on being able to put the individuals concerned into larger classes, classes whose identities were largely determined by their past. The long genealogies that mark Hesiod's *Theogony* and *Catalogue of Women* served to tie together the gods, on the one hand, and the heroes, on the other, but in ways that were very largely bland and carried little significance, simply disposing of figures into past generations. A world where belonging to a particular state or class mattered did not need genealogies but accounts which set out the particular claims that had been made by that state or class.

History, known to us first through the extant works of Herodotos and Thucydides, and even in antiquity effectively shaped by them, provided the stories not written upon the body upon which civic identities rested. Herodotos' fundamental concern, and the reason why his history of the Persian Wars turns to narrative only in its second half, was to distinguish Greek and Persian worlds, to distinguish precisely that which fifth-century Greek states wanted to declare of fundamental importance but which was not written on the body. Thucydides' variously detailed narrative of the events which led up to the long war between Athens and Sparta was similarly concerned to clarify a history that was precisely not visible on any physical inspection of those involved. Patterns of enmity and alliance were dependent on the stories told about past events. Events of the past were tied in to the patterns of current events: just as the cities of the fifth-century Greek world were tied in to patterns of alliance, so all Greek cities were made from their foundation to be linked into networks. Those networks were the product of a fiction that the foundation of every city could be traced to a state decision to send out a chosen body of its own men to found a new community in the image of their 'mother city'. Stories were therefore told in which the settlers were chosen according to their state of origin, or their membership of particular state subgroups, in a carefully planned act; the truth was that most settlements arose because miscellaneous individuals, 'the scum of all the Hellenes', thought that they saw an opportunity to better their lives by

---

[21] R. Osborne (2001a).

moving to greener pastures.[22] More or less random opportunism was not good to think with: political use of the past demands that the past features planning and conspiracy, not impulsive actions and cock-up.

It is well documented that oral histories serve a purpose, and that oral histories change over time as different needs arise.[23] But Herodotos' and Thucydides' histories were written with a purpose too, and though we might debate precisely what that purpose was, namely what lay behind Herodotos' concern that the great deeds of Greeks and Persians should not become blotted out by time, there is no doubt that the purpose of both historians was political. Not only did Herodotos and Thucydides establish political history as what history was, they also established that history worked with and in terms of political categories. The history written on the body was largely irrelevant to their enterprises;[24] that history could and should be written without bodily knowledge has been assumed ever since.

This book has been concerned with the consequences of historical writing taking the history written in texts to be the only history there is. I have tried to point out the ways in which the history written in texts is no guide to the history that was lived and experienced, to the ways in which those texts construct a world in which it is impossible that anyone lived. Athenian chauvinism and the Athenian citizen club need to be put into the context of a city in which the only people with whom one came into daily contact whom one could place inside or outside the supposedly charmed circle of citizens were those about whom one already knew more than could be judged by appearances. By the classical period, the Athenian community had long ceased to be such a community whose members all knew each other's history in that way. What Athenians said, and what Athenians were able to do, were two different things. To write their history on the basis of what they said is to write the history of a fantasy. The community that comes across as so status-conscious in its writings could not in fact make status a determinant of daily behaviour. Whether we are dealing with citizen exclusiveness, slaves being treated as mere tools, pollution being used as a means of exclusion, or gods being left out of everyday actions, the Athenians

---

[22] I make the case against the 'colonial' model of Greek settlement abroad in R. Osborne (1998b); cf. R. Osborne (2008b), (2009). For the phrase, Archilochos fr. 102.

[23] The classic text is Vansina (1985). Cf. also Tonkin (1992). I discuss this further in R. Osborne (2009).

[24] This is a shameless simplification, of course. The whole structure of Herodotos' *Histories*, and in particular his decision to conclude with successive stories of the crucifixion of Artayktes, the mutilation of the wife of Masistes and the effect of soft lands upon the body, reveals his own desire to insist that the body should not be reduced simply to a cipher in a story of diplomacy.

were in no position to act in the ways that their own discourse prescribed. Life in Athens was neither life as described in the Athenian courtroom nor life as described in the Athenian assembly. What men said that they did and what men in fact did were necessarily two different things.

Once we are aware of the gap between verbal prescription and visual enactment we can see that the Athenians were less exclusive than they claimed to be. But it is also the case that the same gap between the visible and the verbalised gave scope for still more arbitrary discrimination. When the qualities which are held to oblige the different treatment of particular individuals and groups are not visible, this actually increases the scope for indiscriminate victimisation. Those who operate on the basis that what you see is what you get are in a position silently to apply prejudices that attach to visible features. I have argued in Chapter 2 that the ideal classical body was not thought of as a muscular body developed in the gymnasium, but that does not mean that the type of the classical body was not an instrument of discrimination. Perhaps the best demonstration of this is the peculiar development, institutionalised when comedy became part of the festival of the City Dionysia in 486, of the specifically comic body (8.1).

All Greek actors were men and all Greek actors wore masks. But whereas actors in tragedy wore individualised character costumes over their own natural body, comic actors wore their costumes over a comic body, constructed from a body stocking, padded buttocks, padded breasts, and, for male characters, an excessive phallus. Comic actors, unlike actors in tragedy, notoriously refer frequently to the fact that they are actors, breaking the dramatic illusion, but they do not make any reference to their comic body.[25] Comic actors' bodies are indeed described by other actors, but the terms of the description are independent of the actual appearance of the body – there is no reason to think that actors alleged to be thin had no padding or those alleged to be fat had extra padding. There were scenes in comedy when the audience's knowledge that the body they saw was made up of padding, not human flesh, made a big difference to how they reacted to what they saw happening. One example of this is when the comic body is beaten. So in Aristophanes' *Frogs* 'Dionysos' and 'Xanthias' are beaten on their padding by Aiakos, who is trying to discover which of them is a god by discovering which one feels pain. Here the fact that the blows, in both cases, fall upon padding is part of what complicates the humour. But neither in this case nor in any other do the actors themselves draw attention to their comic bodies.

---

[25] On tragedy and comedy see Taplin (1986); on the comic body see Foley (2000), Piqueux (2006).

8.1 Terracotta statuette of a comic actor, fourth century BC.

The comic body is all things that the individual Greek, whatever his or her social background, hoped his body was not. It is fat, presents men and women indifferently as to their breasts, and, in the case of men, has outsize genitalia. So grotesque is the comic body that there is little doubt that it was comic in itself: no Greek could be taken seriously whose body looked like that. It is as if everyone in comedy was a Thersites, who bears upon his body the signs of the moral and intellectual degradation that he displays in his disorderly speech.[26] But the comic body is shared by all comic characters; it instantiates the gap between what can be seen and what can be revealed by discourse and action. The result is visually to undermine every verbal claim that is made: given what we can *see* to be true of these characters, how can we believe what they say or is said about them? The gap between the body and the discourse raises the question of whether we should believe the evidence of our eyes or of our ears. Precisely by imagining the whole range of human interaction, virtuous and vicious, taking place between bodies

26 *Iliad* 2.212–19.

that are uniformly ugly, comedy calls into question what we should take to be 'real' in our everyday encounters: can we be so confident that we can 'read' other people's bodies?

The history written on the classical Greek body is not a better history than the history that is written from classical Greek texts. But it is a different history. In the face of historical narratives dominated by politics, of political history dominated by changing institutional rules, and of social and economic histories dominated by laws and legal status, the history written on the classical Greek body is a history that puts lived experience in the foreground. It acknowledges that there is a gap between the world described in verbal discourse and the world perceived by the eyes. Only the deaf and dumb in antiquity will have had to rely on their eyes alone (supplemented no doubt by the nose) and have been innocent of verbal discourse. But all had to live in a world where much of the evidence available at any one time was not encoded in texts but received as visual images.

I have endeavoured in this book to draw attention to some particular areas of life where the gap between the categories forged in verbal discourse and what can be observed in life is particularly marked. I have also attempted to reveal, through analysis of visual images, the themes that were particularly salient in the history written on the body. To understand human relations within the Greek city we need to take into account both what could not be seen and what vision concentrated upon. We need to discard not only claims that the Greeks were obsessed with athletics and the gymnasium, for which there is neither visual nor textual evidence, but also claims that the Athenians were obsessed with who was and was not in the citizen club and with patrolling its exclusions. Just what classical Greeks believed and the way in which they understood what was said to them depended not merely upon the words spoken but upon the appearance presented by the speaker or the object of discourse. We flatten the Greeks into naïve actors unless we take account of the way in which all actions and passions were shaped as much by the world experienced by the eyes as by the world experienced in verbal discourse. We need to give them back their bodies. 'I don't know if this is a happy ending but here we are let loose in open fields.'[27]

---

[27] Winterson (1992) 190.

References

Amelung, W. (1990) ʻΚοινὸν τῶν Σιδωνίων’, *Zeitschrift für Papyrologie und Epigraphik* 81: 189–99.

Annas, J. (1999) *Platonic Ethics Old and New*. Ithaca.

Arnaoutoglou, I. (1998) *Ancient Greek Laws*. London.

Ashmole, B. (1951) ʻDemeter of Cnidus’, *Journal of Hellenic Studies* 71: 13–28.
  (1972) *Architect and Sculptor in Classical Greece*. London.

Austin, M. M. (2006) *The Hellenistic World from Alexander to the Roman Conquest*. 2nd edn. Cambridge.

Bäbler, B. (1998) *Fleissige Thrakerinnen und wehrhafte Skythen: Nichtgriechen im klassischen Athen und ihre archäologische Hinterlassenschaft*. Stuttgart.

Bäbler B. (2005) ʻBobbies or boobies? The Scythian police force in classical Athens’, in Braund (ed.), 114–22.

Barringer, J. M. (2004) ʻSkythian hunters on Athenian vases’, in Marconi (ed.), 13–25.

Baxandall, M. (1972) *Painting and Experience in Fifteenth Century Italy; a Primer in the Social History of Pictorial Style*. Oxford.

Beard, M. (1985) ʻReflections on "Reflections on the Greek revolution"’, *Archaeological Review from Cambridge* 4(2): 207–14.

Beattie A. J. (1947) ʻNotes on an archaic Arcadian inscription concerning Demether Thesmophoros’, *Classical Quarterly* 41: 66–72.

Beazley, J. D. (1911) ʻThe master of the Berlin Amphora’, *Journal of Hellenic Studies* 31: 276–95.
  (1922) ʻCitharoedus’, *Journal of Hellenic Studies* 42: 70–98.

Beiner, R. (ed.) (1995) *Theorizing Citizenship*. New York.

Bendlin, A. (2007) ʻPurity and pollution’, in D. Ogden (ed.), *A Companion to Greek Religion*. Oxford. 178–89.

Bérard, C. (2000) ʻThe image of the Other and the foreign hero’, in B. Cohen (ed.), 390–412 (Eng. trans. of C. Bérard, ʻL'image de l'Autre et le héros étranger’, *Sciences et Racisme* 67 (1985–6) 5–22).

Bérard, C., Bron, C. and Durand, J.-L. *et al.* (1984) *La cité des images. Religion et société en Grèce antique*. Lausanne; Eng. trans. *The City of Images*. Princeton, 1989.

Bergemann, J. (1997) *Demos und Thanatos: Untersuchungen zum Wertsystem der Polis im Spiegel der attischen Grabreliefs des 4. Jahrhunderts v. Chr. und zur Funktion der gleichzeitigen Grabbauten*. Munich.

Berger, J. (1972) *Ways of Seeing*. London.

Best, J. G. P. (1969) *Thracian Peltasts and their Influence on Greek Warfare*. Groningen.

Betz, H. D. (2004) 'God concept and cultic image: the argument in Dio Chrysostom's *Oratio 12 (Olympikos)*', in N. Marinatos (ed.), *Divine Epiphany in the Ancient World* (Special edition of *Illinois Classical Studies* 29). 131–42.

Bianchi Bandinelli, R. (1967) 'Arte Plebeia', *Dialoghi di Archeologia* 1: 7–19.

Bloesch, H. (1943) *Antike Kunst in der Schweiz*. Erlangbach-Zurich.

Blok, J. (2005) 'Becoming citizens. Some notes on the semantics of "citizen" in archaic Greece and classical Athens', *Klio* 87: 7–40.

Boardman, J. (1967) *Excavations in Chios, 1952–1955: Greek Emporio*. London.

Bober, P. P. and Rubinstein, R. (1986) *Renaissance Artists and Antique Sculpture*. Oxford.

Borbein, A. H. (1999) 'Polykleitos', in Palagia and Pollitt (eds.), 66–90.

Bourdieu, P. (1984) *Distinction: a Social Critique of the Judgement of Taste*. London.

Braund, D. C. (ed.) (2005) *Scythians and Greeks: Cultural Interactions in Scythia, Athens and the Early Roman Empire (sixth century BC – first century AD)*. Exeter.

Bremmer, J. N. (1991) 'Walking, standing, and sitting in ancient Greek culture', in J. Bremmer and H. Rodenburg (eds.), *A Cultural History of Gesture. From Antiquity to the Present Day*. Cambridge. 15–35.

  (1994) *Greek Religion* (Greece and Rome New Surveys in the Classics). Oxford.

Brock, R. (2000) 'Sickness in the body politic: medical imagery in the Greek polis', in Hope and Marshall (eds.), 24–34.

  (2006) 'The body as a political organism in Greek thought', in Prost and Wilgaux (eds.), 351–60.

  (2009) 'Citizens and non-citizens in Athenian tragedy', in D. F. Leao, E. M. Harris and P. J. Rhodes (eds.), *Law and Drama in Athens*. London. 94–107.

Bryson, N. and Bal, M. (1991) 'Semiotics and art history', *Art Bulletin* 73: 174–208.

Buck, C. D. (1955) *The Greek Dialects: Grammar, Selected Inscriptions, Glossary*. Chicago.

Buitron-Oliver, D. (1995) *Douris: a Master-painter of Athenian Red-figure Vases*. Mainz.

Burke, P. (2001) *Eyewitnessing: the Uses of Images as Historical Evidence*. London.

Butler, J. (1990) *Gender Trouble: Feminism and the Subversion of Identity*. London.

Cairns, D. (1993) Aidos. *The Psychology and Ethics of Honour and Shame in Ancient Greek Literature*. Oxford.

  (ed.) (2005) *Body Language in the Greek and Roman Worlds*. London.

Carey, C. (2004) 'Offence and procedure in Athenian law', in Harris and Rubinstein (eds.), 111–36.

Carpenter, T. H. (1991) *Art and Myth in Ancient Greece*. London.

Carpenter, T. H. and Faraone, C. A. (eds.) (1993) *Masks of Dionysus*. Ithaca.

Carter, J. B. (1984) *Greek Ivory-carving in the Orientalizing and Archaic Periods.* Ann Arbor.

(1987) 'The masks of Ortheia', *American Journal of Archaeology* 91: 355–83.

Cartledge, P. A. (1993) *The Greeks: a Portrait of Self and Others.* Oxford.

(2001) *Spartan Reflections.* London.

Cartledge, P. A., Millett, P. C. and Todd, S. C. (eds.) (1990) *Nomos: Essays in Athenian Law, Politics and Society.* Cambridge.

Caskey, L. D. and Beazley J. (1954) *Attic Vase Paintings in the Museum of Fine Arts, Boston, Part 2.* Oxford.

Certeau, M. de (1988) *The Writing of History.* New York.

Cesare, M. de (1997) *Le statue in imagine: studi sulle raffigurazioni di statue nella pittura vascolare greca.* Rome.

Christ, M. R. (1992) 'Ostracism, sycophancy, and the deception of the demos: [Arist.] *Ath. Pol.* 43.5', *Classical Quarterly* n.s. 42: 336–46.

(2006) *The Bad Citizen in Classical Athens.* Cambridge.

Cixous, H. (1997[1986]) 'Sorties', in S. Kemp and J. Squires (eds.), *Feminisms.* Oxford. 231–5; reprinted from H. Cixous and C. Clément (eds.), *The Newly Born Woman.* Manchester, 1986.

Clairmont, C. W. (1970) *Gravestone and Epigram: Greek Memorials from the Archaic and Classical Period.* Mainz.

Clark, K. (1956) *The Nude. A Study of Ideal Art.* London.

Clarke, John R. (2003) *Art in the Lives of Ordinary Romans: Visual Representation and Non-elite Viewers in Italy, 100 BC – AD 315.* Berkeley.

Cohen, B. (ed.) (2000) *Not the Classical Ideal. Athens and the Construction of the Other in Great Art.* Leiden.

Cohen, E. E. (ed.) (2000) *The Athenian Nation.* Princeton.

Connelly, J. B. (2007) *Portrait of a Priestess: Women and Ritual in Ancient Greece.* Princeton.

Connor, W. R. (1994) 'The problem of Athenian civic identity', in A. Boegehold and A. Scafuro (eds.), *Athenian Identity and Civic Ideology.* Baltimore. 34–44.

Cooper, J. (1990) 'Political animals and civic friendship' in G. Patzig (ed.), *Aristoteles' 'Politik': Akten des XI. Symposium Aristotelicum.* Göttingen. 220–4.

Corso, A. (2007) *The Art of Praxiteles*, vol. II: *The Mature Years.* Rome.

Coulton, J. J. (1984) 'The Parthenon and Periklean Doric', in E. Berger (ed.), *Parthenon-Kongreß Basel.* 2 vols. Mainz. 40–4, 368–9.

Craik, E. M. (1998) *Hippocrates: Places in Man. Greek Text and Translation with Introduction and Commentary.* Oxford.

Crick, B. (2000) *Essays on Citizenship.* London.

Crowe, D. M. (2004) *Oskar Schindler: the Untold Account of his Life, Wartime Activities, and the True Story behind the List.* Philadelphia.

Daehner, J. (2005) 'Grenzen der Nacktheit', *Jahrbuch des Deutschen Archäologischen Instituts* 120: 155–300.

Davidson, J. (2006) 'Revolutions in human time. Age-class in Athens and the Greek-ness of Greek revolutions', in S. Goldhill and R. Osborne (eds.), *Rethinking Revolutions through Ancient Greece*. Cambridge. 29–67.

(2007) *The Greeks and Greek Love*. London.

Dawkins, R. M. (ed.) (1929) *The Sanctuary of Artemis Orthia at Sparta*. London.

Dawson, D. (1992) *Cities of the Gods: Communist Utopias in Greek Thought*. New York.

Demand, N. (1994) *Birth, Death and Motherhood in Classical Greece*. Baltimore.

Despret, V. (1999) *Ces émotions que nous fabriquent. Ethnopsychologie de l'authenticité*. Paris.

deVries, K. (2000) 'The nearly other: the Attic vision of Phrygians and Lydians', in B. Cohen (ed.), 338–63.

Diggle, J. (2004) *Theophrastus*: Characters. *Edited with Introduction, Translation and Commentary* (Cambridge Classical Texts and Commentaries 43). Cambridge.

Diller, A. (1937) *Race Mixture among the Greeks before Alexander*. Urbana.

Dillon, S. (2006) *Ancient Greek Portrait Sculpture: Contexts, Subjects, and Styles*. Cambridge.

Doepner, D. (2002) *Steine und Pfeiler für die Götter. Weihgeschenkgattungen in westgriechischen Stadtheiligtümern*. Wiesbaden.

Donohue, A. A. (1988) Xoana *and the Origins of Greek Sculpture*. Atlanta.

(1997) 'Greek images of the gods', *Hephaistos* 15: 31–45.

Dougherty, C. and Kurke, L. (eds.) (1993) *Cultural Poetics in Archaic Greece*. Cambridge.

Douglas, M. (1966) *Purity and Danger: an Analysis of Concepts of Pollution and Taboo*. London.

(1975) *Implicit Meanings: Essays in Anthropology*. London.

(1993) *In the Wilderness: the Doctrine of Defilement in the Book of Numbers* (Journal of the Study of the Old Testament, Suppl. Series 158). Sheffield.

Dubois, L (1988) *Recherches sur le dialecte arcadien*. 3 vols. Louvain.

Dyck, A. R. (1996) *A Commentary on Cicero*, De officiis. Ann Arbor.

Dyer, G. (2005) *The Ongoing Moment*. London.

Edwards, C. (1999) 'Lysippus', in Palagia and Pollitt (eds.), 130–53.

Elsner, J. R. (ed.) (1996) *Art and Text in Roman Culture*. Cambridge.

(2006) 'Reflections on the "Greek Revolution" in art: from changes in viewing to the transformation of subjectivity', in S. Goldhill and R. Osborne (eds.), *Rethinking Revolutions through Ancient Greece*. Cambridge. 68–95.

(2007) *Roman Eyes: Visuality and Subjectivity in Art and Text*. Princeton.

Faraone, C. (1992) *Talismans and Trojan Horses*. Oxford.

Ferrari, G. P. (1986) 'Money bags', *American Journal of Archaeology* 90: 218.

(2002) *Figures of Speech: Men and Maidens in Ancient Greece*. Chicago.

Ferrari, G. R. F. (2003) *City and Soul in Plato's* Republic. Sankt Augustin. (Reprinted Chicago, 2005.)

Finley, M. I. (1973) *Democracy Ancient and Modern*. London.

Fisher, N. R. E. (1998) 'World and leisure', in P. A. Cartledge (ed.), *The Cambridge Illustrated History of Ancient Greece*. Cambridge. 193–218.

Fittschen, K. (2001) 'Zur Mantelstatue aus dem Heraion von Samos,' in D. Pandermalis, M. Tiverios and E. Voutiras (eds.), *Agalma: meletes gia ten archaia plastike pros timen tou Giorgou Despine*. Thessaloniki. 325–32.

Fitzhardinge, L. F. (1980) *The Spartans*. London.

Flower, M. A. and Marincola, J. (2002) *Herodotus Histories Book 9*. Cambridge.

Foley, H. (2000) 'The comic body in Greek art and drama', in B. Cohen (ed.), 275–311.

Foucault, M. (2002[1970]) *The Order of Things*. 2nd edn. London (Eng. trans. of *Les mots et les choses*. Paris, 1966).

Frontisi-Ducroux, F. and Lissarrague, F. (1983) 'De l'ambiguité à l'ambivalence sous le signe de Dionysos', *Annalie del Seminario di Studi del Mondo Classico, Archeologia e Storia Antica* 5: 11–32; Eng. trans. 'From ambiguity to ambivalence: a Dionysiac excursion through the "Anakreontic" vases', in Halperin, Winkler and Zeitlin (eds.), 211–56.

Gadamer, H.-G. (1975) *Truth and Method*. 2nd edn. London.

Gaifman, M. (2005) 'Beyond mimesis in Greek religious art: aniconism in the archaic and classical periods.' PhD dissertation, Princeton.

(2006) 'Statue, cult and reproduction', *Art History* 29.2: 258–79.

Graf, F. (2004) 'Trick or treat? On collective epiphanies in antiquity', in N. Marinatos (ed.), *Divine Epiphany in the Ancient World* (Special edition of *Illinois Classical Studies* 29). 111–30.

Garnsey, P. D. A. (1996) *Ideas of Slavery from Aristotle to Augustine*. Cambridge.

Gauthier, P. (1971) 'Les XENOI dans les texts athéniens de la seconde moitié du Ve siècle av. J.-C.', *Revue des Études Grecques* 84: 44–79.

Gauthier, P. (1985) *Les cités grecques et leurs bienfaiteurs*. Paris.

Gill, C., Postlethwaite, N. and Seaford R. (eds.) (1998) *Reciprocity in Ancient Greece*. Oxford.

Gillies, M. M. (1925) 'Purification in Homer', *Classical Quarterly* 19: 71–4.

Giuliani, L. (1986) *Bildnis und Botschaft: Hermeneutische Untersuchungen zur Bildniskunst der römischen Republik*. Frankfurt.

(2003) *Bild und Mythos: Geschichte der Bilderzählung in der griechischen Kunst*. Munich.

Given, M. J. (2004) *The Archaeology of the Colonized*. London.

Goldhill, S. D. (1986) *Reading Greek Tragedy*. Cambridge.

(1994) 'Representing democracy: women at the Great Dionysia', in R. Osborne and S. Hornblower (eds.), *Ritual, Finance, Politics: Athenian Democratic Accounts Presented to David Lewis*. Oxford. 347–69.

Goldhill, S. D. and Osborne, R. (eds.) (1994) *Art and Text in Ancient Greek Culture*. Cambridge.

Gombrich, E. (1960) *Art and Illusion*. London.

Goodman, N. (1969) *Languages of Art: an Approach to a Theory of Symbols*. Oxford.

Gordon, R. L. (1979) 'The real and the imaginary: production and religion in the Graeco-Roman World', *Art History* 2: 5–34; reprinted in Gordon (1996) as ch. 1.

(1980) 'Reality, evocation and boundary in the Mysteries of Mithras', *Journal of Mithraic Studies* 3: 19–99; reprinted in Gordon (1996) as ch. 5.

(1996) *Image and Value in the Graeco-Roman World*. Aldershot.

Gould, J. P. A. (1980) 'Law, custom and myth: aspects of the social position of women in Classical Athens', *Journal of Hellenic Studies* 100: 38–59; reprinted in J. P. A. Gould, *Myth, Ritual, Memory, and Exchange. Essays in Greek Literature and Culture*. Oxford, 2001. 112–57.

Grote, G. (1862) *History of Greece from the Earliest Times to the Close of the Generation Contemporary with Alexander the Great*. 8 vols. London.

Hainsworth, J. B. (1993) *The* Iliad: *a Commentary*, vol. III: *Books 9–12*. Cambridge.

Hall, E. M. (1989) *Inventing the Barbarian: Greek Self-definition through Tragedy*. Oxford.

Hall, J. M. (2002) *Hellenicity: between Ethnicity and Culture*. Chicago.

Hall, J. (2005) *Michelangelo and the Reinvention of the Human Body*. London.

Halperin, D. M., Winkler, J. J. and Zeitlin, F. I. (eds.) (1990) *Before Sexuality: the Construction of Erotic Experience in the Ancient Greek World*. Princeton.

Hansen, M. H. (1991) *The Athenian Democracy in the Age of Demosthenes*. Oxford.

(1997) 'The polis as an urban centre: the literary and epigraphical evidence', in M. H. Hansen (ed.), *The Polis as an Urban Centre and as a Political Community* (Acts of the Copenhagen Polis Centre 4). Copenhagen. 9–86.

Hansen, M. H. and Nielsen, T. H. (eds.) (2006) *An inventory of Ancient Greek City-States*. Oxford.

Harris, E. M. (2002) 'Workshop, marketplace and household: the nature of technical specialization in classical Athens and its influence on the economy', in P. Cartledge, E. E. Cohen and L. Foxhall (eds.), *Money, Labour and Land: Approaches to the Economies of Ancient Greece*. London. 67–99.

Harris, E. M. (2007) 'Who enforced the law in classical Athens?', in E. Cantarella (ed.), *Symposion 2005: Vorträge zur griechischen und hellenistischen Rechtsgeschichte (Salerno, 14–18 September 2005)*. Vienna. 159–76.

Harris, E. M. and Rubinstein, L. (eds.) (2004) *Law and the Courts in Ancient Greece*. London.

Harrison, E. B. (1984) 'Time in the Parthenon Frieze', in E. Berger (ed.), *Parthenon-Kongreß Basel*. 2 vols. Mainz. 230–4, 416–18.

Hartog, F. (1980) *Le miroir d'Hérodote: essai sur la représentation de l'autre*. Paris.

Harvey, D. (1990) 'The sykophant and sycophancy: vexatious redefinition?', in Cartledge, Millett and Todd (eds.), 103–22.

Haubold, J. (2000) *Homer's People. Epic Poetry and Social Formation*. Cambridge.

Hayes, M. (2002) 'Photography and the emergence of the Pacific cruise', in Hight and Sampson (eds.), 172–87.

Heinemann, A. (2000) 'Bilderspiele beim Gelage. Symposiast und Satyr im Athen des 5. Jahrhunderts v. Chr.', in T. Hölscher (ed.), *Gegenwelten zu den Kulturen Griechenlands und Roms in der Antike.* Leipzig. 321–49.

Hermary, A. (2006) 'Le corps colossal et la valeur hiérarchique des tailles dans la littérature et la sculpture grecques archaïques' in Prost and Wilgaux (eds.), 115–31.

Herzog, R. (1897) 'Namensübersetzungen und Verwandtes', *Philologus* 56: 33–70.

Heubeck, A. and Hoekstra, A. (1989) *A Commentary on Homer's* Odyssey, vol. II: *Books 9–16.* Oxford.

Hight, E. M. and Sampson, G. D. (eds.) (2002) *Colonialist Photography: Imag(in)ing Race and Place.* London.

Himmelmann, N. (1967) 'Erzählung und Figur in der archaischen Kunst', *Abhandlungen, Akademie der Wissenschaften und der Literatur, Mainz: Geistes und Sozialwissenschaftliche Klasse* 2. 73–101.

  (1971) *Archäologisches zum Problem der griechischen Sklaverei.* Mainz.

  (1994) *Realistische Themen in der Griechischen Kunst der archaischen und klassischen Zeit* (Jahrbuch des Deutschen Archäologischen Instituts 28. Ergänzungsheft). Berlin.

Hodkinson, S. (2000) *Property and Wealth in Classical Sparta.* London.

Hölkeskamp, K.-J. (1992) 'Written law in archaic Greece', *Proceedings of the Cambridge Philological Society* 38: 87–117.

  (1999) *Schiedsrichter, Gesetzgeber und Gesetzgebung im archaischen Griechenland.* Stuttgart.

Hollein, H.-G. (1988) *Bürgerbild und Bildwelt des attischen Demokratie auf den rotfigurigen Vasen des 6.–4. Jahrhunderts v. Chr.* Frankfurt.

Hope, V. M. and Marshall, E. (eds.) (2000) *Death and Disease in the Ancient City.* London.

Hornblower, S. (1987) *Thucydides.* London.

Hunter, V. (1994) *Policing Athens: Social Control in the Attic Lawsuits, 420–320 BC.* Princeton.

Ichilov O. (1998) 'Patterns of Citizenship in a Changing World', in O. Ichilov (ed.), *Citizenship and Citizenship Education in a Changing World.* London. 11–27.

Ignatieff, Michael (1995) 'The myth of citizenship' in Beiner (ed.), 53–77.

Ivanchik, A. I. (2005) 'Who were the "Scythian" archers on archaic Attic vases?', in Braund (ed.), 100–13.

Janoski, T. (1998) *Citizenship and Civil Society.* Cambridge.

Jay, M. (1993) *Downcast Eyes: the Denigration of Vision in Twentieth-century French Thought.* Berkeley.

Jenkins, I. D. (2007) *The Parthenon Sculptures in the British Museum.* London.

Jiménez, A. (2011) 'Pure hybridism. Late Iron Age sculpture in southern Iberia', *World Archaeology* 43: 102–23.

Johnson-Roehr, C. (2009) 'From visual data to fine art: photography collections at the Kinsey Institute', *Visual Resources* 25: 259–80.

Kampen, N. B. (1981) *Image and Status: Roman Working Women in Ostia.* Berlin.

Keesling, C. (2003) *The Votive Statues of the Athenian Acropolis.* Cambridge.

Kelly, J. (1977) 'Did women have a Renaissance?', in R. Bridenthal and C. Koonz (eds.), *Becoming Visible: Women in European History*, Boston. 137–64; reprinted in J. Kelly, *Women, History and Theory: the Essays of Joan Kelly.* Chicago, 1984. 19–51.

Keyt, D. (2005[1993]) 'Aristotle and Anarchism', in Kraut and Skultety (eds.), 203–22; reprinted from *Reason Papers* 18: 137–57.

Kirk, G. S. (1985) *The* Iliad: *a Commentary*, vol. I: *Books 1–4.* Cambridge.
    (1990) *The* Iliad: *a Commentary*, vol. II: *Books 5–8.* Cambridge.

Kraut, R. and Skultety S. (eds.) (2005) *Aristotle's Politics: Critical Essays.* Lanham.

Kroll, J. H. (1982) 'The ancient image of Athena Polias', in *Studies in Athenian Architecture, Sculpture, and Topography Presented to Homer A. Thompson (Hesperia Supplement 20).* Princeton. 65–76.

Krummeich (1999) *Das Griechische Satyrspiel.* Darmstadt.

Kunisch, N. (1997) *Makron (Kerameus 10).* Mainz.

Kuriyama, S. (1999) *The Expressiveness of the Body and the Divergence of Greek and Chinese Medicine.* New York.

Kurke, L. (1993) 'The Economy of *Kudos*', in Dougherty and Kurke (eds.), 131–63.

Kurtz, D. C. (1983) *The Berlin Painter.* Oxford.
    (1984) 'Vases for the dead, an Attic selection, 750–400 BC', in H. A. G. Brijder (ed.), *Ancient Greek and Related Pottery.* Amsterdam. 314–28.

Kurtz, D. C. and Boardman, J. (1986) 'Booners', *Greek Vases in the J. Paul Getty Museum* 3: 35–70.

Kyle, D. G. (1987) *Athletics in Ancient Athens.* Leiden.

Lambert, S. D. (1993) *The Phratries of Attica.* Ann Arbor.

Lane Fox, R. (1996) 'Theophrastus and the historian', *Proceedings of the Cambridge Philological Society* n.s. 42: 127–70.

Lapatin, K. (2001) *Chryselephantine Statuary in the Ancient Mediterranean World.* Oxford.

Laqueur, T. (1990) *Making Sex: Body and Gender from the Greeks to Freud.* Cambridge, MA.

Laslett, P. (1956) 'The face to face society', in P. Laslett (ed.), *Philosophy, Politics and Society: First Series.* Oxford. 157–84.

Latour, B. (2002) 'Body, cyborgs and the politics of incarnation' in I. Hodder and S. Sweeney (eds.), *The Body.* Cambridge. 127–41.

Layton-Henry, Z. (2001) 'Patterns of privilege: citizenship rights in Britain', in A. Kondo (ed.), *Citizenship in a Global World. Comparing Citizenship Rights for Aliens.* Basingstoke. 116–35.

Leftwich, G. (1995) 'Polykleitos and Hippokratic Medicine', in W. G. Moon (ed.), *Polykleitos, the Doryphoros, and Tradition.* Madison. 38–51.

Leipen, N. (1971) *Athena Parthenos.* Toronto.

Lévy, E. (1985) '*Astos* et *polites* d'Homère à Aristote', *Ktema* 10: 53–66.

Lewis, D. M. (1959) 'Attic Manumissions', *Hesperia* 28: 208–38.

Lewis, S. (2002) *The Athenian Woman: an Iconographic Handbook.* London.

Lissarrague, F. (1987) *Un flot d'images: une esthétique du banquet grec.* Paris; Eng. trans. *The Aesthetics of the Greek Banquet.* Princeton, 1990.

(1990) *L'autre guerrier. Archers, cavaliers, peltastes.* Paris.

(1993) 'On the wildness of satyrs', in Carpenter and Faraone (eds.), 207–20.

(1999) *Vases grecs: les Athéniens et leurs images.* Paris; Eng. trans. *Greek Vases: the Athenians and their Images.* New York, 2001.

Llewellyn-Jones, L. (2002) 'A woman's view? Dress, eroticism and the ideal female body in Athenian art', in L. Llewellyn-Jones (ed.), *Women's Dress in the Ancient Greek World.* Swansea. 171–202.

(2003) *Aphrodite's Tortoise. The Veiled Woman of Ancient Greece.* Swansea.

Lloyd, G. E. R. (1966) *Polarity and Analogy: Two Types of Argumentation in Early Greek Thought.* Cambridge.

Loraux, N. (1981a) *Les enfants d'Athena.* Paris; Eng. trans. *The Children of Athena: Athenian Ideas about Citizenship and the Division between the Sexes.* Princeton, 1993.

(1981b) *L'invention d'Athènes: histoire de l'oraison funèbre dans la 'cité classique'.* Paris; Eng. trans. *The Invention of Athens: the Funeral Oration in the Classical City.* Cambridge, MA, 1986.

(1981c) 'Le lit, la guerre', *L'Homme* 21.1: 37–67; reprinted in N. Loraux, *Les expériences de Tirésias: le féminin et l'homme grec.* Paris, 1989 and Eng. trans. *The Experiences of Tiresias: the Feminine and the Greek Man.* Princeton, 1995, as ch. 1.

Low, P. (2006) 'Commemorating the Spartan war dead', in S. Hodkinson and A. Powell (eds.), *Sparta and War.* Swansea. 85–109.

Lupu, E. (2005) *Greek Sacred Law. A Collection of New Documents.* Leiden.

Mackie, V. (2000) 'The Metropolitan Gaze: Travellers, Bodies and Spaces', *Intersections: Gender, History and Culture in the Asian Context* 4: http://intersections.anu.edu.au/default.htm.

Männlein-Robert, I. (2007) *Stimme, Schrift und Bild: Zum Verhältnis der Künste in der hellenistischen Dichtkunst.* Heidelberg.

Marconi, C. (ed.) (2004) *Greek Vases: Images, Contexts and Controversies.* Leiden.

Marr, J. L. and Rhodes, P. J. (2008) *The 'Old Oligarch': The Constitution of the Athenians Attributed to Xenophon; Edited with an Introduction, Translation and Commentary.* Oxford.

Marrou, H.-I. (1954) *De la connaissance historique.* Paris.

Meier, C. (1990) *The Greek Discovery of Politics.* Harvard.

Métraux, G. P. R. (1995) *Sculptors and Physicians in Fifth-century Greece. A Prelim-inary Study*. Montreal.

Meyer, M. (1988) 'Männer mit Geld', *Jahrbuch des deutschen archäologischen Instituts* 103: 87–125.

Michaelis, A. (1871) *Der Parthenon*. Leipzig.

Miller, M. C. (1991) 'Foreigners at the Greek symposium?', in W. J. Slater (ed.), *Dining in a Classical Context*. Ann Arbor. 59–82.

   (1992) 'The parasol: an oriental status-symbol in late archaic and classical Athens', *Journal of Hellenic Studies* 112: 91–105.

   (1997) *Athens and Persia in the Fifth Century BC: a Study in Cultural Receptivity*. Cambridge.

   (2000) 'The myth of Bousiris: ethnicity and art', in B. Cohen (ed.), 413–42.

Millett, P. C. (2007a) *Theophrastus and his World* (*Proceedings of the Cambridge Philological Society* Suppl. Volume 33). Cambridge.

   (2007b) 'Aristotle and Slavery in Athens', *Greece and Rome* 54: 178–209.

Mitchell, T. J. (1988) *Colonising Egypt*. Cambridge.

Mitchell, W. J. T. (1986) *Iconology: Image, Text, Ideology*. Chicago.

   (1994) *Picture Theory*. Chicago.

Morgan, T. J. (2005) 'The Wisdom of Semonides Fr. 7', *Cambridge Classical Journal* 51: 72–85.

Morris, I. M. (2000) *Archaeology as Cultural History: Words and Things in Iron Age Greece*. Oxford.

Mulvey, L. (1973) 'Fears, fantasies and the male unconscious or "You don't know what is happening Mr Jones?"', *Spare Rib*; reprinted in L. Mulvey, *Visual and Other Pleasures*. Bloomington, 1989: 6–13.

Mylonas, G. (1957) Ὁ Πρωτοαττικός ἀμφορεὺς τῆς Ἐλευσῖνος. Athens.

Naficy, H. (1999) 'Veiled visions, powerful presences', in R. Issa and S. Whitaker (eds.), *Life and Art: the New Iranian Cinema*. London. 44–66.

Napier, A. D. (1986) *Masks, Transformation, and Paradox*. Berkeley.

Neer, R. T. (2002) *Style and Politics in Athenian Vase-painting: the Craft of Democracy, ca. 530–460 BCE*. Cambridge.

Nehamas, A. (2007) *Only a Promise of Happiness: the Place of Beauty in a World of Art*. Princeton.

Neils, J. (1980) 'The group of the Negro alabastra: a study in motif transferal', *Antike Kunst* 23: 13–23.

   (ed.) (1992) *Goddess and Polis: the Panathenaic Festival in Ancient Athens*. Princeton.

Newman, W. (1887–1902) *The* Politics *of Aristotle with an Introduction, Two Prefatory Essays and Notes Critical and Explanatory*. 4 vols. Oxford.

Nick, G. (2002) *Die Athena Parthenos: Studien zum griechischen Kultbild und seiner Rezeption* (Mitteilungen des Deutschen Archäologischen Instituts Athenische Abteilung 19). Mainz.

Nicolet, C. (1980) *The World of the Citizen in Republican Rome*, trans. P. Falla. London.

Nightingale, A. W. (2004) *Spectacles of Truth in Classical Greek Philosophy:* Theoria *in its Cultural Context.* Cambridge.

Nussbaum, M. C. (2004) *Hiding from Humanity: Disgust, Shame, and the Law.* Princeton.

Oakley, J. H. (2000) 'Some "other" members of the Athenian household: maids and their mistresses in fifth-century Athenian art', in B. Cohen (ed.), 227–47.

(2004) *Picturing Death in Classical Athens: the Evidence of the White Lekythoi.* Cambridge.

Ober, J. (1989) *Mass and Elite in Democratic Athens.* Princeton.

Ogden, D. (2002) 'Controlling women's dress: gynaikonomoi', in L. Llewellyn-Jones (ed.), *Women's Dress in the Ancient Greek World*. London. 203–25.

Oliver, G. J. (2000) 'Athenian funerary monuments: style, grandeur and cost', in G. J. Oliver (ed.), *The Epigraphy of Death: Studies in the History and Society of Greece and Rome.* Liverpool. 59–80.

Ollier, F. (1933–43) *Le mirage spartiate: étude sur l'idéalisation de Sparte dans l'antiquité grecque.* 2 vols. Paris.

Osborne, C. (1987) 'The repudiation of representation in Plato's *Republic* and its repercussions', *Proceedings of the Cambridge Philological Society* 33: 53–73.

Osborne, R. (1985a) Demos: *the Discovery of Classical Attika.* Cambridge.

(1985b) 'Law in action in classical Athens', *Journal of Hellenic Studies* 105: 40–58; reprinted with endnote in R. Osborne (2010a).

(1987) 'The viewing and obscuring of the Parthenon frieze', *Journal of Hellenic Studies* 107: 98–105; reprinted with endnote in R. Osborne (2010a).

(1990a) 'The Demos and its divisions in classical Athens' in O. Murray and S. R. F. Price (ed.), *The Greek City from Homer to Alexander.* Oxford. 265–93; reprinted with endnote in R. Osborne (2010a).

(1990b) 'Vexatious litigation in classical Athens: sycophancy and the sykophant', in Cartledge, Millett and Todd (eds.), 83–102; reprinted with endnote in R. Osborne (2010a).

(1991) 'The potential mobility of human populations', *Oxford Journal of Archaeology* 10: 231–52; reprinted with endnote in R. Osborne (2010a).

(1994) 'Looking on Greek style. Does the sculpted girl speak to women too?', in I. M. Morris (ed.), *Classical Greece: Ancient Histories and Modern Archaeologies.* Cambridge. 81–96.

(1996/7) 'Funerary monuments, the democratic citizen and the representation of women', in M. B. Sakellariou (ed.), *Démocratie athénienne et culture.* (Athens, 1996), 229–42; revised and enlarged version published as 'Law, the democratic citizen and the representation of women in classical Athens', *Past and Present* 155 (1997), 3–33; reprinted in R. Osborne (ed.), *Studies in Ancient Greek and Roman Society* (Past and Present Series). (Cambridge, 2004), 38–60 and, with endnote, in R. Osborne (2010a).

(1997a) 'Law and laws: how do we join up the dots?', in L. G. Mitchell and P. J. Rhodes (eds.), *The Development of the Polis in Archaic Greece*. London. 74–82.

(1997b) 'Men without clothes: heroic nakedness and Greek art', *Gender and History* 9.3: 504–28.

(1997c) 'The Spartan Exception', *Caeculus* 3: *Debating Dark Ages*. 19–24.

(1998a) *Archaic and Classical Greek Art*. Oxford.

(1998b) 'Early Greek colonisation? The nature of Greek settlement in the West', in N. Fisher and H. van Wees (eds.), *Archaic Greece: New Approaches and New Evidence*. London. 251–70.

(1998c) 'Sculpted men of Athens: masculinity and power in the field of vision', in L. Foxhall and J. Salmon (eds.), *Thinking Men. Masculinity and its Self Representation in the Classical Tradition*. London. 23–42.

(1999) 'Inscribing Performance', in S. Goldhill and R. Osborne (eds.), *Performance Culture and Athenian Democracy*. Cambridge. 341–58.

(2000a) 'An other view: an essay in political history', in B. Cohen (ed.), 21–42.

(2000b) 'Archaic and classical Greek temple sculpture and the viewer', in B. A. Sparkes and K. Rutter (eds.), *Word and Image*. Edinburgh. 228–46.

(2001a) 'The use of abuse', *Proceedings of the Cambridge Philological Society* 47: 47–64.

(2001b) 'Why did Athenian pots appeal to the Etruscans?', *World Archaeology* 33.2: 277–95.

(2003) Review of E. E. Cohen (2000) in *Classical Philology* 97: 93–8.

(2004a) *The Old Oligarch. Pseudo-Xenophon's* Constitution of the Athenians. LACTOR 2. London.

(2004b) 'Images of a warrior: On a group of Athenian vases and their public', in Marconi (ed.), 41–54.

(2005) 'Monumentality and ritual in archaic Greece', in D. Yatromanolakis and P. Roilos (eds.), *Ritual Poetics* (Center for Hellenic Studies). Washington. 37–55.

(2006) 'Roman poverty in context', in M. Atkins and R. Osborne (eds.), *Poverty in the Roman World*. Cambridge. 1–20.

(ed.) (2008a) *The World of Athens*. Cambridge.

(2008b) 'Colonial cancer', *Journal of Mediterranean Archaeology* 21: 281–4.

(2008c) 'For tradition as an analytic category', *World Archaeology* 40: 281–94.

(2008d) 'Idealism, the body and the beard in classical Greek art', in D. Borić and J. Robb (eds.), *Past Bodies: Body-centred Research in Archaeology*. Oxford. 29–36.

(2009) *Greece in the Making, 1200–479 BC*. 2nd edn. London.

(2010a) *Athens and Athenian Democracy*. Cambridge.

(2010b) 'Democratic ideology, the events of war and the iconography of Attic funerary sculpture', in D. Pritchard (ed.), *War and Democracy in Classical Greece*. 245–65.

(forthcoming) 'Cultures as languages and languages as cultures', in A. Mullen and P. James (eds.), *Multilingualism in the Greco-Roman Worlds.* Cambridge.

Osborne, R. and Alcock S. E. (2007) 'Introduction', in S. E. Alcock and R. Osborne (eds.), *Classical Archaeology.* Oxford. 1–10.

Palagia, O. and Pollitt, J. J. (eds.) (1999) *Personal Styles in Greek Sculpture* (Yale Classical Studies 30). Cambridge.

Parker, R. C. T. (1983) Miasma: *Pollution and Purification in Early Greek Religion.* Oxford.

(2004) 'What are sacred laws?', in Harris and Rubinstein (eds.), 57–70.

Pellegrini, A. (1997) *Performance Anxieties: Staging Psychoanalysis, Staging Race.* London.

Petersen, L. H. (2006) *The Freedman in Roman Art and Art History.* Cambridge.

Pipili, M. (2000) 'Wearing an other hat: workmen in town and country', in E. E. Cohen (ed.), 153–79.

Piqueux A. (2006) 'Rembourrages et image du corps dans la comédie ancienne et moyenne: témoignages archéologiques et textes comiques', in Prost and Wilgaux (eds.), 133–50.

Platt, V. J. (2010) *Facing the Gods. Epiphany and Representation in Graeco-Roman Art, Literature and Religion.* Cambridge.

Pocock, J. G. A. (1995) 'The ideal of citizenship since classical times', in Beiner (ed.), 29–52.

Pollitt, J. J. (1986) *Art in the Hellenistic Age.* Cambridge.

Postrel, V. (2003) *The Substance of Style. How the Rise of Aesthetic Value Is Remaking Commerce, Culture and Consciousness.* New York.

Powell, J. E. (1938) *A Lexicon to Herodotos.* Cambridge.

Pritchard, D. (2003) 'Athletics, education and participation in classical Athens', in D. Phillips and D. Pritchard (eds.), *Sport and Festival in the Ancient Greek World.* London. 293–349.

Prost, F. and Wilgaux J. (eds.), (2006) *Penser et représenter le corps dans l'Antiquité.* Rennes.

Pucci, G. (2005) 'Costruire il bello. Ancora sul Canone di Policleto', in V. Neri (ed.), *Il corpo e lo sguardo. Tredici studi sulla bellezza del corpo nella cultura antica.* Bologna. 41–52.

Raeck, W. (1981) *Zum Barbarenbild in der Kunst Athens im 6. und 5. Jahrhundert v. Chr.* Bonn.

Ramage, E. S. (1973) *Urbanitas: Ancient Sophistication and Refinement.* Norman.

Rausa, F. (1994) *L'immagine del vincitore. L'atleta nella statuaria greca dall' età arcaica all' ellenismo.* Treviso.

Reding, J.-P. (2004) *Comparative Essays in Early Greek and Early Chinese Rational Thinking.* Aldershot.

Reger, G. (2006) 'The Aegean', in M. H. Hansen and T. H. Nielsen (ed.), *An Inventory of Archaic and Classical Poleis.* Oxford. 732–93.

Reusser, C. (2002) *Vasen für Etrurien: Verbreitung und Funktionen attischer Keramik im Etrurien des 6. und 5. Jahrhunderts vor Christus.* Zürich.

Rhodes, P. J. (1981) *A Commentary on the Aristotelian Athenaion Politeia.* Revised edn. 1993. Oxford.

Richardson, N. J. (1974) *The Homeric Hymn to Demeter.* Oxford.
  (1993) *The* Iliad: *a Commentary,* vol. VI: *Books 21–24.* Cambridge.

Richter, G. M. A. (1970) Kouroi: *Archaic Greek Youths. A Study of the Development of the Kouros Type in Greek Sculpture.* 3rd edn. London.

Ridgway, B. S. (1977) *The Archaic Style in Greek Sculpture.* Princeton.
  (1981) *Fifth-century Styles in Greek Sculpture.* Princeton.
  (1997) *Fourth-century Styles in Greek Sculpture.* London.

Rives, J. B. (1999) *Tacitus:* Germania. *Translated with Introduction and Commentary.* Oxford.

Robinson, D. M. (1943) 'A new Arcadian inscription', *Classical Philology* 38: 191–99.

Robinson, R. (1962) *Aristotle's* Politics *Books III and IV. Translated with Introduction and Comments.* Oxford.

Roccos, L. J. (2000) 'Back-mantle and peplos: the special costume of Greek maidens in fourth-century funerary and votive reliefs', *Hesperia* 69: 235–65.

Rosivach, V. J. (1987) 'Autochthony and the Athenians', *Classical Quarterly* 37.2: 294–306.

Rosler, A. (2005) *Political Authority and Obligation in Aristotle.* Oxford.

Said, E. (1978) *Orientalism.* London.

Sandys, J. E. (1893) *Aristotle's* Constitution of Athens. 2nd edn. 1912. London.

Sauer, E. W. (ed.) (2004) *Archaeology and Ancient History.* London.

Schaps, D. M. (1979) *Economic Rights of Women in Ancient Greece.* Edinburgh.

Scheer, T. S. (2000) *Die Gottheit und ihr Bild: Untersuchungen zur Funktion griechischer Kultbilder in Religion und Politik.* Munich.

Schnapp, A. (1988) 'Why did the Greeks need images?', in J. Christiansen and T. Melander (eds.), *Ancient Greek and Related Pottery.* Copenhagen. 568–74.

Schofield, M. (1990) 'Ideology and philosophy in Aristotle's Theory of Slavery', in G. Patzig (ed.), *Aristoteles 'Politik'.* Göttingen. 1–27; reprinted in Schofield (1999) 115–40.
  (ed.) (1999) *Saving the City: Philosopher-kings and Other Classical Paradigms.* London.

Scully, S. (1990) *Homer and the Sacred City.* Ithaca.

Seaford, R. (1994) *Reciprocity and Ritual: Homer and Tragedy in the Developing City-state.* Oxford.

Sedley, D. N. (1999) 'The ideal of godlikeness', in G. Fine (ed.), *Oxford Readings in Plato: Ethics, Politics, Religion and the Soul.* 2 vols. Oxford. II.309–28.
  (2003) *Plato's* Cratylus. Cambridge.

Shear, J. L. (2007) 'Cultural change, space, and the politics of commemoration in Athens', in R. Osborne (ed.), *Debating the Athenian Cultural Revolution: Art, Literature, Philosophy and Politics 430–380 BC.* Cambridge. 91–115.

Sherwin-White, A. N. (1973) *The Roman Citizenship*. 2nd edn. Oxford.

Skinner, Q. and Stråth B. (ed.) (2003) *States and Citizens: History, Theory, Prospects*. Cambridge.

Small, J. P. (2003) *The Parallel Worlds of Classical Art and Text*. Cambridge.

Smith, R. R. R. (2006) 'The use of images: visual history and ancient history', in T. P. Wiseman (ed.), *Classics in Progress: Essays on Ancient Greece and Rome*. Oxford. 59–102.

(2007) 'Pindar, athletes, and the early Greek statue habit', in S. Hornblower and C. Morgan (eds.), *Pindar's Poetry, Patrons and Festivals*. Oxford. 83–139.

Snodgrass, A. M. (1982) *Narration and Allusion in Archaic Greek Art*. Oxford.

(1983) 'Heavy freight in archaic Greece', in P. Garnsey, K. Hopkins and C. R. Whittaker (eds.), *Trade in the Ancient Economy*. London. 16–26.

(1998) *Homer and the Artists: Texts and Pictures in Early Greek Art*. Cambridge.

Sokolowski, F. (1955) *Lois sacrées d'Asie Mineure*. Paris.

(1962) *Lois sacrées des cités grecques supplément*. Paris.

(1969) *Lois sacrées des cités grecques*. Paris.

Sourvinou-Inwood, C. (1988) *Studies in Girls' Transitions: Aspects of the* arkteia *and Age Representation in Attic Iconography*. Athens.

Spivey, N. J. (1995) 'Bionic statues', in A. Powell (ed.), *The Greek World*. London. 442–59.

(1996) *Understanding Greek Sculpture: Ancient Meanings, Modern Readings*. London.

(2005) *How Art Made the World*. London.

Spivey, N. J. and Squire, M. J. (2004) *Panorama of the Classical World*. London.

Squire, M. J. (2009) *Image and Text in Graeco-Roman Antiquity*. Cambridge.

Stager, J. M. S. (2005) '"Let no one wonder at this image": a Phoenician funerary stele in Athens', *Hesperia* 74: 427–49.

Stansbury-O'Donnell, M. (1999) *Pictorial Narrative in Ancient Greek Art*. Cambridge.

Stears, K. (1995) 'Dead women's society: constructing female gender in Classical Athenian funerary sculpture', in N. Spencer (ed.), *Time, Tradition and Society in Greek Archaeology: Bridging the 'Great Divide'*. London. 109–31.

Steiner, D. T. (2001) *Images in Mind: Statues in Archaic and Classical Greek Literature and Thought*. Princeton.

Stevens, A. D. (2002) 'Telling presences: narrating divine epiphany in Homer and beyond'. PhD Thesis, University of Cambridge.

Stevens, G. P. (1955) 'Remarks upon the colossal chryselephantine statue of Athena in the Parthenon', *Hesperia* 24: 240–76.

Stewart, A. (1986) 'When is a kouros not an Apollo? The Tenea "Apollo" revisited', in M. Del Chiaro (ed.), *Corinthiaca: Studies in Honor of Darrell A. Amyx*. Columbia, MO. 54–70.

(1990) *Greek Sculpture: an Exploration*. 2 vols. New Haven.

(1996) *Art, Desire and the Body in Ancient Greece*. Cambridge.

Stewart, A. and Gray, C. (2000) 'Confirming the other: childbirth, aging, and death on an Attic tombstone at Harvard', in B. Cohen (ed.), 248–74.

Stewart, P. (2007) 'Gell's idols and Roman cult', in R. Osborne and J. Tanner (eds.), *Art's Agency and Art History*. Oxford. 158–78.

Stone, L. M. (1981) *Costume in Aristophanic Comedy*. New York.

Stroud, R. S. and Lewis D. M. (1979) 'Athens honors King Evagoras of Salamis', *Hesperia* 48: 180–93.

Tanner, J. J. (2006) *The Invention of Art History in Ancient Greece: Religion, Society and Artistic Rationalisation*. Cambridge.

Taplin, O. (1986) 'Fifth-century tragedy and comedy: a synkrisis', *Journal of Hellenic Studies* 106: 163–74.

(1989) *Greek Fire*. London.

(2007) *Pots and Plays: Interaction between Tragedy and Greek Vase-painting of the Fourth Century BC*. Los Angeles.

Taylor, M. C. (1990) 'Denegating god', *Critical Enquiry* 20: 592–610.

Testart, A. (1991) *Des mythes et des croyances: esquisse d'une théorie générale*. Paris.

Thomas, R. (2000) *Herodotus in Context*. Cambridge.

Todd, S. C. (1993) *The Shape of Athenian Law*. Oxford.

Tonkin, E. (1992) *Narrating our Pasts*. Cambridge.

Trevett, J. C. (1992) *Apollodoros Son of Pasion*. Oxford.

Tsagalis, C. (2008) *Inscribing Sorrow: Fourth-century Attic Funerary Epigrams*. Berlin.

Tsiafakis, D. (2000) 'The allure and repulsion of Thracians in the art of classical Athens', in B. Cohen (ed.), 364–89.

Tueller, M. A. (2008) *Look Who's Talking: Innovations in Voice and Identity in Hellenistic Epigram* (Hellenistica Groningana 13). Leuven.

Turner, S. M. (2009) 'Classical attic grave stelai: gender, death and the viewer'. PhD Thesis. University of Cambridge.

Tzachou-Alexandri, O. (ed.) (1989) *Mind and Body: Athletic Contests in Ancient Greece*. Athens.

Usener, H. (1914) *Kleine Schriften*. Vol. I. Leipzig.

Valeri, V. (2000) *The Forest of Taboos: Morality, Hunting, and Identity among the Huaulu of the Moluccas*. Madison, WI.

Vansina, J. (1985) *Oral Tradition as History*. London.

van Wees, H. (2005) 'Trailing tunics and sheepskin coats: dress and status in early Greece', in L. Cleland, M. Harlow and L. Llewellyn-Jones (eds.), *The Clothed Body in the Ancient World*. Oxford. 44–51.

Vernant, J.-P. (1989[1986]) 'Dim body, Dazzling body', in M. Feher (ed.), *Fragments for a History of the Human Body*. New York. 19–47 (Eng. trans. of 'Corps des dieux', *Le temps de réflexion* 7. Paris, 1986).

Veyne, P. (1961) 'La vie de Trimalcion', *Annales: Économies, Sociétés, Civilisations* 16: 213–47.

Vickers M. (1985) 'Artful crafts. The influence of metalwork on Athenian painted pottery', *Journal of Hellenic Studies* 105: 108–28.

Vickers, M. and Gill, D. (1994) *Artful Crafts: Ancient Greek Silverware and Pottery.* Oxford.

Vidal-Naquet, P. (1970) 'Valeurs religieuses et mythiques de la terre et du sacrifice dans l'*Odyssée*', *Annales ESC* 25: 1278–87; reprinted in M. I. Finley (ed.), *Problèmes de la terre en Grèce ancienne* (The Hague, 1973), 269–92; Eng. trans. in R. Gordon (ed.), *Myth, Religion & Society. Structuralist Essays* (Cambridge, 1981), 80–94.

Vlassopoulos, K. (2007) 'Free spaces: identity, experience and democracy in classical Athens', *Classical Quarterly* 57: 33–52.

Vos, M. F. (1963) *Scythian Archers in Archaic Attic Vase-painting.* Groningen.

Wardy, R. B. (2000) *Aristotle in China. Language, Categories and Translation.* Cambridge.

Webster, T. B. L. (1972) *Potter and Patron in Classical Athens.* London.

Weitmann, P. (2002) 'Götterbild und Götternähe im Spiegel der Entwicklung klassisch griechischer Skulptur', in W-D. Heilmeyer (ed.), *Die griechische Klassik: Idee oder Wirklichkeit.* Mainz. 83–93.

White, H. V. (1978) *Tropics of Discourse: Essays in Cultural Criticism.* Baltimore.

(1987) *The Content of the Form: Narrative Discourse and Historical Representation.* Baltimore.

Whitehead, D. (1986) *The Demes of Attica 508/7–ca. 250 BC.* Princeton.

(1993) 'Cardinal virtues: the language of public approbation in democratic Athens', *Classica et Mediaevalia* 44: 37–75.

Whitley, A. J. (2001) *The Archaeology of Ancient Greece.* Cambridge.

Williams, B. A. O. (1973) 'The analogy of city and soul in Plato's *Republic*', in E. N. Lee, A. P. D. Mourelatos and R. M. Rorty (eds.), *Exegesis and Argument* (*Phronesis* Suppl. 1). 196–206.

(1993) *Shame and Necessity.* Berkeley.

Winckelmann, J. J. (1756) *Gedanken über die Nachahmung der griechischen Werke in der Malerei und Bildhauerkunst.* 2nd edn. Dresden and Leipzig.

(1991) *Réflexions sur l'imitation des oeuvres grecques en peinture et en sculpture: suivi de lettre à propos des réflexions sur l'imitation des oeuvres grecques en peinture et en sculpture: et explication des réflexions sur l'imitation des oeuvres grecques en peinture et en sculpture*, ed. and trans. Marianne Charrière. Nîmes.

Winterson, J. (1992) *Written on the Body.* London.

Wölfflin, H. (1953) *Classic Art: an Introduction to the Italian Renaissance*, trans. P. Murray and L. Murray. London.

Woodford, S. (2003) *Images of Myths in Classical Antiquity.* Cambridge.

Wyke, M. (1999) 'Herculean muscle: the classicizing rhetoric of bodybuilding', in J. I. Porter (ed.), *Constructions of the Classical Body.* Ann Arbor. 355–79.

Young, D. C. (2004) *A Brief History of the Olympic Games.* Oxford.

Zanker, P. (1995) *The Mask of Socrates: the Image of the Intellectual in Antiquity.* Berkeley.

Zeitlin, F. I. (1986) 'Thebes: theater of self and society in Athenian drama', in J. P. Euben (ed.), *Greek Tragedy and Political Theory.* Berkeley. 101–41; reprinted in J. J. Winkler and F. I. Zeitlin (eds.), *Nothing to Do with Dionysos? Athenian Drama in its Social Context.* Princeton, 1990. 130–67.

Index

www.ingramcontent.com/pod-product-compliance
Ingram Content Group UK Ltd.
Pitfield, Milton Keynes, MK11 3LW, UK
UKHW030900150625
459647UK00021B/2712